PROMOTIONAL CULTURE

Theory, Culture & Society

Theory, Culture & Society caters for the resurgence of interest in culture within contemporary social science and the humanities. Building on the heritage of classical social theory, the book series examines ways in which this tradition has been reshaped by a new generation of theorists. It will also publish theoretically informed analyses of everyday life, popular culture, and new intellectual movements.

EDITOR: Mike Featherstone, *Teesside Polytechnic*

EDITORIAL BOARD
Roy Boyne, *Newcastle upon Tyne Polytechnic*
Mike Hepworth, *University of Aberdeen*
Scott Lash, *University of Lancaster*
Roland Robertson, *University of Pittsburgh*
Bryan S. Turner, *University of Essex*

Also in this series

The Body
Social Process and Cultural Theory
edited by Mike Featherstone, Mike Hepworth and Bryan S. Turner

Consumer Culture and Postmodernism
Mike Featherstone

Talcott Parsons
Theorist of Modernity
edited by Roland Robertson and Bryan S. Turner

The Symbol Theory
Norbert Elias

Religion and Social Theory
Bryan S. Turner

Images of Postmodern Society
Social Theory and Contemporary Cinema
Norman K. Denzin

PROMOTIONAL CULTURE

Advertising, ideology and symbolic expression

ANDREW WERNICK

SAGE Publications

London • Newbury Park • New Delhi

First published 1991
Reprinted 1992, 1994

SAGE Publications Ltd
6 Bonhill Street
London EC2A 4PU

SAGE Publications Inc
2455 Teller Road
Newbury Park, California 91320

SAGE Publications India Pvt Ltd
32, M-Block Market
Greater Kailash – I
New Delhi 110 048

British Library Cataloguing in Publication Data

Wernick, Andrew
    Promotional culture: Advertising and ideology in
    late capitalism.
    I. Title
    659.101

    ISBN 0–8039–8390–5
    ISBN 0–8039–8391–3 pbk

Library of Congress catalog card number 91-050676

Typeset by Photoprint, Torquay
Printed and bound in Great Britain by
Biddles Ltd, Guildford and King's Lynn

CONTENTS

PREFACE AND ACKNOWLEDGMENTS

The project underlying this study has been modified considerably since I first began to be interested in the cultural implications of the rise of advertising more than a decade ago.

My initial focus was on commercial advertising and its ideological role; wherein, to correct a synchronic bias, my aim was to introduce a historical dimension into the semiological critique of popular culture pioneered by Barthes (and in a different way McLuhan), and applied to advertising 'texts' themselves, most notably, by Judith Williamson. Besides formal–theoretical concerns, my particular interest, naturally, was in the history I had lived. How had North American advertising in its value appeals on behalf of promotionally imaged products reflected, refracted, and processed the ideological upheavals of the 1960s and 1970s? And what light could that throw on the more general course of hegemonic and counter-hegemonic politics since the Second World War?

Later, I began to see that advertising was not just a commercial phenomenon, nor, as the latter, just the product of a specific communications apparatus. Promotion (my term for advertising and its practices taken in the widest and most generic sense) was a rhetorical form diffused throughout our culture. As such, it had come to shape not only that culture's symbolic and ideological contents, but also its ethos, texture, and constitution as a whole. By the same token, it seemed to me, the place of promotion within the cultural formation of late capitalism was both under-rated and under-theorized.

Two paths opened up. The first led towards a reformulation of certain aspects of the traditional critique of commodified culture developed by the Frankfurt School. The (early) writings of Jean Baudrillard provided a point of departure – though, clearly, a meditation on the promotional (re-)fashioning of late capitalist culture leads in quite different directions from those pointed to in Baudrillard's own analysis of 'general exchange' and 'the political economy of the sign'. The second path led towards an engagement with the growing debate about whether, why, and with what (progressive/regressive) implications late capitalist culture had undergone some kind of postmodern turn. A suggestive hypothesis formed: that the pan-promotionalism of contemporary communications (private as well as public, political, academic, artistic, etc) could itself account for many of the features – intertextuality, de-referentiality, absorption of the real into its image, etc – held to characterize the postmodern. If the latter (in Frederic Jameson's words) has become a new 'cultural dominant', can this aspect of capital's 'cultural logic' help explain why? Is postmodernism, indeed, just the (anti-)aesthetic implied by the rhetoric of the commodity finally coming to cultural power?

In weaving together these not entirely compatible themes, I am painfully aware of the gaps and inconsistencies that remain. I have not tried to hide a partial shift in problematic that occurs between Chapters 4 and 5. To impose coherence, and because I have wanted to examine promotional culture as a total complex, I have followed a narrative order designed to display the logic – historical and structural – of its formation as such. Thus I begin with the imaging of consumer goods, move on to the culture industry and the media, and finish by looking at the promotionalization of non-commercial spheres such as politics and intellectual life. Besides mapping dimensions of the present, this provides a framework for examining the spread of promotion as a process. That is: for tracing out the unfolding relationship between the intensive and extensive development of the market as an organizing principle of social life, and the increasingly diffuse and convoluted forms of promotional communication to which this has given rise.

The reader will note, and perhaps object to, one other thread that runs through the account. Except for some summary reflections in the final chapter, I have consistently emphasized the impact of promotion on the objective side of culture (on what is articulated, produced, circulated or expressed), while ignoring consciousness, subjectivity, and that whole range of issues having to do with reception. This runs the risk of one-sidedness, which would be fatal if the elision were made theoretically absolute. I defend it here only as a tactical choice: a self-limitation that recognizes that all cannot be said at once. The analysis that I offer may stray beyond this mandate, but it remains self-consciously partial in the determinations it chooses to highlight, and stammeringly provisional as a statement about these.

The individuals to whom I am personally indebted for help in stimulating this book, clarifying its ideas, and seeing it through to completion, are too many to count.

The bulk of the writing and editing was done on sabbatical leave in Cambridge. Special thanks are due to Philippa Berry, Maurice Biriotti, and the staff of King's College for making my mid-life return there so reviving and productive. My gratitude to colleagues, staff, and students at Trent University is unbounded, and I apologize if my (paradigmatic) references to Trent in Chapter 7 in any way suggest otherwise. It is invidious to single out names, but among colleagues I will especially mention John Fekete, John Hillman, and Jonathan Bordo whose conversations, challenges, and ideas have been crucial. Nor can I forget, whether as individuals or as a milieu, the succeeding generations of 'mass media and society' students whose engaged enthusiasm has sustained my own, and who have provided a bracing medium within which to test out ideas.

For critical feedback at various stages of the manuscript itself I must thank Arthur Kroker, Heather Jon Maroney, Mike Featherstone, and Stephen Barr. For help with the visual materials, I thank Susan Wheeler of the Trent Communications Department, Tadek Jarski of London Solidarity for Solidarity, and (over several years) the staff of the Trent Institute for the Study of Popular Culture, especially Peter Clayton, Ken Orenstein, and Frances Enns. I am also grateful for the help and copyright permissions granted by IBM (Canada), *Penthouse* International Ltd, Volkswagen, GM/Oldsmobile, the British Museum, the Wedgwood Museum (Barlaston), Toyota (US), the *Observer*, and Vauxhall (UK).

Chapters 2, 3, and 4 are revised versions of previously published essays. They appeared, respectively, as: 'Advertising and ideology: an interpretative model', in *Theory, Culture & Society*, Vol. 3, No. 1, 1984; 'From voyeur to narcissist: the shifting image of men in postwar advertising', in Kaufman (ed.) (1987) *Beyond Patriarchy: Men on Pleasure and Power*, Toronto: Oxford; and 'Vehicles for myth: the shifting image of the modern car', in Jhally and Angus (eds) (1989) *Cultural Politics in Contemporary America*, New York: Routledge. Editorial permissions by Mike Featherstone, Ian Angus and Sut Jhally, and Michael Kaufman are gratefully acknowledged.

My most incalculable debt, however, is to Heather Jon Maroney who has borne with this project from start to finish and, whatever the weather, has provided continuous commentary, suggestions, and support. It is to her, with all their imperfections, that I dedicate the results.

1

IMAGING COMMODITIES

It seems absolutely necessary for the increase of our sales that some means must be unremittingly made use of to keep up the attention of the world to the fine things we are making and doing for them.

Josiah Wedgwood to Thomas Bentley (1 March 1779)

An artefact and its double

One of the most celebrated exhibits at the British Museum is an eighteen-inch high, blue-black and white Roman glassware pot known as the Barberini or Portland Vase.

Dating, it is now thought, from the last half century of the Roman Republic,[1] and originally manufactured in Alexandria, the vase was rediscovered during the pontificate of Urban VIII (1623–44). Urban was a Barberini, and under the benign gaze of St Peter the prize soon passed into his family's private hands. There it stayed until 1784 when it was acquired by the British envoy (and antiquities collector) Sir William Hamilton through whom it was re-sold, first to the Duchess of Portland and then, after her death shortly after, to the Duke. With the rest of the Portland collection, it was subsequently loaned to the British Museum, with whom it has remained ever since.

The vase, an exquisite artefact, has long been famous as a high watermark of classical ceramics. As such, it still helps to draw visitors – these days to a public institution – and, needless to say, it is one of the icons which graces the postcards sold in the Museum's lobby to publicize the collections and raise a little extra cash. A visitor to the Museum in the autumn or winter of 1988 would not, however, have been able actually to see the vase, for it was being restored. Not that the display case was empty. In place of the original, Museum staff had temporarily mounted an almost equally celebrated copy: one of a limited series by Josiah Wedgwood, and a companion piece to one just like it which is regularly displayed in another section of the Museum devoted to the more recent history of pottery in Britain.[2] A curious substitution. What made it possible was the fact that the Wedgwood (scrupulously labelled by the Museum as such) is so close a replica of the original. To the casual observer, they are virtually impossible to tell apart. Thus while it could not *be* the original – the Roman vase the visitor expected to see – Wedgwood's copy could at least serve to bring the original's physical details to mind.

In this borrowed setting, of course, the copy serves only *as* a copy. Its

own significance – historical, cultural, aesthetic, etc – is eclipsed by what it faithfully and self-effacingly represents. It is quite otherwise in the section of the Museum which houses the British ceramics collection, where Wedgwood's version is exhibited as a masterpiece in itself. There it is a chapter in another story: the unfolding of British artistic and technical genius; and what we are led to admire is Josiah Wedgwood's achievement in having been able to make such a perfect copy at all.

Now when we enquire into how this copy came to be made[3] we discover an interesting fact. The task was encouraged by the Duke of Portland himself, from whom Wedgwood borrowed the original only three days after the Duke had bought it at the auction of his wife's estate. Nor was it just a whimsical idea, for they both realized that the combined celebrity of the Portland Vase and of England's master potter, then at the height of his fame, guaranteed that others in the aristocracy would want just such a replica for themselves. The technical challenge was prodigious, and it took five and a half years for Wedgwood to produce an object he felt confident enough about to place on public view. Besides the difficulties in making a good mould (for which Wedgwood employed Henry Webber, head of his ornamental wares department and perhaps the best such craftsman of his day) the greatest challenge was to replicate in earthenware the iridescent blue-black material from which the body of the pot was made. Knowledge of how Roman craftsmen achieved their effect[4] had died with them, and it was only after years of experimenting with various admixtures to clay that Wedgwood found the match he sought. Compounding matters, his brief from Hamilton was to produce a perfect resemblance, including all defects of age or execution in the original vase's colouring, figuration, and form. A specimen of the results, after Wedgwood had given a private showing to the Queen, was finally submitted to the Society of Antiquaries in 1790 and then certified as a 'correct and faithful imitation' by no less an authority than Sir Joshua Reynolds, in his capacity as President of the Royal Society.

If Josiah Wedgwood had been only a supplier of customized craft ceramics to the stately homes of late Georgian England, the story would end there. To readers of Walter Benjamin's 'The work of art in an age of mechanical reproduction' (1970)[5] its significance would lie primarily, perhaps, in the contrast it illustrates between an auratic original and its de-auratized simulacrum. In these terms, in fact, the Wedgwood replica represents a fascinating hybrid. The model from which the series was made (principally the mould, but also the experimentally arrived at mix of in-gredients) is itself an example of what Benjamin meant by a copy – a mimetic product of hand and eye which, unlike a photograph or sound recording, retains the quality of being a specific product of concrete human labour. The actual members of the series, on the other hand, being made from the same mould, process, and mixture, are related to one another more as simulacra. The mutual similitude of these latter, however, was itself only approximate; for in their firing and finishing, Wedgwood's series of Portland vases were still individually crafted. Altogether, then, the starkness of the Benjaminian distinction is here quite blurred. Indeed, before becoming, through an accident of history, the 'Barberini' and then the 'Portland' vase, the ceramic masterpiece Wedgwood was copying had itself, we may assume, been part of a series.[6]

Still, the distinction between the two artefacts does not thereby collapse. The second was intended to simulate the first; and its significance is correspondingly of quite a different order. But here, too, there is an ambiguity. The vase Wedgwood copied had already become an exhibition piece, and so it by no means had the same cultural status as the ceremonial object scholars say it once was.[7] In its original usage, the mythological allusion made by its decorative white figures would have been clear and direct. Presumably, too, that allusion would have been tied to a living tradition of ritual and belief. For the vase's new British owners and viewers, however, like the Barberinis before them, classical Roman culture was long dead. In that context, the details of the vase's design were less significant than what they generally connoted: as second-order signifiers for classical antiquity and all that term conjured up in the aesthetic sensibility of the time. By 1785, moreover, when Wedgwood began his work, no-one even knew who the figures were, nor to what scene or story the whole mythological tableau was meant to refer.[8]

The original that Wedgwood copied, in other words, was one whose aura had already decayed; and in his replication of it, the discontinuity between its initial and contemporary meaning-in-use was simply presupposed. What remained of the difference was only that Wedgwood's copy had never been nor meant anything else. As an iconic representation of a Roman icon, it had only ever been a once-removed and conventionalized sign.

Of course, the two switched objects are embedded in a socioeconomic history as well. It was what they came to share in that regard, as private property privately donated, that made it possible for them both to be exhibited in the Museum. Equally, the fact that both the original and its copy were esteemed by contemporaries as Art shows the intimate connection between the historical institution of that category and the process of commodification which simultaneously set both vases into commercial circulation. Wedgwood's production of the copy, in parallel with the Portland family's purchase of the original, came just at the point where the Renaissance ideal of craft-based humanist art was beginning to be rendered problematic by the extension of capitalist principles to that sphere. What has been temporarily substituted in the Museum, then, is not just an archaic original by its modern copy, but one deracinated artefact which (thereby) became a commodity by another which, in imitating so brilliantly the physical appearance of what it copied, had instantly become a valuable collector's item – and investment good – in its own right.

But the significance of the copied vase is hardly exhausted by the terms of such an account. Wedgwood was not just a maker of up-market art. He was a capitalist entrepreneur of the first rank, a pioneer of industrialism who introduced an advanced division of labour into his Staffordshire works, who developed new commercial methods and technical processes (including his own invention: the pyrometer[9]), and whose manufactures became the premier supplier of tableware not just for the aristocracy but for the growing middle classes of Britain and, indeed, of parts of Europe and North America as well.[10] A mainstay of his operation was the 'creamware' dinner sets which he perfected in the 1770s, and of which in his lifetime many thousands were sold. Other items produced in similarly vast quantities included tea and coffee services, salt and pepper shakers, busts of famous people and everyday accessories, from watch-cases and snuff boxes to ear-rings, brooches, and buttons. As Meteyard, his nineteenth-century biographer, pointed out: 'It was this sale of ordinary ware which enabled Wedgwood to spend so much in ornamental art. Had he lived upon the fruits of his cameos and bas-reliefs he would have died a poor, if not an insolvent man' (Meteyard, 1865, Vol. I: 481–2).

Not surprisingly, then, when Wedgwood acceded to the urgings of would-be subscribers and took on the project, he made clear that he did so reluctantly, with little prospect of immediate gain. 'I do not' he wrote to his patron in the summer of 1785 'think £5000 for the execution of such a vase, supposing our better artists to be capable of such work, would be at all equal to their gains from the works they are now employed in.'[11] Considering that this estimate, even if padded, took no account of fixed costs, nor of his own labour, and that the Duke of Portland had acquired the original for £1029, it can be seen that supply and demand curves were unlikely to intersect for what inevitably had to be, as a one-off batch of labour-intensive luxury goods, a strictly limited edition. Eventually, some few dozen were actually sold[12] at an asking price of £50 each. Evidently he made a loss. Why, then, did he take it on? What was there to gain?

That the time and money Wedgwood devoted to the project was no mere indulgence, that – like everything else he did – it fitted coherently into the overall pattern of his business activities, is clear from what he did with the vase as soon as its status as a true copy had been officially certified. His first step was to place it on special public display. Set among his finest ornamental pieces, including other classical-style ones made from the same 'Jasperware' process, the vase was given pride of place in the company's London showrooms in Greek Street. The opening itself was publicized in the press, and staged as a (tickets-only) gala event to which the cream of society was invited, and flocked. Three months later, the vase, along with other choice items from the show, was taken on tour by his son (Thomas) and nephew (Thomas Byerley) to Holland and Germany. Starting at The Hague, and with the Greek Street gala as a model, this was similarly orchestrated as a glittering string of society events. 'All the first people that are at the Hague were there', reported Thomas of the tour's opening in a letter to his father. 'The Prince and Princess with their daughter, who is to be married to the Duke of Brunswick . . . . They said everything that was to be expected.'[13] And to complete the operation, at each stop along the way an agency was established offering the full range of Wedgwood wares.

Wedgwood's stunning achievement in producing a true copy of the Portland Vase was employed, in short, as a marketing device. Most immediately, the vase exhibited in London and elsewhere drew potential clients for further copies of the vase itself. In turn, as the centrepiece of a travelling upper-class roadshow, which itself generated secondary publicity through newspapers and word of mouth, the vase anchored a whole sales campaign on behalf of Wedgwood's latest line – 'Jasperware' – together with his wider range of ornamental goods. Finally, this campaign itself served to publicize the name and produce of Wedgwood more generally, gaining notice as well for his largest selling lines.

Altogether then, the vase and its attendant publicity was used to generate and focus demand for four distinct kinds of Wedgwood product: for (other) copies of the vase, for other cameos in the Jasper line, for still other items in the ornamental/luxury class, and for the more middle-class oriented 'usefull wares' which made up the bulk of company sales. Each of these is evidently a commodity, or class of commodities, in its own right. But, be it noted, they also constitute an ordered series, functionally differentiated according to their place within the overall logic of Wedgwood sales.

To see this, we can picture the overall Wedgwood catalogue as a kind of pyramid, with the items that were most limited in number, labour-intensive, and dear at the top, and those which were most numerous, capital-intensive, and cheap at the base. As we move up the pyramid profitability decreases, since the profits from ornamental ware were lower than those for ordinary ware, and the most exclusive pieces were actually sold at a loss. What increases, at the same time, is the relative significance of each product category as advertising for the higher profit goods in the categories below. Overall, then, the direct profits to be made from the sale of a particular product line were inversely related to its promotional value; and the production costs of the luxury pieces were subsidized by revenues from the sale of ordinary ware in return for the their power to promote.[14] At the apex of this whole construct, its splendid and promotional capping stone, stood (on its plinth) the copied Portland Vase itself.

The promotional commodity

What we are confronted with, then, is a curious kind of object. An early instance of 'art in an age of mechanical production', certainly: but with the peculiarity that it was a copied artefact whose original had been re-contextualized as 'great art' and whose own aesthetic value hinged precisely on its (unprecedented) perfection as a copy. The object is also, and in just this setting, a commodity: but again, not a commodity in the ordinary sense. For, beyond serving as a consumer good that could command, as such, its own market price, its exchange-value to the capitalist who produced it was amplified by – indeed, depended on – the enhanced sales of other goods which its exhibition value enabled it to stimulate. From this vantage point, what is particularly striking is the way that the vase's symbolic meaning articulates with its rhetorical function precisely as an ad.

The basic operation involved is easily described. Its overall point was to help construct a powerfully positive cultural identity for Wedgwood, his company and its hallmarked produce. In effect, as a standard-bearer for these latter, the Wedgwood copy is equated with what both it and its original mean metaphorically, in their contemporary reception as works of art and craft. There are four main moves.

First, and most obviously, as a copy of the already existing and already admired Portland Vase Wedgwood's faithful replica borrows all the lustre and cultural associations which cling to the original. To Wedgwood's contemporaries that original epitomized what it embodied. It was not just *a* Roman vase, but *the* Roman vase. By virtue of the grace and proportion of its design, and of its supreme craftsmanship, cognoscenti like Hamilton judged it one of the finest pieces of Roman antiquity still extant. The publicity surrounding its sale and transfer from Italy to London ensured, in addition, that it was canonized as such, converting it into a natural but conventionalized sign of the best in the aesthetic tradition to which it belonged.

All this was set against the background of a Renaissance-derived view of European history which saw the classical Mediterranean world as not just a revered ancestor (whence the first stirrings of philosophy, law, and a global order based on reason) but as a pinnacle of civilization whose cultural achievements remained a perennial challenge to the moderns. This was particularly so in the area of architecture and the plastic arts where, in a burst of revivalism that followed the archaeological discoveries at Herculaneum,[15] the prosperous classes of late eighteenth-century England could not procure enough environing objects, whether original or not, made in this style.

Several factors underpinned this renewed round of classical revival. Besides the excitement generated by the new discoveries themselves, these included the birth of a romantic nostalgia for the pre-industrial, and indeed pre-Christian, which stimulated a new passion for history and its exotica; the beginnings of an international trade in antique *objets d'art*; and a growing prosperity which sought status expression in the show and accoutrements of a grand style.

In that context, the vogue for classicism, like the baroque it ousted, had a class meaning, too. Both were assimilated to the vocabulary of power, the baroque through a leisured and luxurious ostentatiousness, classical revival through grandeur, proportionality, and restraint. It is not hard to see here an analogue of the difference between an *ancien régime*'s sumptuary alliance of court and nobility, now sinking into decline, and the more puritanical and rationalistic ethos of the mercantile and professional classes which had already ousted it in Britain and, with much bloodshed, were about to do the same in France. The period from antiquity, moreover, which exercised the greatest fascination was early Imperial

Rome – to which period the vase itself was thought to belong. In the mirror of the Augustan age, with its austere civicism, artistic patronage, and civilizing conquests, the gentry, merchants, manufacturers, military leaders, administrators, and statesmen who guided Europe's – and, pre-eminently, Britain's – own rise to global power were able to see a flattering and ennobling picture of themselves.

In its new setting, at the same time, classicism was not just slavishly revived. Borrowings were selective, and in the fashioning of new artefacts the style itself was modified so as to fit the idioms of the old to the particularities of those who, in drastically different historical circumstances, sought to express their own identities through it. The key medium for this neo-classical translation was architecture, particularly as relayed through the proselytizing ideas of Robert and Joseph Adam. The Adam brothers' stylistic approach represented, in effect, a re-adaptation of the Palladian principles which Italian architects had extracted from their contemplation of Roman ruins a century before.[16] The main change concerned private house design, particularly with respect to their interiors. In place of the presumed Roman severity (derived from the remains of temples and palaces, and which the excavations at Herculaneum had shown to be misconstrued) was substituted an intimate sense of domestic space. Adam's drawing and dining rooms, with their human scale and uncluttered adornment, mediated between a need for prestigeful entertainment and a need for a family-centred private zone which expressed the taste and refinement of those who lived there. While patronized by the rich, such ideas could evidently be adapted to fit a variety of income and property situations. You did not have to buy the whole architectural and lifestyle package. Neo-classicism was sufficiently malleable, then, to exert stylistic appeal downwards: from what Wedgwood termed the 'Great People' to the 'Middling Class . . . which we know are vastly, I had almost said infinitely superior, in numbers'.[17] As a proto-industrialist of the machine age it was to the latter that his own produce was massively directed.

The fact that the precise meaning of the vase's white decorative figures was now unknown[18] only facilitated its conversion into a general signifier for this cluster of classical and neo-classical values. It gave the vase a mysterious quality, an exotic strangeness which clothed the distant past it came from, like faraway places in travellers' tales, in a sheen of strangeness and magic. Of course, what Joshua Reynolds declared a true likeness could only represent the late eighteenth-century's idea of the classical iconically; whereas the original could do so indexically, by actually being a Roman vase. Nor was this indexicality – in Benjamin's sense, its aura – itself transferable. But the original artefact's haze of connotations, communicated semiotically by the vase's replicable form, certainly could be so transferred, albeit at one remove and without the same power of being a material trace.

At a second level, the copied vase connoted the labour and knowhow which went into its own making as a copy. Today we marvel less, but such skill in ceramic reproduction, including the discovery of how to achieve, through new techniques, the material texture of a form of ancient stoneware whose production secret was lost, had never been seen before.

Here, too, a chain of secondary cultural associations enveloped what Wedgwood had done. There was, to begin with, the very fact that this creation, unlike its anonymous double, could be identified with an individual creator. It was, to use the Enlightenment/Romantic cliché, a work of genius. Besides the cult of the individual it evoked, more particularly, the idealized figure of the individual craftsman, seen as the very type of *homo faber*, the shaper and improver of Nature. It did so, moreover, in the twin forms – as Engineer (Inventor) and Artist – in which that figure was most celebrated in the bourgeois culture of industrial capitalism's initial take-off phase. Thus the copied vase embodied not just individual genius, but the genius of Wedgwood and, through his example, that synthesis of Art and Science that marked the peculiar genius of a world which, through a providential progress, had evolved into essential harmony with itself.[19]

The third move was to tie these two meanings together. The Wedgwood was not just a supremely successful copy, but a copy of this particular Roman vase. And it was not just a stand-in for the latter, but a brilliant rendition in itself. Its total meaning, therefore, is a composite of what is signified by both.

As a first approximation, we can say that the first meaning (classicalness) elevates the second (the craft genius of Wedgwood) by virtue of the way the copy, in its fidelity to the original, implies their identity with one another. Thus the Wedgwood presents the modern production values it embodies as simply continuous with those signified by its antique original. But there is a twist. If the moderns, through Wedgwood, had caught up with the ancients, and could be regarded here and now, in this vase, as their equals, it was with wholly new methods of production. Far from being ancient and time-honoured, these methods rested on unprecedented advances in the physico-chemical sciences. Wedgwood himself was a member of the Royal Society. Of equal importance, these methods also involved an industrially organized production process whose expansionist activities were geared to maximizing the value of the capital employed. In other words, the values of individual craftsmanship connoted at so many levels by Wedgwood's duplicate pot covered over the fact that this artefact, and still more the regular produce of Wedgwood's factory, was the outcome of a very different process: one, indeed, that spelt the end for craft production as such. If Wedgwood himself, as his company's polytechnic boss, could and did engage in every aspect of what his factories made, his company's hired hands, subject to a rigid division of labour, most assuredly could not. Correspondingly, while Wedgwood's promotional cameos were customized, time-consuming, and individually made, his more ordinary plates and saucers were turned out in stylized and standardized batches of several dozen at a time. He was, in short, a mass manufacturer of high-grade kitsch.

The contradiction between the ideology and the reality of what, and how, Wedgwood produced was buried in the copied vase's archaic reference to classical Rome. But it was not wholly suppressed. In the initial publicity the copy did announce the novelty of at least the experimentally derived substance – 'Jasper' – of which it was physically made. As such, it tacitly represented the present as having not just caught up with the best of the ancient world, but as now being in a position (given the inevitability of further progress) to surpass it. The copied vase could present itself, then, as not just equivalent to the best in classical pottery, but as evidence that Wedgwood and his company were its legitimate heirs. More: the living head of a tradition which they had become able to transcend.

Finally, by being presented as the centrepiece and summation of Josiah Wedgwood's ceramic art, all the symbolic associations which Wedgwood's version of the Portland Vase evoked were transferred on to himself as its creator, on to the company he headed, and finally on to all its manufactured goods. In effect, then, the copied vase helped to supply a meaning for the Wedgwood name – and thence for a brand which was stamped, literally, on all his produce, and whose associated image defined and differentiated whatever was produced or distributed under that sign.[20]

In this, of course, the Portland Vase project did not stand alone. It was part of a broader imaging strategy which extended to every aspect of Wedgwood's business operation. This was evident even in the name – Etruria – selected for the model factory he built at Burslem in 1768–9, at first to produce his ornamental specialities, and then, after 1774, his entire product range. In addition to the Etruria works, he further memorialized the fabled pre-Roman cradle of Italian ceramics[21] in the neo-classically designed Etruria Hall which became, in 1770, his principal family home. This was no mere private affectation. At Etruria's grand opening, on 13 June 1769, the highlight was provided by Josiah himself, spryly hopping around on his wooden leg, as he threw on the wheel the first six ceremonial vases. Each was subsequently inscribed with the date, a picture of (the Etruscan) Hercules and his companions in the garden of Hesperides, and the motto: *Artes Etruriae Renascentur* ('the arts of Etruria are reborn'). The factory itself, moreover, was laid out not just as an exemplary production site, with an eye to workforce order and morale; but also as a showcase for potential purchasers (with salesroom attached) to impress the Etruscan comparison on visiting clients and dignitaries.[22]

The same strategy can be seen in the design of Wedgwood's actual produce, starting with the ornamental ware itself. At first this had been just a sideline. But, following his collaboration (from 1762 onwards) and partnership (in 1769) with Thomas Bentley, he took their production increasingly seriously[23] and the Etruria works was dedicated to this side of the business. Whence, spurred on by Bentley, Wedgwood set about satisfying the burgeoning demand for antique-looking vases, chimney-pieces and other such ornaments to embellish the interiors of the classical revival dwellings and estates which had come to be in vogue.[24] At the top of the line, and as much for show as for sale, were the demonstration pieces which, together with Adam and his followers in architecture, placed Wedgwood and his pottery at the forefront of neo-classical style.

Some of these, like the Portland Vase, were exact replicas of well-known originals.[25] Most, however, were adaptations of classical style rather than exact renditions. 'I only pretend to have attempted to copy the antique forms', he wrote in 1789, 'but not with absolute servility. I have endeavoured to preserve the style and spirit, or if you please the elegant simplicity of antique forms, and so doing introduce all the variety I was able.'[26]

Such 'variety' was also dictated by the market. Keenly aware that women were the effective purchasing agents, he always, according to his own testimony, tried out new creations on his wife first.[27] There was, besides, a problem with Greek and Roman figuration of any kind that made some adaptation essential. In reply to a suggestion from Flaxman, one of his principal modellers, he noted that

> The history of Orestes is an excellent subject . . ., but there is one objection which I fear is insurmountable and that is the nakedness of the figures. To clothe them would not only be a great increase of labour, but would require the hand of an experienced master in the art, and besides then the piece would not be a copy from the antique . . . . The nude is so general in the works of the ancients that it will be very difficult to avoid the introduction of naked figures. On the other hand it is absolutely necessary to do so . . . for none either male or female of the present generation will take or apply them as furniture if the figures are naked.[28]

The absolute necessity of which he spoke was evidently commercial. To ensure that his products had the widest possible appeal their design had to be consonant not only with the dictates of neo-classical style, but also with whatever other values prevailed among those making up the bulk of his market.

If in a more simplified and standardized fashion, finally, the same stylistic inspiration can be seen in the development of Wedgwood's ordinary ware as well.[29] After initial efforts in green glaze and tortoiseshell (themselves a mix of English country garden vernacular and gilded rococo) his dinner services shed their heavily decorated look and affected the elegant simplicity which was the hallmark of neo-classicism's reaction to the baroque. Here, too, the company's sales campaign had been spear headed by a show case commissioned work: the 952-piece Russian banquet service, decorated with scenes from the Great Houses of the English gentry, which in 1774 had been delivered to Catherine the Great. Prior to delivery, the service, like the later Portland Vase, was made the subject of a special exhibit at the Soho showrooms.[30] This generated a stream of follow-up orders for its cheaper version which, in yet another promotional move, was dubbed 'Queensware' after a specially decorated set of it was commissioned by the British royal house.[31]

To the extent that 'Queensware', and all the other ordinary items which graced the tables and cabinets of the merely well-to-do, also helped sustain the imagistic association with the neo-classical that gave Wedgwood produce its special stylistic edge, it too was part of the broader promotional effort. And this is just the point. All Wedgwood's produce had a promotional element in it. While the functions were in different proportions in different products, all served both as commodities, in the immediate sense, and as advertisements at a second order. What is extraordinary about the copied Portland Vase, in this regard, is only the relative weight of the promotional within its functional mix. It approaches the limiting case of the product which is not itself sold, but is wholly paid for from the proceeds of other goods: a pure advertisement, circulating only as a promotional sign.

We can now see that the two Portland vases displayed in the Museum, Wedgwood's and the original, are not only physically similar, but similar in their pragmatic functions as well. Both, in that setting, are promotional: the original in relation to the Museum itself, its copy in relation to the Wedgwood company. Since 1791, moreover, the year of the latter's completion, their respective publicity values have been deeply intertwined. Each artefact, and each organization, has helped promote the other. In which respect, too, Wedgwood's rendition has a distinctly modern face. For, as we shall see, the mutual entanglement of promotional signs in one domain with those in another has become a pervasive feature of our whole produced symbolic world.

Production/advertising/design: the Wedgwood matrix

From an historical standpoint, what the dense web of promotion surrounding Wedgwood's copy of the Portland Vase illustrates is not just that the familiar forms of modern marketing can be traced back to the late eighteenth century,[32] but how integral they were, from the very beginnings of industrial capitalism, to the mass production of consumer goods.

It is a matter for debate to what extent this new combination of production and promotion was the product of a purely economic necessity. For the pottery masters of Staffordshire – and a similar story could be told about the iron masters of Birmingham or the mill owners of Manchester – rising competition due to improved techniques and economies of scale no doubt served, from the 1720s onwards, as a general force pushing the most enterprising of them to expand their marketing efforts beyond their local bailiwick. The saturation of British markets by the late 1760s, and the ensuing slump, reproduced the same pressures on a larger scale.[33] That it was Wedgwood who was most successful in making the turn, and that he was able to take such unparalleled advantage of the national and international markets which had opened up, makes him both intriguing as a pioneer and important as a paradigm case.

The personal attributes that singled Wedgwood out have been traced by biographers to his practical and non-conformist upbringing, to a toughening childhood bout with smallpox, and to an exacting apprenticeship with his older brother. His launchpad was a five-year partnership with Thomas Whieldon, who financed his experiments and whose other proteges included Thomas Spode; following which, at the self-confident age of twenty-nine[34] he acquired a small manufactory and set up on his own. And to all the technical and commercial skills he rapidly displayed we must also add the social ones. From the start, these enabled him not only to manage his employees with a minimum of repression and a maximum of loyalty, but also to move with ease through all the social circles that mattered. An inveterate networker and backstage political organizer,[35] he steadily acquired among his friends and contacts all the leading industrialists, scientists, visual artists, and society notables of his day.

It goes without saying that Wedgwood's ascendancy would have been impossible to attain had the goods themselves not been of leading quality. Wedgwood's boast that the Etruscan arts had been reborn in his factories was not entirely without foundation. But it is equally clear that, past the point of purely local production, the fact that Wedgwood's produce had to get to market physically, and that there had to be orders and sales once (indeed before) they arrived, entailed a secondary level of organization. Wedgwood's success in establishing this was crucial to his commercial success.[36]

First, and leaving aside his strenuous efforts to improve canal and turnpike transportation to and from his factories, indeed in the North Midlands region as a whole,[37] we may note that Wedgwood established a vast and thorough system for distributing what he produced. This went beyond the usual wholesaling arrangements with merchant middlemen,[38] and beyond the partnership he entered into with Bentley himself.[39] He also went out of his way to secure direct retail access. Permanent showrooms were set up in London, Bath, Buxton, Liverpool, and Dublin, complemented by the living theme park of Etruria itself. He also introduced (in 1777) a system of travelling salesmen, 'riders', who crisscrossed the countryside and, armed with samples and pattern boxes, visited the private homes in the shires that his urban outlets could not penetrate. Overseas, supplied by Bentley's ships from Liverpool, a string of permanent agencies, each with its own network of salesmen and supplemented by travelling exhibits, was similarly set up; and access to these markets was also secured by working closely with British embassies, through whom Wedgwood lobbied vigorously both for tariff reduction and for special orders from the aristocratic circles in the host countries to which the ambassadors belonged.[40]

Even with effective distribution, however, Wedgwood produce could not simply sell itself. The more far-flung his operations the heavier the competition he had to face. In England, besides smaller manufacturers (and cheap imitators), he was rapidly up against such early industrial giants as Thomas Derby and, in the fashion accessories market, Matthew Boulton. In Europe, despite tariff barriers, he also had to compete with Dresden, Delft and Sèvres – not to mention all the other ornamental potteries and china-works that the princes and princelings of Europe had set up, and subsidized, to the greater glory of their courts and realms.[41] Nor was price and quality competition the only problem. The further these markets were from Wedgwood's home base, the more that demand for his own products had to depend not on direct impressions of their quality, nor even on word of mouth, but on a reputation indirectly communicated from afar.

In part, the distribution system itself provided the requisite promotional channel. Wedgwood's network of salesmen, salesrooms, and agencies served as a conduit not only for goods, but for information to customers about them. But such communication was not simply left to chance. Like Etruria, the London showrooms were visually laid out with great care and, a century before Macy's and *Galeries Lafayette*, Wedgwood was explicit about the importance of retail display. A great 'variety of setts of Vases should decorate the Walle' he wrote in a letter to Bentley (May 1767), and

> these articles may, every few days, be so altered, reversed and transformed so as to render the whole a new scene, even to the same Company, every time they shall bring their friends to visit us. *I need not tell you the very good effects this must produce, when business and amusement can be made to go hand in hand* [emphasis added].[42]

Agents, envoys, and salesmen were also provided with an illustrated catalogue; and with Bentley's help a sixty-page first edition was produced in 1773, followed by periodic revisions and further editions in French.[43] In 1790, his travelling salesmen were furnished with a 'Traveller's Book' which provided not only information about roads and routes but also detailed instructions on customer etiquette and approach.[44]

This carefully organized retail operation was also supplemented by direct advertising. While he eschewed handbills as too down-market, and for the same reason was reluctant to use paid advertising in the newspaper press (alongside ads by medical quacks and the like), he did encourage 'puffs' and even placed paid notices in both British and European publications drawing attention to new lines of ware, especially, as in 1774 and 1790, when linked to a special promotional event. In short, both in the staging and scripting of the selling process, and through the generation – both in-house and through the press – of additional publicity materials, Wedgwood developed a whole communicative strategy for competitively strengthening demand.

Nor was this – though it was certainly part of the picture – just a question of hyping, orally, in print and pictorially, the virtues of the products for sale. The sales drive was topped off, indeed led, by all the publicity assiduously cultivated around his showcase ornamental work. And the not-so-hidden commercial point of campaigns like those which surrounded the Russian service and the Portland Vase was not merely to gain attention. It was to ensure that this work's quality profiling of Wedgwood – enhanced by the way it identified him with the best in the classical tradition – rubbed off on his ordinary ware.

The overall aim, in short, was imagistic: to identify Wedgwood produce within the international tableware and ornaments market as the very acme of contemporary ceramic art. Everything communicated in the name of the company, from exhibitions to sales patter, was designed to impress that message. Indeed, not only was it the clear subtext of showroom presentation at the point of purchase. To complete the promotional circle, the same message was projected by the very appearance of the produce itself. In which respect, the vaunted quality which gave even the humblest Wedgwood artefacts cachet as possessions was more than just a matter of their being well made. Their perceived high quality was also a function of what their purity of line and texture, their elegant decoration, and their overall fidelity to the neo-classical spirit symbolized stylistically: as the very embodiment of up-to-date good taste.

At this level, the substance, shape and ornamentation of Wedgwood's plates and vases was continuous with how they were promoted for sale. And conversely: their sign-value as advertising was indistinguishable from what these products materially were. The promotional practices through which Wedgwood sought to enhance the demand for his goods was not at all, then, just an external complement to the primary activity of production. Through the intermediary of market-oriented design, production and promotion were integrally conjoined. Wherewith, in terms of pre-industrial methods, their order became reversed. Rather than produce, then sell, promotional requirements were taken account of before production even began. The goods that left the factory gate were already imaged to give them sales appeal, and this image was manufactured at the same time, and in the same act, as the manufacture of the goods themselves. In the Wedgwood organization, this was reflected in a decision flow in which new models were conceived, on the basis of customer feedback, from above, by Wedgwood and Bentley themselves; while the moulders, painters, etc, who actually performed the art work were subordinate cogs in the machine. The new Etruria heralded the arrival, then, not only of science-based production and the factory system but, in an equally significant break from the craft tradition, of artificial semiosis: the industrial manufacture of meaning and myth.

Artificial semiosis is a multiple practice which occurs at all the points in production, distribution, and exchange at which the commodity imaging process takes shape. These imaging sites can be thought of as ranged along a line whose two endpoints define both the object and mechanism of the whole promotional process. At one end – not only in the form of advertisements, but also through packaging and presentation, the staging of media events, the use of 'name' sponsorships, etc – we have the completely separated *promotional sign*. At the other, we have the composite entity comprised by the commodity itself, together with the significations imparted to it through advertising and design. Advertising transfers meanings on to a product from the outside, through repeated imagistic association. Through design, on the other hand, that same signification is stamped on to it materially. The result is a dual-character object, the *commodity-sign*, which functions in circulation both as an object-to-be-sold and as the bearer of a promotional message. As the latter, it serves to advertise both itself (on the shelf) and (wherever displayed) all the other produce to which, by brand and style, it is imagistically linked.

In this integrated system of production/promotion, the commodity and its double – the commodity-sign and the promotional sign – are deployed together in a mutually referring and self-confirming way. That interacting duality is condensed in Wedgwood's copy of the Portland Vase. But it has been rendered virtually invisible in the British Museum (where Wedgwood made no secret of wishing his work ultimately displayed[45]) by the copied vase's hallowing as a treasure of Heritage and Craft.[46] The outcome, if mystifying, is a triumph for its maker's commercial intent. In the face of this we do well to remind ourselves that the significance of the copied vase as a symbolic construct is only fully grasped when taken in conjunction with the more mundane articles it was originally displayed to promote. In this commercial setting, the remarkable interplay of commodity and sign which the copied vase incarnates makes it emblematic of something less exalted than what it means in the Museum, but arguably more real: the general form, from then till now, of the mass produced and mass marketed consumer good.

What was innovative in the Wedgwood matrix, it should be stressed, was neither the symbolic character of artefacts as such, nor the mere fact of their being advertised. As for the first, we need hardly go beyond the original Portland Vase itself to see that human artefacts have always had – and always been produced with the recognition that they have – cultural meanings which go beyond their purely practical use. Use itself can rarely be reduced to the utilitarian and is frequently, even in the most de-ritualized of societies, embedded in ceremonial. Nowhere is this more evident than in the genteel practices of eating and drinking which so many Wedgwood products were themselves designed to serve. Animals feed; human beings have meals. The novelty lies only – though it is a big only – in the manner in which, through manufacture, such symbolic associations came to be conferred. No longer, as in the staider practices of the pottery industry before its explosive mid-eighteenth-century growth, were the shapes and decorative appurtenances of domestic crockery just an idiosyncratic rendition of what was pre-given by custom in the context of a slow-moving stylistic tradition. Instead, in response not only to demand but also to the exigencies of supply, the semiotic and aesthetic fashioning of objects became instrumentalized: a matter for systematic and hard-headed calculation about what would maximize customer appeal and, therefore, sales. What Wedgwood and other early pioneers of mass production initiated was the rationalization of product symbolism through the promotionalization of design.

Whatever its (autonomizing) impact on the development of 'art', this loosening of aesthetic traditionalism in the mainstream of commercial production neither liberated individual creativity from the hold of convention nor freed it from the past. What did occur, though, was a decisive change in register. Under the aegis of a purely commercial logic, the process of cultural expression through objects became systematically instrumental and other-directed, a question of orienting to whatever, given the proclivities of the target market, was currently valued and desired.

The effects were ambiguous. Spurred by status competition among consumers, manufacturers' heightened attention to fashion accelerated the turnover of styles. Set against the decorative extravagance which had previously dominated taste, the recycled classicism of Wedgwood and Bentley must have seemed itself, at first, voguishly new. At the same time, what was presented and promoted in such terms was commercially constrained to keep within the bounds of majority values. Hence, as in Wedgwood's adoption of classicism with clothes on, conventionalism itself, if by a circuitous route, was still assured. Moreover, as the mood of archaic revivalism catered to by Wedgwood attests, the new could itself be represented via a sign for the old. So long as the market demanded time-honoured design, that is just what it continued to get. Of course, there was an important modification. If the late eighteenth-century ceramics market demanded tradition, what was delivered in its name – and exactly the same could be said of the apparently opposite ideas of the 'modern' and the 'new' which became stylistic hallmarks a century or so later – was not that tradition as a living force, but 'tradition' as a manufactured signifier: a 'tradition' which had no necessary or organic relation either to any wider process of symbolization, or to any particular object to which it was affixed.[47]

A similarly qualified point can be made about Wedgwood's innovative place in the history of advertising. Commercial communication between buyers and sellers is an inherent feature of commodity exchange and without it no market can function. Given any degree of competition at all, sellers must actively solicit customers by, in some fashion or another, hawking their wares. In this basic sense, the large-scale selling campaigns conducted by Wedgwood played exactly the same function as the come-ons, street cries, and haggling that swirled round the stalls of a medieval market or, still today, a Cairo bazaar. This is not to deny the considerable differences between them. It is just to emphasize that the histories of advertising and commodities completely coincide, and that what distinguished Wedgwood from his pre-industrial predecessors was not the sheer fact of promotion, but the type and modality of promotion deployed.

Even here there were continuities. The marketing of Wedgwood produce still involved oral salesmanship at the local point of purchase. However, this was now orchestrated as part of a system which was organized from above; and in that system's dispersed communicative reach the flow of product information was anything but face-to-face. It was, that is to say, mediatized, i.e. converted into fixed forms which could be mass disseminated from a distance: self-explicitly, through sales brochures, newspaper ads, and free media; but also, tacitly, through the use of stylized and standardized goods (in conjunction with one-off specials) as a mass medium in itself. What this meant, in either case, was the propagation of promotional messages which could not be answered back. There is no way to interact with an objectified image nor to intervene in the construction of an ad. Feedback from consumers can only occur passively, through revealed preference and market research – areas whose eventual rationalization Wedgwood's own more intuitive and non-statistical approach to demand analysis plainly foreshadowed.

An important corollary of mediatization was that promotional discourse was set free from the immediacies of buying and selling to develop a life of its own. And on this basis, as advertising, packaging, and public relations, promotion became more systematically involved in the definition to consumers of what the proffered goods were. In turn, this opened up the possibility of pre-defining what needs and desires they might satisfy, and what, through the inescapably fictive process of representation, they could be taken to mean. In sum: by becoming a distinct and strategized level of business practice, by becoming unilateral and communicatively detached, and finally by re-involving itself with production through product design, promotion was able to become an independently acting force in the social construction of commodities on their whole symbolic side.

The commercialization of craft-work and the development of promotion were inherent tendencies of a commodification process which itself spanned centuries. The change that came about in the industrial revolution as a result of the geographical expansion of the market and the inception of mass production was nevertheless decisive. Symbolic manufacture and advertising fused. This was the change signalled by Wedgwood's Etruria, whose very name bespeaks what that change implies: that in the consumer goods sector of industrial capitalism, image-making becomes a central and integrated element of the production process itself. In this advanced form, that is as artificial semiosis, promotion shows itself as a strangely transformative, even engulfing, practice. What enters production, enters commodities. It is no innocent addition. Both by transferring cultural associations on to products propagandistically, and by inscribing them into their actual body, the promotion of mass-produced consumer goods transfigures what it ostensibly helps only to sell. What industrial capitalism ushers in, then, is not just more goods, more commodities. It introduces, in increasing plenitude, *a new kind of product* whose peculiarity it is to be indissolubly linked to a new kind of cultural expression as well: mass-mediated advertising in symbiosis with the commodity-sign.

To this, finally, there is an important rider at the level of social structure as a whole. The birth of commodity imaging in the cradle of early industrialism heralded the beginnings of a change in the very constitution of market society. It is a change which went unnoticed by Adam Smith and was ignored by Marx as well. Only at a much more advanced stage of capitalist development have its larger implications begun to be apparent.

Chief among these is that the expanded role of promotion, indeed of the circulation process as a whole, has led to a mutation in the relation between economic 'base' and cultural 'superstructure' such that the latter has become absorbed into the former – as the zone of circulation and exchange – while the former – as the zone of production – has itself become a major cultural apparatus.

Notes

1. Until the late nineteenth century, and following a legend built up in the Barberini family, the Portland Vase was thought to date from three centuries later. The story was that it had been discovered in Monte de Grano, outside Naples, inside the sarcophagus of Emperor Alexander Severus, who died in 235 AD, and that it was, in fact, a funerary urn containing the ashes of the Emperor and his mother. For a detailed account of the vase's actual provenance, and of the legend which obscured it, see Mankowitz (1952: 51–60).

2. Other members of the original series are currently displayed at the Wedgwood Museum in Barlaston, Staffordshire.

3. The story is told in Meteyard (1865, Vol. II: 575 et seq.), Thomas (1971: 131–2), Forty (1986: 16 et seq.), and Mankowitz (1952: 19–34).

4. Wedgwood is now credited as being correct in his surmise that the original vase was made in a double process in which the basic body, of blue-black glass, was coated with a second layer of white glass which was, in turn, cut away to leave the white figures which surround it in paper-thin relief. See Mankowitz (1952: 17–18).

5. Susan Buck-Morss (1989) has less misleadingly translated Benjamin's title for this essay as 'The work of art in an age of technical reproducibility'.

6. To compound matters, the original today is a complete restoration and its continuity with the original original (as it were) a matter for scholarly debate. In 1845, the latter was smashed to pieces in its Museum display case by a drunken artist, William Lloyd. It was restored to its current state on the basis of drawings and plaster models made of it while it had still been intact. During this first period of repair, the British Museum had substituted yet another copy, this one made from a mould by Giovanni Pichler. Wedgwood's own copy was rejected for this task on the grounds that it 'is only a modern copy, and not cast from the original' (see Mankowitz, 1952: 16).

7. Having demolished the idea that the vase was an incinerary urn, Mankowitz (1952: 56–9) supports Erasmus Darwin's late eighteenth-century speculation that it was probably used in the rituals attaching to an esoteric cult like that of the Eleusinian mysteries.

8. For a listing of the various theories, see Mankowitz (1952: 55–60).

9. It was the invention of the pyrometer, a bar of layered alloys whose differential rates of expansion made it possible to measure high temperatures, which earned Wedgwood his election to the Royal Society. He published two papers on the instrument, in 1782 and 1783, and it was following the publication of the second that he was made a Fellow. See Meteyard (1865, Vol. II: 465).

10. For Wedgwood's economic significance as a pioneer of the industrial revolution see Thomas (1971: 104–32), McKendrick (1960) and McKendrick et al. (1982).

11. Letter from Josiah Wedgwood to William Hamilton, June 1786, cited in Meteyard (1865, Vol. I: 578–9).

12. Thomas (1971: 131) says twenty; Meteyard (1865, Vol. I: 595) cites a figure of about fifty.

13. 26 July 1790. Cited in Thomas (1971: 113–14).

14. In noting the unprofitability of ornamental wares, Thomas (1971: 130), however, competely misses this commercial point: 'It is surprising that a business man like Wedgwood had not yet learnt [!] the doctrine for effective and progressive salesmanship – to sell at lower

prices the increasing output of mass production, and still maintain the quality of the product.' Compare this with Wedgwood's own argument for maintaining his expensive ornamental wares production in the face of cheap, imitative, competition: 'This would certainly procure us the good will of our best customers, and place us in a very advantageous light to the Public eye. We should no doubt be esteemed as *antique*, and as great *curiositys* as any of the vases we fabricate, and perhaps upon the whole, this scheme might bring us as much *profitt* as *loss*.' Letter from Wedgwood to Bentley, 27 September 1769, cited in Finer and Savage (1965: 81).

15. The site was opened up in the mid-eighteeenth century and first visited by Robert Adam in 1755. For this visit and its impact on Adam's architectural ideas, see Fleming (1962: 155–6 et seq.), and Kelly(1965: 17–20).

16. For an account of Palladian principles, and how these were modified in the neo-classical movement of the late eighteenth century, see Kelly (1965: 15–17).

17. It was 'Wedgwood's genius', notes Meteyard (1865, Vol. I: 441) in a characteristically gushing passage, 'to unite the principles of utility and beauty'.

18. Letter from Wedgwood to Bentley, 23 August 1772, cited in Finer and Savage (1965: 131).

19. According to the current British Museum description, the figures disporting themselves under a winged Cupid are now thought to be Peleus, on the left, Doris or Tetheus in the centre, and Nereno or Oceanus on the right.

20. 'It will be absolutely necessary for us to mark them, and advertise that mark.' Letter from Wedgwood to Bentley, 7 June 1773, cited in McKendrick et al. (1982: 117).

21. The vogue for Etruria particularly followed the publication of Hamilton's *Etruscan Antiquities*, concerning which Mankowitz (1952: 77–8) notes: 'The antiquities were not Etruscan at all, but the name can be used to cover almost any classical find.'

22. The Etruria factory was built in 1768–9, and Etruria Hall in 1779. The opening is described in Meteyard (1865, Vol. II: 112–4).

23. Bentley, a Liverpool-based exporter who specialized in the American trade, was also an art connoisseur whose antennae were finely tuned to the shifting currents of fashionable taste. For Bentley's role in Wedgwood's enterprise see Forty (1986: 22–4), and Meteyard (1865, Vol. I: 305–7).

24. 'Vases are furniture for a chimney-piece. Bough-pots for a hearth, under a slab or marble table. I think they can never be used instead of another; and I apprehend one reason why we have not made our dressing flower-pots to please has been by adapting them to chimney-pieces.' Wedgwood to Bentley, 29 July 1772, cited in Meteyard (1865, Vol. II: 157).

25. In such work, Wedgwood's main sources were illustrated books: the Comte de Caylus's *Recueil d'Antiquités*, Winckelmann's *Gedanken uber die Nachahmung der griechischen Werke*, and D'Hancaville's guide to the Hamilton collection. He also despatched modellers to Italy to make copies direct (Kelly, 1965, 18–19).

26. Josiah Wedgwood to Dr Darwin, 28 June 1789; cited in Meteyard (1865, Vol. II: 524–5).

27. 'I speak from experience in Female taste, without which I should have made but a poor figure among my Potts; not one of which of any consequence is finished without the approbation of my Sally.' Josiah Wedgwood to Thomas Bentley, 8 June 1770; cited in Meteyard (1865, Vol. II: 156).

28. Wedgwood to Flaxman, 11 February 1790; cited in Meteyard (1865, Vol. II: 589).

29. For a discussion of Wedgwood's adaptation of neo-classical style to the production demands of standardization see Forty (1986: 29–41).

30. As with the later Portland Vase exhibition, admission was by ticket, and the opening was advertised in the press. Meteyard (1865, Vol. II: 293) mentions ads in the *St James Gazeteer*, the *St James Chronicle* and the *Public Advertiser*. For an account of Wedgwood's Russian service, which is in the Hermitage in Leningrad, see Williamson (1909).

31. Wedgwood well understood the importance of such prestige naming. '*Fashion* is infinitely superior to *merit* in many respects and it is plain from a thousand instances that if you have a favourite child and wish the public to fondle and take notice of it you have only to make choice of proper sponsers [sic].' Josiah Wedgwood to Thomas Bentley, 19 June 1779 [emphasis in original]; cited in McKendrick et al. (1982: 100).

32. See Thomas (1971: 125–6). Most Staffordshire potters favoured the lowering of prices, but Wedgwood rejected this: 'Low prices will beget contempt, neglect and disuse, and there is an end to trade' (letter from Josiah Wedgwood to Thomas Bentley, 14 April 1773). Of course, the principle was even more important for explicitly luxury produce. Later that year, in another letter to Bentley, Wedgwood further noted: 'A great price is at first necessary to make the vases esteemed Ornaments for Palaces' (Wedgwood to Bentley, 19 June 1773, cited in McKendrick et al. 1982: 106).

33. This is the principal thesis of the studies in McKendrick et al. (1982).

34. But without much capital. His father, though a master potter, was not prosperous. Josiah was willed £20, but after Josiah senior's death in 1739 it is not clear that his son ever got it.

35. As an outgrowth of a lobby to maintain tariffs on Irish imports, for example, Wedgwood was instrumental in establishing the General Chamber of Manufacturers in 1784.

36. For Wedgwood's role in the improvement of transportation in north-west England see Burton (1976: 52–60) and Meteyard (1865, Vol. I: 428 et seq.).

37. See especially McKendrick (1960).

38. Hulme and Walmesley, Boulton and Fothergill, Bentley and Bardman were the main ones. See Thomas (1971: 120–1).

39. According to its terms Wedgwood and Bentley split the profits of ornamental ware production 50/50, with Josiah's nephew Thomas having a similar partnership with regard to 'usefull Ware'. The latter was defined in a letter Josiah wrote to Thomas Bentley on 3 September 1770: 'May not usefull fare be comprehended under this simple definition, of such vessels as are *made use of at meals*?' [emphasis in original]. Cited in Meteyard (1865, Vol. II: 192–3).

40. In the lead-up to the famous banquet service order from Catherine the Great, he reported: 'I have waited on Lord Cathcart, the Russian Ambassador, to bring about the plan we settled of introducing our manufacture at the Court of Russia. The Ambassador and his Lady came into my measures with the utmost readiness, and I am to get done a plate by way of a specimen with the Russian arms and an edging round the plate.' Josiah Wedgwood to Matthew Boulton, 19 March 1768, cited in Thomas (1971: 114).

41. For the porcelain and pottery mania of the early eighteenth century see Plumb (1973) and Thomas (1971: 104–7). In England, one factor stimulating the demand for tableware was the growing popularity of tea. Between 1728 and 1767, according to Thomas's figures, annual tea consumption went from 1,493,626 lb to 3,762,800 lb. By 1833 it had reached 31,829,620 lb.

42. Cited in Meteyard (1865, Vol. II: 33).

43. According to Meteyard (1865, Vol. II: 76, 355) the idea had been suggested by Matthew Boulton as early as 1767. In the course of a correspondence about advertising Boulton had advised 'printed sheets containing engraved examples of various articles' plus 'price-lists and other particulars'.

44. McKendrick et al. (1982: 115–16). On the outfitting of special 'travelling vans' see Thomas (1971: 120–21).

45. See Meteyard (1865, Vol. II: 158).

46. The same effect is achieved in the display of the vase, together with other works, in the Wedgwood Museum. There it is inserted into the story of the Wedgwood company from the beginning till now. The company itself was bought by the Waterford Group in the early 1980s, but the new owners had every interest in perpetuating the mystique of the original marque.

47. For the invention of tradition in this culturally constructed sense, see Hobsbawm (1983).

2
ADVERTISING AS IDEOLOGY

The steady trend in advertising is to manifest the product as an integral part of large social purposes and processes.

Marshall McLuhan (1967: 202)

White soap

An English Pears' soap advertisement of 1910[1] is divided into two panels. The top one shows a little black boy in a cast-iron bath tub about to be soaped and scrubbed by a young white nursemaid. In the panel below, her look of happy amazement registers the effects of what has evidently been a miracle. Where Pears has been applied the boy's skin has changed colour from black to white.

To the advertiser and audience of the time, we can well imagine that this would seem just a harmless figure of speech (not without a certain humour) which graphically presses home – look, it works! – the product's excellence as soap. Eighty years later it is hard to get past something else. The ad's selling point relies entirely on a casual, and taken-for-granted, identification of whiteness with cleanliness and blackness with dirt.

Racism, as we have learned to call it, has historically come in many guises. Here it is protective, British Imperial, Kiplingesque. The rule of white civilization over the less fortunate is likened to an act of charity in which a substitute-mother supervises the bathing of a friendly little piccaninny. No accident, of course, that the ministering angel at the centre of this touching little scene (perhaps the boy is a foundling) is dressed so vaguely in terms of her social station: she could be anything from a domestic servant to Lady Bountiful herself. For the ad is aimed at 'the British housewife', both middle- and working-class. The point of the Pears campaign was to promote the product as an everyday household staple for use by all in the British market. The white pride Pears appeals to similarly cuts across class lines. Indeed, it offers the subordinate a compensatory sense of superiority – which they can express, among other ways, by buying, often, the proffered soap.

I cite this example not in order to make an obvious point about the prevalence of racial prejudice in pre-1914 Britain. But because the very obviousness (to us) of the assumptions on which the advertisement relies makes it a vivid illustration of the way in which the brand-imaging of mass produced consumer goods links them symbolically to the whole world of social values. That relation, we should immediately note, is two-way. Not only does the ad use the ideology of white superiority to sell soap. To accept the selling message is to accept the values it presupposes. By representing such values as just part of the visual furniture the ad naturalizes them, and to that extent reinforces their hold.

We have seen something similar in the imaging operation conducted by Wedgwood. There, however, the imperialist associations which were transferred, via references to classical antiquity, on to his pottery, were only tacitly expressed. They blurred, as style, into the aesthetics of the commodity-object itself. In the Pears' case the ideological element is blatant and stands on its own. What makes that element so easy to see, moreover, is that (official) attitudes to racial difference have changed. Today, such an ad could not be shown. Not only would its pitch fail to have broad appeal, it would be positively divisive. Under most Western jurisdictions it would even be illegal, violating laws against discrimination, not to mention new definitions of the nation-state as a 'multicultural community'. The bias of contemporary advertising is much harder to spot. In line with an identical marketing logic, the values it expresses are updated and, in a moving present, continuous with our own. Benetton's 'Colours of the World' campaign makes a liberal virtue out of its cosmopolitan ambition to capture a global market for its kiddie fashion clothes. For the affluent, new, middle-class stratum at which it is aimed, its vapid, feel-good colour-blindness will not, perhaps, seem ideological at all.

But 'ideology' is an ambiguous and contested word, so I must immediately make two things clear. The first is semantic. In the present context, 'ideology' refers simply to that level of reality, at once individual and collective, subjective and objective, at which people orient meaningfully to their world.[2] At the social level, this means symbols and cosmologies, values, norms and ideals, plus the systems and partial systems into which these are culturally arranged. At the level of the individual: cognitive and affective maps on the one hand, and modes of self-identification on the other. Such a definition is both universal – ideology as an irreducible element of all collective and individual life – and neutral. It carries no assumption about illusoriness, nor does it pejoratively counterpose ideology to illumination, science or truth. Nor is ideology exclusively identified, here, with dominant or dominated consciousness. Oppositional and critical perspectives from whatever quarter are themselves forms of ideology. Nor, finally, is there any suggestion that the values and symbols which make up a society's public ideological life are necessarily or exclusively to be understood as the expressions of particular class interests. This is to leave open, for example, the relation between orientations to property and those towards sexuality, gender, technology, and death. If the word 'orientation' could form compounds in English, and if it could swiftly call to mind all the dimensions – moral, aesthetic, political, class, sexual, etc – in which individual and collective orientation is framed, then it would do as well.

My intent in neutralizing the term, however, is not to ditch altogether the Marx-derived model of culture and society to which the purged associations are tied. It is rather – and this is my second point – to facilitate an analysis of the relation of advertising to ideology, and of both to the maintenance of capitalist order, which can take account of the particular way that advertising articulates with social values and, through that, with the wider processes of social reproduction. As a myriad examples would show, there is no question that imagistic promotion is value-laden,[3] and that the values expressed are in some sense socially conservative. The question is how and why.

Among recent writers, perhaps the boldest attempt to examine the bias of advertising in terms of this larger problematic is Stuart Ewen's *Captains of Consciousness* (1976).[4] Ewen traces the acquisition by advertising of a conservative ideological function – which he takes to have been decisive for the maintenance of American capitalism ever since – to its establishment as a full-scale industry in the 1910s and 1920s. For him, the dramatic rise of advertising in that period was both economically caused and economically necessary. It was, indeed, an essential aspect of capitalism's transition to an advanced, corporate stage. Most immediately, Ewen links the establishment of the advertising industry to the introduction of assembly line production on the one hand, and to the boom in the production of consumer durables, from cars to fridges, on the other. In this, he follows the line of analysis pursued by Galbraith and others,[5] according to which the new capitalism required 'demand management'. However, he takes the argument two steps further.

First, stimulating sufficient demand to absorb the (costly) new cornucopia required not only massive publicity but also radical changes in household habits, spending patterns, and family values. The family had to become a centre of consumption rather than production, attitudes to thrift had to change, and a premium was placed on being modern and young. To help consumers adapt – and so *become* consumers – advertisers were obliged to address directly the cultural turmoil that urbanization and the techno-economic transformation of the household were provoking on the domestic front. In short, by becoming crucial (in tandem with consumer credit) to the heightening and maintenance of effective demand, advertising was driven to adopt a pedagogical stance. At the same time, the introduction of mass production – and linked to that, of Taylorism and 'scientific management' – transformed work relations and provoked severe industrial unrest. As a counter, advertising provided the captains of industry with an ideal propaganda vehicle. Its every message pointed to the consumer affluence which mass production promised. Through such blandishments, the disaffected of the 1920s could be persuaded to abandon their dreams of worker-controlled production in favour of safer, more individualist aspirations. And if the real-life realization of these proved elusive, at least their psychological substitute could be provided in the promoted patina of purchased goods.

Overall, then, the commercial requirements of cultural adaptation and the political requirements of social control combined to make advertising strategic not only in the management of consumer demand, but in the management of consciousness. For the same reasons, moreover, advertisers (both agencies and manufacturers) were led to become self-conscious about this role as well.

At a time when semiological approaches to advertising had eclipsed attention both to the historicity of promotional texts and to their contextual dimension,[6] Ewen's historical emphasis was refreshing. He certainly demonstrated an uncanny degree of fit between the Youth/ Glamour/Success values prominent in 1920s advertising and the contemporary exigencies of maintaining capitalist control. Yet his overall formula for what happened – that the captains of industry became the 'captains of consciousness'[7] – is haunted by a mechanical model of how ideological hegemony operates. This model has never fitted well the case of quasi-autonomous institutions like churches and, despite the less mediated class ties, it is no less misleading here. It seems to imply that because corporate owners and managers use advertising commercially, they do so politically; and that behind the ideological bias of their ads lies a directing intelligence which seeks deliberately to secure loyalty to the system they rule.[8]

This is not to deny that, on occasion, corporate sponsors do directly propagandize on behalf of their sectional or general class interests. In Canada, one thinks of the early 1980s oil company campaign against nationalization, or the use of billboards and customer billings during the 1980 Quebec referendum campaign. More recently, British newspaper readers have been treated to a spate of one-pagers identifying the Anglo-American Corporation (which monopolizes the gold mines and much else in South Africa) with the cause of a democratic non-racial South Africa. But these instances, like the anti-Bolshevik panic of the early 1920s to which Ewen's own study refers, are situationally specific. It is hard to identify the mediating mechanisms through which such considerations could be routinely introduced into the selling process (as Lenin would say) 'from the outside'. Normally, and in the overwhelming majority of instances, brand-name ads, like all others, have one single aim: to sell commodities. So whatever seemingly surplus signifying material they contain needs to be understood, in the first instance, in terms of how they discharge that promotional function.

As a major (if not, today, *the* major) institution for the circulation and distribution of ideological values, modern advertising marks, in fact, a crucial departure. Unlike previously dominant institutions of this kind, like churches, schools, and the ceremonials of Law and State, its raison d'etre is not as a socializing or propagandizing agency at all. Those who shape and transmit its symbolic material have no intrinsic interest in what, ideologically, that material might mean. Advertising is an entirely instrumental process. You promote to sell. You sell to get money, in turn to get more money or else to exchange for something else. In this, the mobilization of affect through the invocation of values is strictly a tool, an incidental side-effect of what advertising is instrumental for. The task of unravelling the advertising industry's wider relation to the processes of social reproduction and control must begin, then, with its immediate economic role. That is: with the way in which advertising's first-order function as promotion leads it to engage with the values, norms, goals, and dreams of those to whom it is addressed.

For ease of exposition, and to provide a concrete point of reference, I want to pursue this question by examining, in detail, a one-page glossy for Eves cigarettes* which appeared, among other places, in the July 1975 issue of *Cosmopolitan*. Besides its general representativeness as an instance of TV-age commodity imaging, this ad holds particular interest because the values it plays with touch on one of our period's most sensitive cultural issues: the status and identity of women. To look at how post-1960s advertising has dealt with gender is evidently a strategic point of entry into the way in which it has come to represent, and re-configure, the ideological world as a whole. From the point of view of cultural dynamics, moreover, an examination of how advertising has responded to a situation of deep value conflict, as opposed to one of unruffled consensus, can tell us a great deal about the kind of ideological intervention which advertising, precisely *as* advertising, is compelled to make. The fact, finally, that the ad is both culturally marked as belonging to a previous moment ('the seventies') yet still thematically resonant (the gender issue has not been resolved) enhances its exemplary value. The historicity of its codings will be plain, while not so starkly that a hermeneutic chasm has to be crossed in order to disclose what, in context, they ideologically mean.

---

* Regrettably, readers will have to imagine what the Eve advertisement looks like on the basis of the description below, since the Liggett Group Inc. (the parent company and owner of the ad's copyright) point-blank refused permission to reproduce it. Liggett was the only company organization which responded in this way, an exceptionalism which evidently reflects the strategic dilemma facing the industry rather than any concern about the specific impact of its appearance here on sales. The strength of the anti-smoking movement (which, for all its benefits, is linked to a wider 'health'-based authoritarianism to which I do not subscribe) has presumably made the company hyper-sensitive to any publicity for its publicity which it does not directly control. By a curious coincidence, on the very day that Liggett's letter of refusal was received, the Quebec Superior Court, in response to a suit brought by a group of cigarette manufacturers, struck down as unconstitutional a federal Canadian law banning tobacco advertising in the Canadian mass media. The legal ground given was that the law violated the Charter of Rights and Freedoms by unreasonably restricting free speech.

The selling pitch

While combining elements of information and art, advertising, strictly speaking, is neither. It belongs, rather, to that special branch of communicative arts the ancient world called rhetoric.[9] The factual knowledge which ads transmit, and the aesthetics of their construction, are subordinate ends in the teleology of salesmanship. In this respect it makes no difference whether advertising employs rational or irrational arguments. The point is always the same: to persuade potential customers that the publicized product or service is worth at least the price of purchase. This is the underlying logic of any sales pitch; and if we want to understand how an ad can simultaneously function as an ideological message, we must examine how such a logic can generate statements pitched in that register which at once derive from, but transcend, the purely commercial relation between consumer and producer.

Let us begin by considering, then, how advertising operates in its most rationally transparent form. That is: in the limit case, where the ad consists entirely of take-it-or-leave-it factual information. Take, for example, the following classified ad for a second-hand car: '78 Rabbit, champagne, 4 dr., AM/FM, 5 position stick shift, 46,000 ml., cert., $4,900. Tel. ...–.... Days'.[10] The text consists entirely of precise technical data about the car, its conditions of sale, its price (subject, presumably, to negotiation) and how to contact the vendor. The only claims made are empirical. Indeed the complete absence of rhetorical flourish at first conceals that it is rhetoric at all. Yet even here the information presented has both a demonstrative meaning (notice this car: it's for sale!) and an evidential function within an argument (to the effect that, at the stated price, this car is worth buying).

To simplify, let us leave aside the ad's attention-seeking aspect and just concentrate on its character as an argument. Implicit in the data presented, first, is a minimum commercial claim: that the satisfaction to be derived from purchasing this 1978 Rabbit, by those in the market for a second-hand car of this type, is greater than the potential satisfaction foregone by the money and effort that would have to be expended to buy it. Evidently, the proposition has a subjective component, and its proof could only be established *post facto*. But there is a further step. To be effective, the ad must also position the advertised commodity favourably against the competition. In the first instance, this means other second-hand cars, many of which the reader can check out for him or herself in all the other ads on the page. But the vendor has also to contend with substitute products (such as new cars, or motorbikes), and indirectly, as well, with unrelated discretionary purchases which compete for the same purchasing dollar.

From this trivial instance we can already see the outlines of a more general formula; one that applies, indeed, to all advertising, including the kind which substitutes symbolic valorization for hard information about how the product performs. To use the language of marginalist economics: an ad for a product will generally seek to persuade us that the net utility of purchasing it is higher than what is foregone through purchase, and at least equal to the satisfaction to be derived from making alternative and equivalent expenditures.

Let us now turn to the much more complicated case represented by the Eves ad: an ad that operates, not with performance and price data spelled out in cold print, but evocatively, through an emotively laden combination of pictures and slogans.

Consider, first, the ad's pictorial elements. A single scene covers the page. In the foreground, and dominating the left-hand side, is a fresh-faced conventionally attractive brunette, in her middle-to-late twenties. She is kneeling on a sandy beach with one hand resting coquettishly on her head, which is cocked to one side as she flashes a Farrah Fawcett smile. Her other hand is holding up, between index finger and thumb, an unlit cigarette. On the right, larger than life and perched on a mound of leafy shrubs, two fresh packs of Eve lean together. The one marked 'Menthol' is unopened, while the other containing 'Filters' has three cigarettes protruding, invitingly, upwards. The same motif of wild flowers which decorates their filter ends (olive green, flecked with yellow and red), is clearly visible on the outside of each pack. It also reappears in the material of her sun-hat and blouse, which is open at the top and casually tied at the waist. The Eve floral design stands out sharply against the dazzling white of the woman's other clothes – the whiteness of which is mirrored most brightly of all in the dazzle of her smile.

Across the top of the picture a caption proclaims: 'There's a little Eve in every woman.' In smaller print, nestling next to the exposed filter tips and extending over the two packs of Eve, we further read:

Try today's Eve.
Flowers on the outside.
Flavor on the inside.

In still smaller print – and in obedience to government regulations – a white box in the bottom left-hand corner carries the message: 'Warning: The Surgeon-general Has Determined That Smoking Is Dangerous To Your Health.' As the eye moves along the bottom edge, and further to the right, it encounters a final statement, printed so small as to be almost invisible. 'Eve Filters and Menthol. 18mg "tar". 1.3mg nicotine per cigarette by FTC Method.'

As an expression of sales rhetoric, this ad differs from the classified in three major respects.

First, in what it omits: namely, any reference to price or indeed to any other aspect of purchase. Given the widespread retail availability of cigarettes, and the regional standardization of their price, such information would doubtless be redundant. But as with many other consumer goods, price-competition between brands is in any case subsidiary to the struggle to establish the product's unique selling feature. It is through this that Eve seeks to position itself against all the other (and similar) brands available to the relevant market (women smokers). In addition to the emphasis such promotion places on the image of the product, the absence of any reference to its exchange-value eliminates as well the only sign by which it is distinguished as a commodity. The commercial nexus which every advertising text presupposes, and which was explicitly acknowledged in the classified ad, is here completely elided.

Secondly, the Eve ad describes the product as an object of human value in a strikingly different way. The second-hand Rabbit is presented as an ensemble of specific performance characteristics (product-type, mileage, accessories, etc). The only non-material attributes referred to (and at that, only by implication) are those already associated in the buyer's mind with the brand-name 'Rabbit' itself. Since the symbolic aura of an economy car (unlike that of antiques and design classics) evaporates with time, and second-hand ones are primarily evaluated according to their mechanical and physical condition, we may say that the mythical resonance of the object presented in the classified is minimal. In contrast, the Eve ad portrays its product primarily as an idea. Eves are shown as the embodiment of a certain – mid-1970s, socially independent but safely fashionable and ideologically compromising – conception of femininity.

What references there are to the product's tangible properties (for example as a relaxant) are subordinated to a display of its psycho-cultural significance. The woman in the picture has not even lit the cigarette she is holding. Indeed, besides showing us that Eves come in two varieties, regular and menthol, the only technical data in the ad are hidden in the tiny black print that runs unobtrusively along the lower edge. More detailed information would be superfluous. Unlike the second-hand Rabbit, which is one of a kind, but like what that car originally was, a mechanically reproduced member of a homogenized series, Eves cigarettes are all individually the same. Moreover, American cigarette tobacco comes in standard types and flavours. For consumers, the only material difference between brands is in the amounts of (carcinogenous) tar and (psychotropic/ addictive) nicotine they contain. As it happens, Eves have a comparatively high tar-to-nicotine ratio, so there is good reason to bury this information at the bottom of the page. It should be added that by the mid-1970s, while tobacco advertising in the mass media was not yet banned, the performance characteristics of tobacco were indelibly associated in the public mind with disease and death. Except where low tar was a distinct selling feature, then, cigarette manufacturers had no interest in mentioning the physical content of their products, and only did so (as in the Eves ad) because legally compelled.

Thirdly, the two ads differ markedly in their modes of address. The classified is strictly impersonal. Its dry factuality is aimed at those with a prior interest in the kind of information it conveys, and the ad addresses potential customers solely at this level. To filter out the audience and attract the selective attention of those really in the market, the Rabbit ad quite naturally abstracts from all the social, cultural, and personal characteristics of the individuals who comprise it. With just one article for sale, a specification of its performance characteristics is all that is needed to connect with relevant others. With the Eves ad the situation is reversed. Everybody and nobody might want the product, since there is materially so little to differentiate it. The cigarette advertiser is thus moved to make a personalized appeal on behalf of a product which is itself infused with all the pathos, and distinctiveness, of a myth. In fact, these strategies converge. The self invited to try Eves is the same as the one whose fantasy ideal is projected on to the product; and she is also the same as the woman who smiles back to us, in person, from the mirror-like surface of the page.[11]

The tone of this appeal is warm, not to say seductive. The image of me/ you-as-Woman-as-Eve is alluringly portrayed by the product presenter[12] whose eyes meet ours. As the ad suggestively remarks, 'There's a little Eve in every woman'; and it is always easy to fall for an idealized image of ourselves. The Eve myth itself sanctions this narcissism. Given our sinful inheritance, it is only natural that we should all enjoy succumbing, now and again, to a little temptation.

In short, in order to summon the relevant audience and persuade them to try the product, the Eve ad sets out to construct a personal and social identity for its potential users. And it simultaneously grafts this identity – 'Today's Eve' – on to the daintily decorated cigarettes which bear that name. It should be added that the glamorization of a gender identity which equates femininity with self-love and moral weakness rests on giving it social as well as sex appeal. In the true spirit of *Cosmopolitan*'s New Woman, the Eve figure in the ad is independent, self-assured, affluent, and white. At leisure on the beach, she exhibits all the conventional signs of status and success. Thus the ad's alter ego is addressed simultaneously in class and gender terms. To be successful, chic and still, in the traditional sense, feminine, smoke Eves. Of course such a message speaks mainly to aspiration. Really independent women with professional or business careers would not get very far if their development were arrested at the stage of coy self-indulgence and pretty flowers.

Each of these respects in which the Eve ad differs from the classified – no reference to price, mythicizing the product, and reliance on psycho-cultural appeal – has the same general effect. In terms of the basic sales argument (buy this, it's worth it), they are all so many ways of increasing the relative desirability of the commodity for those reached by the text.

Symbolic advertising does more, then, even on the economic plane, than just facilitate, through persuasion, the circulation of commodities. To the extent that the commodity is successfully (re-)coded as a desirable psycho-ideological sign, imagistic promotion increases the symbolic gratification to be gained from consuming/having/displaying the product. It thus enhances the product's actual use-value.[13] In this, of course, Eve is not alone. Its competitors, indeed all major advertisers, are engaged in a similar effort. Whatever the competitive edge this gives them, however, either against one another or, collectively, against new market entrants, it may be wondered what the aggregate effect really is. On the one hand, investing consumer goods with symbolic significance increases, vis-a-vis the unbranded, the subjective worth of brand-name products as such. But on the other, systematically associating cultural symbols with the profane world of commerce also cheapens those symbols as a medium of communicative exchange. If Coke is the 'real thing', what is 'real'?

The ideological dimension: a model

All advertising, even the most informational and rationalistic, is ideological, if only in the formal sense that it places its audience in the role of buyer/consumer and seeks to dispose that audience favourably towards what is for sale. But ads of the Eve type, which infuse their products with cultural and psychological appeal, also impinge on more particular dimensions of their addressees' sense of identity, orientation, and purpose. The commodity they project as the object of desire is simultaneously presented as a cultural symbol charged with social significance; and the ego they seek to engage as the subject of desire is induced to adopt the socio-cultural identity attributed to those who already use the product. Such advertising is thus ideological in a concrete sense as well. And it is so just by virtue of the selling pitch it employs.

If we want to grasp the place of ideology in the modern imagistic ad, then, we must examine how, and with what orientational implications, its text lines up an *attributed consumer-ego* (the 'you' to which the ad speaks) with a *symbolized commodity*. In fact, these two terms decompose into three. The product for sale is represented in such a way that it doubles as a signifier for the special significance with which it is promotionally endowed. Thus 'Eve' is both a cigarette that we can buy and smoke, and a sign with mythical and psychological value. The symbolized commodity in which they are united is a textual achievement, that is, a fiction. It is, moreover, a fiction which seeks to validate itself by becoming a matter of cultural fact. In a particular advertising text, the symbolic meaning the ad wishes to associate with a product may be signified by the same signifiers – for example the brand-name, or a picture of the decorated package – as those which denote the product itself. More often these meanings are also independently represented, as through the beach scene into which the Eve presenter is set. Nevertheless, there are always two referents, and two signifying operations: one for the product and a second for what it is made to mean. It is the peculiar genius of imagistic advertising to fuse, and confuse, these two meanings. But however condensed and cross-referenced they may be, they must be prised apart if their arranged promotional union is to be deciphered for what it is.[14]

Just as the symbolized commodity is an irreducible duality of product and sign, so the ego projected as needing/desiring/esteeming it necessarily

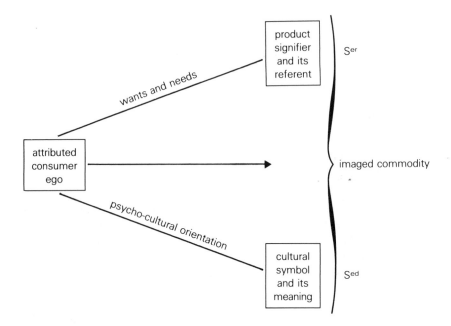

Figure 2.1   *Terms and relations of imagistic ads*

combines elements of orientation towards each of these respects in which it holds significance and value. Altogether, then, there are three fundamental relations to disentangle: (1) between the commodity and its artificial symbolic meaning; (2) between the attributed self and the (pre-symbolized) object it is supposed to want or need; and (3) between that same self and the frame of reference within which the object (through promotion) is symbolically valorized. These three terms and relations are set out diagrammatically in Figure 2.1.

The arrow at the centre represents the surface level at which the ad hooks the consumer and attracts her/him towards the symbolized product. What the figure is designed to highlight, however, is that the apparently single and unilinear relation between reader and advertised product is actually a complex of three distinct relations, each of which is mediated by the other two. To see how the Eve ad is constructed as an ideological message let us look at it, then, from each side of this triadic structure.

The product and its meaning

It is almost as difficult in the real world to make a rigorous distinction between the commodity and its manufactured symbolic aura as in the advertising text. What complicates the distinction is that products, even physical and practical ones, are inseparable from language (including visual language) and from patterns of use that are overlaid with ceremonial and cultural significance. Prior to, and independently of, the Eve campaign, cigarettes and cigarette smoking were already heavy with cultural associations. And these had themselves been shaped by an inextricable combination of previous social and marketing history.[15] Yet there is obviously a difference not only between cigarettes as smoked and cigarettes as marks of gender, status, generation, etc; but also between the latter as generic conventions that have culturally taken root, and the specific identities advertisers construct to distinguish their particular brands.

This supplementary and differential meaning is not introduced by advertising alone, but as part of a larger process of mass marketing which includes design, packaging, and retail display. Advertising is, nevertheless, a crucial link in the chain. Through it, as carried by mass media, the imaging process reaches the consumer, publicly and privately, wherever he or she happens to be. If we think of the commodity imaging process as emanating from production, and then spreading to the point of sale, advertising is indeed its furthest extension outwards towards the consumer. As its end-point, it reflects all the other stages like a Hegelian totality. In the Eve ad, a number of discrete cultural signifiers – the beach, the floral motif, the woman and her clothes, the name 'Eve' itself – are woven together to produce a tailored and updated version of the biblical temptation myth. Alongside them, photographic representations of the cigarette and its package are also displayed as sign-vehicles for that same mythic complex. The cigarette with a springtime floral motif around its filter was a concept from the start. Sometimes, the marketing of the added symbolic meaning is so successful that independently represented cultural signifiers become unnecessary to keep it alive. Chanel Number 5, which was promoted during the 1960s as the essence of Parisian chic (epitomized by Catherine Deneuve) was promoted in the 1970s by ads which eliminated all visual imagery except the bottle and its name. The scent itself was transparent, as invisible as the glamorous associations which the mere sight of its package was deemed sufficient to evoke. Eve, on the other hand, was not an established product and so its designated meaning had to be spelled out in full.

That spelling begins with the product's very name: 'Eve'. Of course, whether linked to cigarettes or not, this name can be nuanced in many different ways. It is the other signs on the page, pictorial and verbal, which tell us precisely how to read it. What we are presented with, overall, is not just biblical Eve, the first woman in her primal temptation scene, but 'the new Eve', a new woman for a new cigarette.

Naming a product both facilitates the pinning of a borrowed meaning to it, and fixes its association as a sign. It also connects the product to its manufacturer. Indeed the first function has followed from the second. Brand-names developed out of patents as a way to lay title, against stealers and forgers, to the personal ownership of the formula, invention or design embodied in a product. But from the start (as we have seen with Wedgwood) they also doubled as an element of publicity, serving at once to identify that product, and to guarantee its quality to the prospective buyer. This latter role has evidently been built on as the site upon which to construct a promotional image. With the development of capitalism, moreover, has come yet a further change. Capital has been depersonalized, so that the brand-name of products has been progressively detached from that of their actual producer/owner. Individual entrepreneurship has been replaced by family capital, family capital by the corporation, and the latter, finally, by a magma of conglomerates and finance pools in which hallmarks are traded like cigarette cards and the autonomy and identity of producing units has itself become just a promotional fiction. At the limit, the brand-name becomes a wholly arbitrary sign – Coca-Cola – which can even transfer its name back from the product itself to the enterprise which makes or distributes it. With 'Eve', and almost universally where a brand-name is an *ex-nihilo* marketing creation, the parent company (here, the American tobacco giant Liggett and Myers) is not separately mentioned, creating the illusion that the brand-name is its name too.

Whatever the precise relation, naming a product after – or as if after – its producer serves to personalize that shadowy presence. It does so, moreover, with a very particular inflection. Like a child's surname, the brand-name names the father. As such, it both provides a screen for infant–parent projection and gives imaginary force to an archaic and paternalist ideology of commodity production as creation, authorship, and service. A Union Carbide campaign in the 1950s (a company-to-company affair conducted mainly in the pages of business weeklies like *Fortune*) used as its central motif a gigantic hand which proffered various Union Carbide products to a grateful world below. Deification of the corporation, here explicitly, transforms the commodity into a gift from on high.

If the meaning of the brand-name can extend outward towards a myth of capitalist production, it can also extend inward towards the psyche of the consumer. In the mirror of the ad, you, the reader, are Eve. The object bearing this name is your own essence, and by consuming it you would be indicating your membership in the communion of all those who share it with you. The narcissistic binding of ego to product, as an act of individual and collective self-celebration, converts consumption into a sacrificial rite. Given that it is the self which is perpetually on the altar, such advertising gives a bizarre twist to the Hobbesian vision of Man as a being of infinite appetite.[16]

The ego and the product: wants and needs

What an ad says about why we should want or need a particular commodity never stands alone. It brings into play both the intended symbolic meaning of the product and the whole range of attributed needs, desires and values which that meaning serves to define. For the same reason, the ad's discourse about needs also serves to define them in relation to the world of objects in general. Indeed, the symbolic ad encodes certain fundamental assumptions about the character of wants and needs just by being an advertisement. Let us take these points in reverse order and work our way back to the specific case at hand.

By addressing individuals always as potential customers, and so attributing to them *a priori* a social identity linked firmly to that role, advertising builds the standpoint of consumption into the design of its every text. Partly under the influence of advertising, this standpoint has even become a powerful ideological force in its own right: an apolitical egalitarianism which, in disregard of differential wealth and power, is grounded in our common status as consumers. In their imagistic elaborations, symbolic ads like those for Eves absolutize this matrix into a full vision of a world without work, social conflict, or indeed any socially negative features at all.

The consumerist address imprisons the subjectivity it projects in a totally commodified ontology. Being is reduced to having, desire to lack. No needs or desires are speakable without a commodity to satisfy them; no commodity without at least an imagined place for it in our affections. Satisfaction is always mediated by an object or programmed experience, which inevitably (if politely passed over) has a price. In the world of the imagistic ad, even 'natural' objects – sky, trees, horse, streets, sandy shore – lose their autonomous significance to the commodities whose mere stage setting they become. The meadow receives the automobile and the mountain lake its bottle of rye without resistance or surprise. Production as human praxis – the satisfaction of human need through non-alienated self-activity – is obliterated as a thinkable thought. The happy consumers ads display are becalmed in a sea of reification. Their bliss is as static as the objects through which it is magically conferred, while the images of well-being which promote the product encode the desire to consume it within a whole paradigm of passive gratification. Given the nebulousness of what image advertising promises, and its dissolution of any clear distinction between need and want, all this can assume a positively anti-rational character. The desire advertising constantly stimulates bypasses all rational criteria (material, moral, aesthetic, political) by which it might be assessed.

The consumerist orientation an ad projects, however, is always focused in terms of a particular promotional pitch. And the more targeted the market, the more specific the ad must be in its socio-cultural definitions of consumer and product.

In plain commercial terms, the overall objective of the Eve campaign was to cut into the fast-growing market of women smokers.[17] As a gender-identified brand – itself just one of a mixed bag of marketing strategies Liggett and Myers employed to package tobacco – the product had to compete both against other female-identified brands (chiefly Virginia Slims), as well as against those which, with whatever overlay of masculinism, were marketed to both sexes. In relation to the latter, it had to present female identity as something women smokers would actually want to assert through their brand, and against the former it had to develop a rival or complementary basis for female self-identification. Given that the steady increase in women smokers since the First World War both reflected the way in which women had come to experience the same everyday stresses and strains as men, and had also come to be defined as an index of their correlative aspiration for equal social status, finding an ideologically appropriate way to define a cigarette as female was not, however, a straightforward task. Why should North American female smokers in the liberated 1970s want a 'female' cigarette at all? General considerations aside, differential gender-identity had become increasingly controversial with the relaunch of a mass women's movement at the end of the 1960s. By 1975,[18] when feminist agitation for legal equality, sexual autonomy, and an end to workplace discrimination was at its height, any traditional marking of male/female difference was hotly contested as a contributory factor in continuing inequalities of condition and power. Nor, in such matters, were women simply and collectively pitted against men. The turmoil in gender relations and definitions divided women as well. It also affected different classes, ethnicities, and generations differently, and was reflected, among women as among men, in ambivalence and internalized role conflict as much as in sharpened gender politics.

The solution adopted by both Eves and Virginia Slims was to construct an ambiguous image of female-ness which encapsulated the ambivalence of those women most likely to be drawn towards a gender-marked cigarette. At its heart was a compromise formula in which old (patriarchal) and new (liberal–egalitarian) conceptions of female gender identity were both given a place. The Virginia Slims campaign, which ran from the early 1970s to the mid-1980s, gave this ambiguity an ostensibly feminist face. The brand was identified, triumphantly, with women's progress towards equality. Each ad in the campaign typically contrasted two pictures. One, in sepia and white like an old photograph, depicted some example of the exploitation, bullying and social exclusion women were subject to in the Victorian bad old days. The other, in glorious colour, showed a supremely self-confident, independent, and successful woman of today. However, this celebration of the movement towards female self-empowerment was immediately cancelled by the patronizingly male, loverboy tone in which it was greeted: 'You've come a long way, baby!'

The Eve ad positions itself against Virginia Slims by offering a traditionalist version of exactly the same ambivalence. Here, though, it is a patriarchal definition of femininity which is pushed to the fore – Adam's rib, poised daintily on the edge of temptation – while the Independent Woman quality of the presenting figure is introduced as a counterbalance. In both cases, but in different ways, the very appearance of the product-presenters embodies the ambiguity in gender definition their products are designed to represent. The woman in the Eves ad wears a unisex hat, blouse, and pants. But the patterning is floral, and the pants are designer culottes, which end just above the knees. The same duality is communicated by her body language: boyish, carefree, and happily alone – but also kneeling, and with head canted submissively to the side.[19] By contrast, the Virginia Slims figure is always standing. It is her assertiveness which is emphasized. At the same time, her long hair, make-up, and elegant attire are marks of an older femininity; a qualification which is reinforced above all by who, and what, we instantly recognize her to be. Cheryl Tiegs: internationally famous fashion model, and cover-girl superstar. Needless to say, to take that occupation as a paradigm of female independence, mobility and achievement is as much a gender-political compromise as the pseudo-feminism it helps associate with the cigarette.

Even as a promotionally constructed sign, however, the cigarette remains a cigarette: a mild stimulant and relaxant on which half the world's adult population are physically and neurotically hooked. Here, though, is another marketing problem. Since the cancer scare of the 1950s (and leaving aside government regulation itself), growing disquiet about the health risks of smoking had made even mentioning the physical properties that draw people to it a risky venture. Accentuating the positive, in such circumstances, implies a veritable transvaluation. In the Eves ad it is subtly done. The Eve woman's shining eyes and radiant smile vibrate with a natural vitality that seems to flow organically from the sun, sea, sand, and leaves that surround her. The setting and colours are calm and mellifluous. This Eve, tantalizingly on the line between innocence and sin, is in transit between here and the garden to which we long to return. She is a siren, gently urging surrender to desire. Try today's Eve. You know it's bad for you, but it makes you feel better. Indeed, besides calming your nerves, it really makes you come alive.

This whole mise-en-scene both speaks to the actual stress which smoking helps alleviate, and rationalizes its self-destructive character as a peccadillo which, paradoxically, leads to Paradise. Being tempted to 'try Eves' returns us to the primal moral dilemma Eve herself faced. And wanting Paradise, we will want to face it with her, from the other side. On this level, the ad is counter-propaganda to attract new smokers and sustain old ones in their habit. Daring to acknowledge the product's negativity – smoking equals sin (and we all know what the wages of sin are) – enables the ad both to exorcise the hidden fears and to neutralize the explicit health warning that the advertiser is compelled to display. The whole construct would evidently collapse if the woman in the ad had actually started to smoke the unlit cigarette she is holding.

The ego and the symbolic: ideology and the cultural code

It would be impossible to valorize products symbolically if the symbolism employed to that end were itself unintelligible or without ideological appeal. Symbolic ads must therefore not only find effective pictorial and verbal devices by which to link the commodity with a significance. They must also build up significance from elements of an understood cultural code; and in such a way that the values in terms of which the product is endorsed are themselves endorsed by those to whom they make appeal. The tautological structure within which symbolic advertising attempts to pull off this textual coup is the same as the one in which it attempts to validate the product as an object of need. Consumer and commodity must be defined in such a way that their respective attributes perfectly match.

At first sight this seems unproblematic. If the cap fits, it will be worn. All advertising has to do, surely, is to bring its proffered attributions into line with the actual self-identifications, needs, and values which consumers experience as their own.[20] But the inevitable selectivity of typifications (is that really me?), plus the need to ensure a two-way fit between consumer subjectivity and brand image, rules out a purely passive approach. The circular logic of attribution masks the leap of faith the reader must make to get into the picture. Potential consumers must be positively induced to embrace what the product is made to mean. On the plane of ideological orientation, as on that of wants and needs, symbolic advertising has at the very least to affirm the code of values to which it makes appeal.

Where the ideological consensus appealed to is strong and stable, so that its shibboleths are unambiguous and have the status of common sense, mere illusion will suffice. Positively coded symbols lie readily to hand and their cultural power is easy to invoke. The extensive use of Madonna-and-child imagery in ads of the 1950s, for example, rested on the secure assumption that for contemporary women ('housewives' all) motherhood and babies were unambiguously Good. Just flashing the icon was enough to valorize the product. But what does the advertiser do if the consensus behind such a conventional value begins to fall apart?

This, of course, is exactly what happened in the field of sex and gender from the late 1950s onwards. At first, the malaise suffered by many of those who tried to live up to the mother/housewife ideal remained (to use Betty Friedan's 1963 term) 'nameless'. During this initial phase, the prevailing gender ideology held, and gathering unease among women could be defined by advertising (as by sociology and medicine) as a mere role-strain which commodities themselves could magically resolve. (A 1959 ad for Jergens hand-lotion shows a pair of silk-skinned and beautifully manicured hands. In the prayer position, but presumably over a sink, they delicately enclose a half-peeled potato.) But once the malaise broke surface, the whole feminine/domestic mystique lost its hold, becoming indeed a matter of deep division both between women and men, and between women (divided along class, age, and ideological lines) themselves.

Under the circumstances – and evidently, in the 1960s and 1970s it was not only the sex/gender code that was shaken up – advertisers could no longer rely on the force of a taken for granted ideological consensus at all. This dictated both caution and creativity. Caution because, with so many land mines strewn about, product images had to be crafted very precisely in relation to the demographic and psychographic profiles of their relevant product markets. Creativity, because advertisers had virtually to manufacture an ideological consensus, if only in the fictional world of their ads, in order to provide a symbolic setting within which their imaged products could be given stable identities and a focused appeal.

It is in just these terms that the symbolic operation conducted by the Eves ad is to be understood. The problem it had to solve was how to depict, in an image of force and appeal, the compromise vision of womanhood (neither too feminine nor too feminist) which, for marketing reasons (only the cross-pressured would want the product), had to be identified with its 'female' cigarette. Such a task was formidable, for this composite ideal had to be emotively and ideologically valorized in the very act of being assembled. However, symbolic advertising has two main strategies open to it, and the Eves ad conducts them both with a virtuosity that makes it something of a set-piece.

First, even if the final mythic meaning to which the ad makes appeal cannot be invoked by simple allusion, its ideological equivalent can always be manufactured from conventional elements of the fractured code which are themselves still resonant and entrenched. The carefully ambiguous image of Woman which the Eves ad seeks to identify with its brand of cigarette is collaged together out of many such elements – including nature symbols (beach, ocean, sky, shrubs, floral patterns), gestural signs (the model's pose and facial expression, her clothes and how she wears them), and biblical references (Genesis, Book I, Ch 6) – each replete with their own elemental cultural associations.

Myth, in fact, which Barthes defined as 'second-order speech', is raised here to a second power. The symbolic elements just mentioned are themselves second-order signs. The beach on which the scene is set is a figure, at once, for the Carefree Existence and the Origins of Life; while the floral motif, the word 'Eve' and the opened pack offered as something we might be tempted to try, provide a setting within which that beach also becomes Paradise. In that context as well, the woman facing us, cigarette in hand, becomes a signifier for the biblical Eve. And in being about to try the product, we catch her, in an echo of that archetypal scene, in the moment of Temptation itself. The same woman also doubles as the product's 'presenter', and as such represents the ideal–typical modern consumer with whom the reader herself, in turn, is invited to identify. The mirror position, gaze meeting gaze, encourages this identification, which is further facilitated by the desirable-but-not-unattainable paradigm of cheery, middle-class young womanhood she seems to embody. Finally, as a result of the multiple semiotic roles played by this image, the biblical myth of Eve combines with recognizably contemporary socio-cultural ideals to constitute a new mythical signified: Everywoman as 'today's Eve'. In its perfect blend of old and new conceptions of female sexuality ad identity, this revised mythological figure converts the unstable compromise actually lived by the secretaries, nurses, elementary teachers, housewives, etc, who make up the Eves market into a fashionable, coherent-seeming, ideal.

Completing this whole construct, and likewise endowed with a multiple significance, is the product itself. In relation to the Genesis story, the proffered cigarettes stand at once for Temptation (the apple), the Tempter (the snake) and – via their name – for Eve, the Tempted One, herself. In the revised version, as 'today's Eve', they also signify the same revised myth complex as the woman presenter cast before our eyes in that role. The slogan over the two packs on the right ('flowers on the outside, flavor on the inside') refers both to the cigarettes and to that woman, and so draws them together: ideal consumer and branded product, identified with one another as embodiments of the same myth, and through that myth jointly standing as signifiers for what the ad hopes the reader/consumer will take herself to be (see Figure 2.2).

If the first strategy is to create a new myth out of the old, the second is to infuse the results with erotic appeal. Symbols can encode desires as well as cultural values. And since the pleasure principle validates itself (explicitly so in the Me-Generation libertarianism of the mid-1970s), the synthesis of moribund metaphors with desire can give them a cathectic charge they

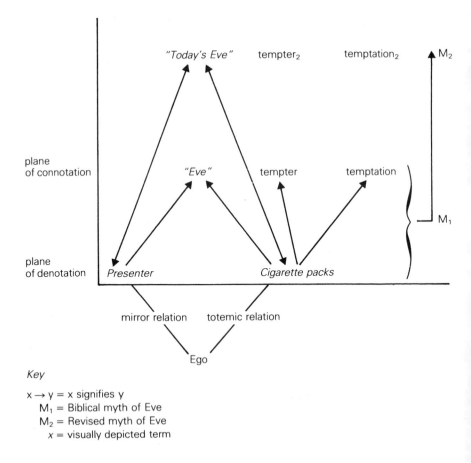

Key

$x \rightarrow y$ = x signifies y
M_1 = Biblical myth of Eve
M_2 = Revised myth of Eve
x = visually depicted term

Figure 2.2 *Semiotic structure of Eve ad*

would otherwise lack. In fact these strategies are deeply intertwined, and it is precisely by deciphering the erotic meaning of the ad that we can see the ideological implications of the revised myth it constructs.

The story of Eve, to be sure, was already invested with a sexual significance before its appropriation by the ad. According to the prevailing interpretation,[21] Eve's forbidden fruit represented sexual pleasure. It was her desires that provoked her, frail woman that she was, to disobey the patriarchal God and break his taboo. The snake is a carnal symbol. But whereas in the biblical version Eve's lust is punished as a sin, the ad's version sanctions it by rewarding her with re-entry to Paradise. Through her example, and playfully taking the role of the Evil One itself, the ad invites the 'little Eve in every woman' to similarly succumb.

This accentuation of erotic load in relation to the anti-erotic prohibition of the original is no mere detail. In order to accommodate the pleasure principle more fully, the structure of the story is decisively altered. Indeed, and not only by siding with temptation, it transforms the entire meaning of the myth. In the ad there is no jealous Jahweh; nor is there any Adam, as Eve's lord and master, to mediate His commands. The punishing father has vanished, leaving Eve alone with the fascinating object of her desire. Patriarchy is over if you want it. All a woman has to do is repossess the phallic signifier,[22] and use it as an object of her own pleasure. The repressive dimension of biblical Eve's situation – her domination and punishment by males – evaporates in the very act of disobedience in which she yields to (auto-erotic) temptation. The only remaining trace of the patriarchate is in the cigarette, at once a boy-toy, a breast substitute, and a mild psychotropic in which today's Eve feels secure enough to indulge.

The infantilism and heterosexual dependency deeply embedded in this vision of the eternal woman belie its surface statement of female self-sufficiency. The ad's allegory of patriarchy overcome and Paradise regained not only wishes away the threat of punishment. It palliates the disturbing impulse from which real rebellion might spring, and cuts out of the picture the struggle and conflict which any genuine process of emancipation would involve.

Nor is this only a modification with respect to the (elided) contradictions of male/female power. In Genesis, what tempts Eve is 'the fruit of the tree of Good and Evil'. Here, too, Eve is enticed by an oral pleasure, but it comes from a suck not a bite. Through it, moreover, comes not pain and suffering, but innocence regained. Not only is this revised message – 'try Eve', and blissfully regress – perfectly attuned to the fantasy gratification implicit in a cigarette. It also resonates, and with a suitably qualifying biblical overtone, with the confused mood of boundary-breaking sexual freedom which the late 1960s upheaval left in its hedonistic wake. In this respect too, the Eves ad perfectly complements the campaign for Virginia Slims against which its product is positioned. In Cheryl Tiegs the compromise figure of the new woman is placed in a work setting: fashion plate as independent career lady. Here she is at play: the new Eve as consumer, with consumption itself projected as an orally gratifying experience.

In the ad's psychological subtext we can see the distance travelled by advertising since its coming out party as a proselytizer for consumer culture in the period examined by Ewen. The good news of happiness through commodities is now an old story – as old as the Fall. Moreover, and despite the warnings of moralists, when we gaze at the 'liberated' fantasy-subject of post-1960s mass consumption we see immediately that its repressively de-sublimated Eros[23] will not threaten the existing order. Today's Eve, like yesterday's motherhood, is totally acceptable.

The bias of advertising

Defenders of the market like to depict it as a mechanism for delivering to consumers – for better or worse – the goods and services they want. This view can be extended to the imagistic side of commodities, too. Here, indeed, it seems especially appropriate, considering that the point of such imaging is to identify the product with what targeted consumers are known already to cherish or desire. We might well suppose, then, that the symbolization of products through advertising (and other means) simply delivers back to people the culture and values that are their own. And, correspondingly, that the intervention of advertising into the formation of consciousness is neutral, a kind of inert gas. At most: a reinforcement of whatever ideological codes and conditions have, for other reasons, come to prevail.

This may do as a first approximation. But as the Eves example suggests, the fact that such reflection is part of a process whose aim is to sell implies definite limits on what orientations and values advertising will actually mirror, and at what angle. Both in the values appealed to and in the symbols deployed, there is a deep bias towards the conventional and the most widely diffused. Promotion, moreover, is determinedly positive and upbeat. Within the field of polarities which make up the codes of culture, the product is identified with good not bad, comedy not tragedy, life not death. Nor is this just a matter of selective emphasis. In projecting commodities as the road to happiness, ads redefine as soluble through consumption any negativity which clings to the process of capitalist production as such. Related to which, finally, the message presupposes a consumerist orientation – the world is my oyster, for money – in its very mode of address. In short, imagistic advertising may build on the values, desires and symbologies that are already out there, but by no means does it simply reflect them. It typifies what is diverse, filters out what is antagonistic or depressing, and naturalizes the role and standpoint of consumption as such. The picture of the world it presents, accordingly, is flat, one-dimensional, incorporative, and normalized.

But the Eve case illustrates a further point. In its effort to construct the precise ideological focus most appropriate to a given marketing situation, and by building up dense semiological systems out of the bits and pieces of prevailing culture, commodity imaging can, to a degree, be ideologically creative. It may even, as with the Eve ad's modification of the Fall, bring about a real symbological mutation. In fact, under conditions of dissensus and conflict, it is forced to do so.

Where, for example with gender, sexuality, and work/family roles, there is no agreed code of cultural categories, nor agreement about how they should be affectively mapped, straightforward appeals to what is consensual and taken-for-granted no longer work. And the larger and more socially diverse the market aimed at the greater the difficulty, for the harder it becomes to pick a message and mode of address that will not alienate some part of the market, nor touch on matters about which potential customers feel awkward or ambivalent. The solution is to appeal over the heads of the combatants and beyond their incompatibilities to whatever, nevertheless, can be expected to unite them all. That is: to their lowest common ideological denominator. The problem is that the degree of ideological consensus fluctuates. And the sharper the conflict, and the more fractured the code, the less even such vague and spongy social universals as motherhood can be leaned on as the basis for an imagistic pitch. Under such circumstances, the lowest common ideological denominator has to be constructed afresh, out of the contradictory elements currently in play. The result is a compromise: one that is either positively constituted at the point of overlap, or which is in the form of a both/and that reduces the inconsistency of what is assembled in a vague blend that allows different readings to be simultaneously possible.

Modern advertising, then, has a functionally determined affinity for the middle of the road – a middle, where necessary, that it will not hesitate to invent. It is this, rather than any particular ideological commitment, which is the constant in its bias. Nor, if the outcome is consistent with the requirements of social control, should these requirements be mistaken for the cause. The conservatism (vis-a-vis capital) of the advertising meta-message is the blind effect of a commercial averaging which projects consensual typifications into the affirmative pseudo-totality of a utopia which has apparently already arrived. In such a world, the safe compromise, the false unity of irreconcilable perspectives, is represented as our deepest and most natural desire. The soft sell which prevails in the market would enfold everyone in its happy embrace. Only a Scrooge or a porcupine would resist. The Eve ad, which conducts this integrative operation with brilliance, manages to reconcile instinct and renunciation, feminism and femininity; to personify this in the image of a happy, well-adjusted, insipid, young, white-collar consumer; and then pass off the whole construct as a figure for Paradise regained. The irony of its milquetoast invitation to 'try Eve' is that that in the case of cigarette smoking seduction is truly a dangerous game. However, through a symbolic manoeuvre which crosses danger with pleasure, the glaring contradiction between promise and delivery, and between the social forces pressing for public health and those thwarting it, is just absorbed as well into the general euphoria of opposites dissolved.

The particular compromise which 'today's Eve' represents is evidently a child of its place and times. Its patriarchal anti-patriarchalism and controlled concession to sexual freedom pick a consensualist path through the contrarieties of mid-1970s North America. One might even hypothesize that the middle of the road mechanism it exemplifies provides a key to the more general process of re-normalization which, during the 1970s, brought the ideological turmoil of the previous decade to an end.[24] If so, the significance of that mechanism can be couched in still more general terms. For the cycle of rebellion/normalization to which the Eve ad pertains is neither without precedent, nor incapable of a kind of return. It is rooted in a long-term cultural dynamic which is likely to persist as long as the marketplace itself.

From the very start, as Marx put it, capitalism has been 'a revolutionary mode of production'. Its inbuilt developmental drive (an organicist term which hardly begins to capture the conflict and turmoil involved) has constantly disequilibriated social life, and not just with respect to the relations of production. Cultural contradictions have been endemic, too. For Daniel Bell (1976), a major cause of instability in capitalism's 'post-industrial' phase has been that the 'axial principles' underlying the spheres of production and consumption have increasingly come into collision. Indeed, the antagonism has reached the point where the ethos of capitalist consumption – individualist, anarchic, pleasure-oriented – threatens to undermine completely the work/rationality complex necessary for the functioning of the productive economy. I would formulate the same polarity in different terms. The real provocateur has been not consumerist culture, in devilish alliance with an antinomian hedonism pioneered by romanticism and modernism in the arts, but the disruptive pressures of commodification itself.

An expanding market requires that more and more aspects of life are free to circulate in commercial exchange. But the prying loose of things, services, and people from pre-commercial ties and institutions continually comes up against entrenched patterns and codes that not only have weight in themselves but are defended by their guardians as the form and level of impulse and behaviour control essential to the reproduction of society as such. Periodically, as in the cultural upheavals of the 1920s and 1960s, the lagged development of the one and the accumulated pressures of the other provoke a full-scale battle in which boundaries get shifted, and values 'modernized'. A prime example is provided by the sex–gender upheaval to which the Eve ad itself was addressed. The large-scale entry of women into the workforce entailed the commodification of their labour power and their corresponding emancipation from the restrictive conditions of family-centred domesticity. Culturally entrenched barriers to the greater mobility of women came under attack, which inevitably provoked conflict, inside and outside the labour market, over the rules of their circulation, indeed over the very definition of female-ness itself. By the end of the 1970s, anticipated (one is tempted to say guided) by a flood of Eves-type imagery in the organs of publicity, a new, if more loosely defined, equilibrium had been established. Women were still the more marked, and subordinated, gender-defining term; but anti-sexism and male–female equality had entered the rules governing public speech. Modified patriarchy had been modified, at least symbolically, one further notch.

Overall, then, whether during periods of relative ideological calm or during bouts of conflict, what advertising has continually to negotiate is a cultural tension which is neither contingent on the vagaries of cultural history nor reducible (as in an older model) to class, but which arises from the dynamics of the always expanding and intensifying market itself. Thus a clearer picture of advertising's ideological role begins to emerge. In the images promotionally given to products, advertising produces a continual stream of totemic, market unifying, second-order cultural messages. It does so, however, in constant interaction with the shifting moods, codes and cross-currents of the culture that surrounds it, so that advertising reprocesses and, where necessary, reconciles whatever core values and symbols have currency. In turn, finally, this reconciliation has to be conducted in the face of an ideological tension (reductively expressed as a clash between liberal/modern values and conservative/traditional ones) which capitalist development itself engenders: a tension which expresses the contradiction, which can never be permanently resolved, between the free trade impetus of commodification and the restrictive requirements, in a still multiply hierarchical society, of social control.

As a determinate element, then, of the economy whose cultural disturbances it promotionally mediates, advertising operates as a kind of cultural gyroscope. Since controlled experiments are impossible to conduct, there is no empirical way to disentangle, from among all the other environmental influences which impinge on the formation of consciousness, the specific impact, as such, that advertising has. Sceptics might think it negligible. It has become a matter of common sense, after all, that ads are cynical constructs; in recognition of which they have increasingly come to deliver even their ideological appeals with a certain knowing tongue-in-cheek.

Yet advertising has retained a power to provoke, and not only in its target markets. Its messages circulate widely in the public domain. Unavoidably, then, it comes into contact with that wider process of cultural politics in media, courts, and legislatures, through which official values are fought over and policed. In the aftermath of the 1960s, the same conflicts over race and gender to which advertising had to respond in any specific market made advertising itself controversial and the target of political campaigns. In the 1980s, similar interventions have come from the Right – for example when Pepsi was forced by the fundamentalist lobby in the US to withdraw its heralded 'Madonna' commercial on the grounds that her music-video, *Like a Prayer*, was blasphemous.

All this can be taken as at least negative evidence that the ideological codings of ads do have real force. However, a different (though not opposing) conclusion can be drawn. Through the activities of lobby groups, regulatory bodies and intra-industry voluntary codes, the middle-of-the road character of imagistic advertising, its inherent disinclination to offend any sizable sector of its potential audience/market, has been politically institutionalized. As an ideological vehicle, then, advertising today is not just constrained by the logic of what it is to hug the middle of the road. In becoming subject to the pushes and pulls of ordinary cultural politics, it is also steered from without, but not by capital, if it blunders too far off that track.

Notes

1. Reproduced in de Vreis et al. (1968).

2. A similar definition is developed in Althusser (1971), which itself derives from Durkheim's notion of the *conscience collective*. Durkheim, however, retained from Comte the notion of 'ideology' as false (teleological, metaphysical) consciousness. Raymond Williams (1976) catalogued six (principal) different meanings which have attached to the term.

3. See, for example, Williamson (1978), Leymore (1975), and Leiss et al. (1986).

4. Large-scale socio-historical approaches have also been developed by Smythe (1981) and Haug (1986). Smythe, self-consciously 'materialist', dismisses ideology-critique as idealist, preferring to explore the way in which advertising exploits the labour of its audience. This thesis has been refined by Jhally and Levant (Jhally, 1987: 64–120). Haug focuses on the distorting effect of 'commodity aesthetics' on the shaping of wants and needs.

5. For a Marxist version of Galbraith's (1971) argument about mass production and managed demand, see Baran and Sweezey (1968: 115–31).

6. Several different interpretative strategies and frameworks were deployed. McLuhan's (1967) myth-analysis was part intuitive, part derived from New Criticism; Barthes' (1972, 1978) approach, elaborated by Williamson (1978), derived from Saussure and Beneviste; Leymore (1975) took her structuralist inspiration from Lévi-Strauss and Leach; while Andren et al. (1978) employed the empirical/inductive techniques of an older style of 'content analysis'. For all the immense theoretical sophistication displayed, none paid more than scant attention to the temporal dimension of the ads they set about decoding. Leiss et al. (1986) however, have attempted to rectify the static bias by combining a study of the diachronic and synchronic elements in a large sample of magazine advertisements.

7. '. . . [T]he business community . . . attempted to present an affirmative vision – a new mechanism – of social order in the realm of daily life to confront the resistance of people whose work lives were increasingly defined by the rigid parameters of industrial production and their corporate bureaucracies . . . . Beyond standing at the helm of the industrial machines, businessmen understood the social nature of their hegemony . . . . They aspired to become captains of consciousness' (Ewen, 1976: 18–19).

8. A problem with Ewen's evidence is that it is almost entirely drawn from sources like *Printer's Ink* which represent advertising on behalf of the advertising industry itself.

9. In the *Gorgias* and the *Phaedrus* Plato characterizes rhetoric as the science of persuasion by speech. In the *Phaedrus*, it may be noted, Socrates takes as his initial example the case of one man trying to sell another a horse (Plato, 1973: 72). Neither, however, has seen one, which sets the stage for an attempt by the first to sell the second a donkey, on the specious grounds that horses are recognizable by their long ears. Advertising, as the false promotion of the Good, is a prototype here for rhetoric as such.

10. The *Toronto Star*, 8 May 1980.

11. Williamson (1978: 60–7) relates this mechanism to Althusser's notion of 'interpellation', and to the mirror-phase of Lacan. The magical quality of the mirror is beautifully illustrated

by a 1960 perfume ad for Chanel. Its caption (under a gauzy black and white photograph of an elegant, darkly dressed, Catherine Deneuve) was 'Chanel *becomes* the woman you are'.

12. The figure of the 'presenter' in ads is discussed in Kline and Leiss (1978: 22–3).

13. Haug (1986) makes a similar point, but by arguing that the promotional symbolization of commodities, like the seductive attire of a prostitute, only creates the illusion of enhanced use-value, and turns use-value itself into an abstraction, he holds fast to an ultimately reductive view of what use-value is. For the implications of Sahlins' (1976) and others' insistence that the symbolic dimension of human exchange items must be treated as a material reality, see Baudrillard's critique of the classical Marxist notion of use-value (Baudrillard, 1981: especially 123–63).

14. The prototypical analysis of this mechanism, at a textual level, is Barthes (1978), and it has been further developed, and formalized, in Williamson (1978).

15. For a good account of the symbolic history of cigarette smoking, from their mass market launch in the 1880s to the inter-war rise of women smokers, see Schudson (1986: 178–208).

16. The totemic aspect of brand-name consumer goods is discussed in Jhally (1987: 10, 202). See also Leiss et al. (1986), and Douglas and Isherwood (1979). The totemic function of consumer brands is also the main premise of the movie *Children of a Lesser God*.

17. The campaign was evidently a success. According to the summer 1988 issue of *Tobacco News*, Liggett and Myers' in-house publication, the product was first test-marketed in 1970. Growth of sales was steady throughout the 1970s. By 1988 it had reached '1.2 billion units', and by 1988 2 billion. While there were changes in packaging design and advertising copy, the basic theme remained the same: the floral motif, printed on the cigarette tip itself, which, in the words of Paul Kopf, the original brand-manager, 'positioned it as a feminine product'.

18. According to the previously cited article in *Tobacco News*, two changes in promotional imagery were made in 1975. First, the Eve face (drawn, stylized, innocent, Victorian) was removed from the pack. Secondly, 'Eve became a real-life model appearing in newspaper and magazine ads and point-of-sale displays.'

19. For a discussion of body language in ads see Goffman (1979).

20. McLuhan (1967: 202) sees this perfect fit as advertising's biggest danger: 'To put the matter abruptly, the advertising industry is a crude attempt to extend the principles of automation to every aspect of society. Ideally, advertising aims at the goal of a programmed harmony among all human impulses and aspirations and endeavours. When all production and all consumption are brought into a pre-established harmony with all desire and all effort, then advertising will have liquidated itself by its own success.' For the idea that, to be effective, ads should 'resonate' with their audience members' existing values and desires, see Schwartz (1974).

21. The symbol of the Tree also has an esoteric history. In Jewish apocalyptic thought it came to stand for the Second Law which would be revealed in the Messianic days, and which would suspend the prohibitions of the First Law (the Torah). See Scholem (1974: 180).

22. The continuing taboo on the public display of the male organ is a visible/invisible index of patriarchy's symbolic survival. This literal absence continues to be compensated for by the plethora of symbolic substitutes distributed architecturally, for example, throughout the urban landscape. The cultural place of symbolized female sexuality is the exact obverse in both respects: the stock-in-trade of visual pornography, vaginal symbols are hard to find in the built environment.

23. For a sympathetic reconsideration of Marcuse's (1969) notions of surplus repression and repressive sublimation, see Horowitz (1977).

24. Among ads in a full backlash vein, a particularly stark instance was a 1978 *Newsweek* glossy for 'Tradition' whiskey. It boldly announced, over a tawny bottle of its high-grade product, 'A Return to Traditional Values'.

3

(RE-)IMAGING GENDER:
THE CASE OF MEN

Researchers are beginning to urge advertisers to segment the estimated 500,000 males in Canada and nine million males in the United States who live alone and are worthy targets of homecare products, according to Baker Lovick Ltd of Toronto. They point to the vast numbers of men who live alone – or at least without a female helpmate – and take care and some pride in their cooking, shopping, cleaning and even laundry. The agency reports the segment is in the 30 to 65 age range and would include potential buyers of microwave ovens, frozen foods and drip-dry shirts. Whatever the reasons, they live alone and like it. The research reports there are subtle suggestions that advertisers should show men in a more favourable light so far as laundry is concerned and take it easy on such appeals as 'detergents for your finest washables' while showing lacy lingerie.

Toronto *Globe and Mail*, 9 January 1985

Shaking up the gender code

The Eves ad, which ran in the mid-1970s, would have been inconceivable a decade earlier. If, today, its main motifs do not seem wholly out of date (the flower-tipped cigarette continues to be sold), this is because the ideological compromise 'Eve' embodies has been a fixture in the flux that gender relations have been in throughout the post-1960s period: ever since, that is, changed social conditions and the rebirth of the women's movement brought the post-war restoration of a family-centred (and breast-centred) 'feminine mystique' explosively into question.

As reflected in advertising imagery itself, the results of that upheaval have evidently been mixed. By no means has an egalitarian, emancipated definition of womanhood simply ousted an obsolete cluster of older ones. What has happened, rather, is that under conditions of unresolved gender conflict and partial reform, contradictory definitions of womanhood have come to coexist, often (as in the Eve case) in the space of the same visual image. This, however, is only half the story. Sex/gender codes build on a duality. To get a fuller picture of the way that advertising has revised its gender codings over the past thirty years it is important to consider as well what has happened to the representation of men.

That development is more complex than it seems. In the first place, there has been a change in the relation of men to advertising itself. As a counterpoint to the much more commented upon entry of women into the workforce, men of all classes have become increasingly involved in everyday consumption activities which, only a generation ago, were defined as properly the province of women. The acquisition by women of outside roles has made an older and more rigid division of labour untenable. Even if slow to adapt,[1] male partners have gradually been forced to take greater responsibility for domestic chores so that few of either sex are now unfamiliar with the joys of supermarkets and shopping malls. In addition, the growth in the number of students, the rise in age at first marriage, the increase in divorce rates, and the open emergence of gay households have enlarged the category of men who, from the standpoint of day-to-day consumption, effectively live apart from women. Advertisers of everything from toothpaste and tissues to light bulbs and pasta have thus increasingly had to take into account that men, too, are potential buyers, and so must be treated as part of the 'you' they address.

Beyond the general extension to men of consumer status, there has also been an extension in the range of commodities aimed especially at them. In the 1950s a list of such goods would have been confined to cars, alcohol, certain brands of cigarettes, mechanical tools, and life insurance. To some degree it would also have included men's clothing, though with the assumption that their purchase was primarily a mother's affair before marriage, and at least partly a wife's thereafter. The list, today, is much longer. Men confront an ever-increasing array of leisure goods (including erotica); their clothing has been fully incorporated into the world of fashion; and mounting efforts have been made to sell them all manner of personal-care products and accessories, from jewellery and athletic trainers, to bath-oil, deodorants, and hair-dye. Seventy years after women went through something similar, men as private people, in short, have been targeted for economic development. How ads have come to encode masculinity (and, correspondingly, femininity), then, partly reflects the way advertising has sought to secure men's identification, in sometimes unprecedented contexts, with the standpoint of consumption itself.

What has complicated the advertisers' task is that the definition of masculinity in terms of which to couch such an address has become problematic and confused. To some degree this is a disruptive consequence of consumerization itself. The promotion of fragrance to heterosexual males, for example, involves a break with the formula that men hunt, women attract – not to mention the need to obviate homophobic panic. The very act of enticing men into shops can raise emasculating fears. The exaggerated sexism of images like the one which graced the front cover of the January 1981 issue of *Audio Scene* can be interpreted, in this context, as talismanic. It shows an alluring, slim, teenage blonde, dressed in a pure white outfit of T-shirt and shorts. With mouth half-open and innocent eyes turned towards the reader, she is holding on to a shopping cart, which is piled high with stereo gear. But not just holding. For when we look more closely we can see that she is leaning right into it, as if discreetly feeling up the goods. On the surface, she is herself the consumer, caught by the camera in the very moment of choice. But the address is evidently to the other sex, for whom the equation is reassuringly made not only between audio products and the idea of Technology as a congerie of male-identified sex-machines, but also between supermarket goods in general and virginal young women as themselves consumables on display.

But consumerization has not been the only cause of disturbance. Male gender identity has also been shaken – in private as well as in public – by the more general sex/gender upheaval associated with the rise of feminism itself. Men still predominate within the public sphere, but they have begun to lose their automatic privilege. Men still earn more than women, but they are no longer defined as the exclusive breadwinners. Men are still the more predatory, but they have increasingly had to cope with being prey. Heterosexuality is still the norm, but homosexuality, in the liberal jargon of the market, is becoming an acceptable lifestyle. All in all, the puritan–patriarchal complex, restored to official favour in the corporatist heyday of the Cold War, has lost its self-certainty. All its assumptions about sexuality, the family, and what distinguishes men from women have been hotly contested, dividing the sexes among themselves as well as from one another. For gay men the fissuring of the code has had a liberating side, permitting, even if against great resistance (which the AIDS crisis has reinforced), new social identities to be forged. For the straight majority the benefits have not been so clear. What compensates for loss of gender privilege? What, indeed, does it mean, these days, to be a man?

Not only men but advertisers have had to grapple with that question. They have had to do so, moreover, in a manner which accords with the full spectrum of sex/gender identities and orientations currently alive within their markets. As we slide ambiguously, then, towards a world of greater gender equality, we might well wonder not only how advertising has adapted to this process, but also how, in responding to the complexities and inconsistencies of post-1960s male self-identification, it has redefined for its own purposes the category of masculinity itself.

Men in post-war ads: towards equivalence

Even a cursory glance at what has happened to the representation of men in North American advertising since the mid-1950s reveals a significant, if contradictory, shift. As in the case of women, the old patriarchal codings have in obvious ways survived. Business, Science, and the Military continue to be represented as so many forms and aspects of masculine power. But the sexual turmoil of the 1960s and 1970s has also left its mark. Thus advertisers have had to negotiate such divergent models of masculinity as those arising, on the one hand, from the macho/playboy protest against 'momism' traced by Barbara Ehrenreich in *Hearts of Men* (1983) and, on the other, from gender-bending pop stars and the coming out of gays.

Cutting across this diversification, patriarchal symbolism in advertising has also been weakened by a tendency which points, in the end, to its dissolution altogether. In certain respects advertisers have begun to treat male and female, for all their marked biological differences, as formally interchangeable terms. Measured against the sex/gender system that prevailed during the Eisenhower years there are, in fact, three ways in which the promotional imaging of men has softened in that direction. These concern, respectively, men's depicted relation to their social milieu, to the world of things, and to sexuality. Changes in one area of representation have doubtless had implications, as well, for the other two. But before we can elucidate the modified masculinity they have combined to effect, it may be useful to disentangle, first, the way that the imaging of men has shifted with respect to each.

Men and others

In the ads of the 1950s, the well-nigh universal touchstone for defining social roles and identities was the family. Not just any family, of course, but the nuclear, role-divided (he works, she nurtures), two-to-three-children middle-class ideal – with advertiser attention fixed firmly on the nest-building couple at its purchasing centre. Male, no less than female, consumers were automatically presumed to belong to such a structure and were rarely presented outside its cheery frame. Shirt-wearers, pipe-smokers, television buyers, car drivers (invariably male), all appear as so many hubbies, dads, and career-striving family providers. The automobile itself was promoted as a family vehicle – with the woman in the passenger seat and the kids in the back a virtual emblem, indeed, of the domestic set-up for which it was designed. The further back we go the clearer this pattern becomes. A general trade promotion by the National Tea Council in the October 1950 issue of *Colliers* advises its readers: 'If he comes home "under pressure" give him tea'. From the same issue, another ad has a cutesy infant, snow white against powder blue, gurgling: 'I should say not! My Dad would never smoke anything but Marlboro'.

If there was a counter-trend, it was in the sometimes wildly romantic imagery used in women's fashion ads, particularly for cosmetics. The fantasy male waiting in the wings (usually unshown) to dance attendance on the wearer of Givenchy or Charles of the Ritz could be her actual husband. But he could also be her pre- or extra-marital lover. And in this exotic stranger (Prince Charming? Don Juan? Napoleon?) there is more than a trace of the Bad Man who, like the Bad Woman, has long been an important element of Western sexual mythology. Such a figure, grafted on to screen-hero images of male sexual adventure, for which the Western, *film noir* and swashbuckling period epics provided variant models, increasingly came to appear as well in ads aimed at men. An anodyne version was 'the bold look' touted in the late 1940s by Camp socks. More rakishly came the trench-coated Bogart type used by later Marlboro ads, and the black eye-patch of Hathaway.

Nonetheless, romantic love was – and, if less ritualized, still is – the sanctioned basis for marriage, and even its subversive side was neutralized in such ads by a certain blandness. For all his shady intensity, the trilby-hatted Marlboro Man has clean-cut features and may just be phoning his wife. Besides, at least till the late 1950s, these devil-may-care anti-Dagwood poses jostled side by side with images of an unabashed familial-ism. A 1957 bathrobe ad shows an awkward-looking (because tall, dark, and handsome) father holding an infant. Off-stage, a voice reminds him: 'It's your turn to bath the baby tonight, darling.' Daddy's wry smile may express humour at the incongruity, but there is not a trace, here, of protest or refusal.

By contrast, while the family has made something of a comeback during the 1980s, the overall post-war trend has been away from depicting men in fixed family roles. For example, in the mid-July 1986 issue of *Time*, only one of the eight male figures shown in thirteen full-page ads gives any sign of family ties – and even here, the man himself is not pictorially shown. The comparable figures for July 1971 were five out of twelve, and for July 1956 ten out of twelve. Similar calculations for other consumer magazines, from *Cosmopolitan* to *Sports Illustrated*, would show the same tendency. Except in publications which are explicitly family-oriented, it has become unusual for display ads even to mention the family status of the individuals they depict.

In the majority of cases, where humans are shown at all, the need for such information is in any case reduced because the people shown are shown alone. Combined with close-ups and truncated shots, this simplifi-cation is partly just a device to avoid visual clutter. But it also permits ambiguity, letting the consumers place themselves in an ad from a variety of positions, in keeping with whatever roles and arrangements they may actually live. In two respects, moreover, the absence of ties has come to be presented, particularly for men, as a desirable condition in itself. In the transitional sense, first, of the not-yet-married, 'singles' emerged at the beginning of the 1980s as not just a commercially important demographic group (the product of prolonged middle-class schooling) but as a sign, when placed in a suitably affluent setting, of general upward mobility. Hence that great cliche of Reagan Age promotion, the single young exec, eternally in his early thirties and dressed for success – a figure which has wholly replaced the older, married, and more established business type in the Good Life imagery held out before aspiring men. Some ads, like Camel's long-running 'one of a kind' series, went even further, crossing the Lone Man theme with frontier myths of rugged individualism to produce visions of total male self-sufficiency. Rendered in this more absolute way, the condition of being without ties is converted into an existential imperative and then equated, in all its anti-social glory, with masculinity itself.

Even where men are shown with others, the family frame per se is generally absent. The commonest grouping, to be sure, is the young mixed couple, a figure which points to a new family and, stripped down to its barest essential, is a figure for the family itself. However, couples are usually shown in dating situations, or even at the moment of first encounter, with commitment not yet settled and the marital context, if any, left vague. Other configurations, from the male–male twosome (rare, but no longer absolutely tabooed), to the three-plus male peer group, are still further removed from the family. And the cosy aggregation in which they culminate, the mixed group of age peers, has itself come to assume one of the side-lined family's main roles: to provide personal identity with its primary social anchor. The elevation of the peer group has been particularly evident in ads which push their products as symbols of a wider social belonging. In the most generalized and youth-oriented versions of this theme – one thinks of Coke and Pepsi – solidarity with a whole generation is invoked. In a more adult and careerist mode the emphasis is on interpersonal support. 'Smirnoff', says the text of a 1985 ad over a wood-panelled bar full of elegant neighbourhood yuppies, 'means friends.'

Whatever the similarities, however, the peer groups depicted are different from kin. They are uni-generational and have no fixed roles nor, indeed, individually essential members. Like the empty landscapes surrounding Camel's Man-the-Adventurer, such groups present themselves, rather, as an ego-site in which the consuming subject is free to roam around at will. And this is just the point. The displacement of males from fixed family roles in recent advertising has had as its reverse side the rise of a sign system which highlights the fluidity of social bonding and associates the pleasures of consumption with the sexual, status or existential rewards to be obtained from exercising individual freedom in that setting. Desire itself is defined as an attribute of detachment, with male socio-sexual success being defined in terms of either the status of the females drawn into his orbit or of what, from his affluent or prestigeful appearance, we can assume he has renounced in that regard by splendidly isolating himself from the contest.[2]

Cosmic man

A second set of changes has concerned the more general construction of masculinity as a symbolic term. If patriarchal codings have been weakened by the disappearance of images depicting the literal family, there has also been a disappearance of what one might call the metaphorical family: that parallel set of father-dominant relations which advertising has conventionally projected, through gender-coded goods, nature, and production, on to its pictures of the material world.

As many commentators have pointed out,[3] such a complex in one form or another has helped sustain and legitimize the West's industrial drive at least since the Renaissance. Combining elements of archaic myth with a newer worship of the labouring subject, its central motifs were classically embodied in updated versions of Prometheus and Adam. Through the former, progress based on science was depicted as the heroic strivings of a demigod. Through the latter, industrial Man was made Lord of the Earth.

Linked to this whole androcentric amalgam, moreover, whose literary expression can be traced from Francis Bacon to Marinetti, has been a powerful sexual phantasm – warrior man subjugating woman nature – which in turn renders capitalist technology as an extension of the male organ and its penetrations of the environment as a series of sexual acts. Nature, in this primal scene, is the emphatically dominated bride and we ourselves, arms outstretched to receive the gifts of life from above, the grateful children. But we are not the only progeny. Consumer goods are products of the Nature/Technology union too. And unconsciously, at least, our consumption of these – sibs eating sibs, as it were – can even be regarded as a kind of incestuous sacrifice designed to keep the father-god of production happy and alive.

Fuelled by urban redevelopment, an electronics boom and the arms race, the 1950s was a period of heady technological optimism. It was also, with soldiers returned to the domestic fold and traditional gender lines restored, a period of renewed family-centredness. From both sides, then, the elements of an older patriarchal techno-worship were strongly reinforced, and in the advertising of the time its themes and images came dramatically to the fore.

At the symbolic summit was technological Man himself, represented most clearly in a recurrent image best described as 'the hand of God'. Union Carbide based a whole campaign round this theme. In one such ad the hand – huge, male, reaching from the clouds – offers titanium, in another hydrocarbons, in another whole fighter planes built from the minerals plucked Superman-style from the mountains nearby. A 1955 promotion for Morgan Guaranty Trust uses the same device. Here the hook is air-conditioning systems, a breakthrough made possible (according to the small print) by the money put up by Morgan. 'At the touch of a finger', boasts the headline, 'man-made climate that's better than nature's.' To illustrate which, a strong but gentle male hand, palm down, stretches horizontally across the page. Above, a fierce storm is raging. Below, bathed in a light which seems to be emanating from the hand itself, Mum (sewing), Dad (smoking), and little girl (playing) luxuriate in the protective warmth of their domestic circle. In the background, office clerks (female) work happily away, equally oblivious to the tempest from which the new technology delivers them all. The hand is evidently divine, but its connection with more earthly powers is not concealed. Just visible where the arm enters the page is a hint of immaculate black sleeve and white cuff. The Big Guy is corporate: Our Father as President of the Board.

Such ads move back and forth, in fact, between emphasizing the fatherly qualities of 'technology' and of the business enterprise which controls it. Rendering the company in paternalistic terms was not itself particularly new. But even here, besides the technicist inflection, there was the difference that not before the 1950s had consumers – as opposed to workers – been so explicitly portrayed as dependants of capital in this familial sense. The analogy invoked was not only to parents and children. The benign power of Technology and corporations was presented in marital terms as well. A 1957 ad for New England Life shows a pipe-smoking husband, somewhere in his thirties, confidently watching his wife through a window as she gathers flowers in the garden. 'A better life for her', comments the text – implying not just that she is to him as he is to the insurance company, but also that securing the larger protection of the company is indispensable if he is to live up to his own protective role. An even more direct example, but on the parent/child side, is provided by a 1954 ad for Texas and Pacific Railway. A little girl holds the hand of a doll which looks exactly like herself, while both stare reverently into the sunset. Over an unctuous credo that links freedom to capitalism, and both to the American Founding Fathers, hovers the operative word that ties it, us, and the figures in the picture all together: Faith.

The sexual aspect of this masculinist cosmology was also much in evidence. Indeed, with space exploration (Kennedy's 'New Frontier') as its most spectacular external embodiment, and car design as its main expression in the consumerist sphere, the phallic character of modern technological striving was almost obsessively emphasized in the promotion of the period. The sleek, thrusting, venturesome profile of rocket ships was a particularly common motif, both as immediately bound up with aerospace products (as in defence industry ads) and as a more abstract symbol for futuristic progress. As the latter, it was promotionally affixed to all manner of goods from cars and tyres to railway travel and kitchenware. Even such 'low tech' artefacts as fountain pens were imaged in this fashion. One from 1956 shows a porthole shot of a lunar landscape, dominated by a smooth launchfield, with various space vehicles dotted about. Front and centre, pointing vertically to the stars, is a huge red and gold Parker '61': a bizarre image which equates the erect quill of print man with the projectile being readied, in the electric age, to shoot him into space.

Not surprisingly, the Nature depicted as corresponding to this triumphal-ist masculine reverie was passive, subordinate, and without threat. Nature in the raw – the nature we are part of and that can destroy us – was as absent from the promotional picture as female rage from the pages of *Playboy*. Even when acknowledged, which was rare, the forces of chaos were kept firmly outside the gates. Nor, of course, do 1950s ads show us the messy (and implicitly sexual) activity of subjugation/appropriation itself. The action is always over. Nature is already 'cooked': and cooked indeed to look like nature in precisely this compliant, that is verdant, tranquil, and orderly, sense.

Here, as elsewhere, promotion and the spontaneous symbolism of everyday life came to intersect. The post-war dream of suburbanization had as one of its core elements the tamed wilderness in every backyard. Through window shots of neatly trimmed lawns, etc, some ads (especially for household durables) simply played this figure back. Others projected it on to the larger canvas of the Great Outdoors. Where foregrounded in leisure-identified contexts (for example in a 1954, Canada = fishing, ad for Dominion Ten Whiskey) such landscapes could occasionally acquire a siren-like power of their own. But for the most part feminized nature knew her place: either as a bountiful source of raw materials or as a picturesque backdrop for the world of private plenty Promethean Man was proudly ushering in.

To a contemporary sensibility, such images seem inflated to the point of parody. It is not that capitalism, male dominance, and ecologically insensitive forms of industrial development have gone away. What has happened, rather, is that the cultural upheavals, economic dislocations, and technological implosion[4] of the past two decades have changed how industrial technology is experienced, and darkened the celebratory mood.

Advertisers, of necessity, have tacked with these winds. The corporate father-god has been scaled down, where not effaced. His former pretensions even became the butt of the occasional joke. 'Marriages', declares a 1979 Hilton ad over a breathtaking cloudscape, 'are made in heaven – why not hold the reception here?' The phallic styling of consumer goods has similarly gone out of vogue, and its main vehicle, rocketry, has virtually disappeared. Power-between-the-legs appeal is still important to the marketing of speed-machines like outboards, motorbikes and snow-mobiles. But the new signage of technological progress, which derives from computers and video screens, has come to stress operation over motion, not the body of the contraption but its control panel face.

Of course, as a mix of both modes, even so quintessential a machine age product as the car has always been ambiguously gendered. But the rise of electronic, communication-related goods has confounded the equation of techno-power and masculinity to the point where the gender identity of the former has become virtually indeterminate. Thus, while stereos promise power and wars are fought by keyboard, home-entertainment equipment (including computers) presents itself as user-friendly and is often con-toured along soft, feminine lines. Even here, moreover, there is scope for variance. In the first round of micro-computer marketing, IBM PCs, as befitted their male-oriented business market, were straight, functional, and angular. Apples, by contrast, according to trade-lore originally designed for women, were cute, cuddly, and round.

But the (relative) decoupling of phallic and frontier masculinity from symbols of technological progress in the advertising images of the 1970s and 1980s has reflected more than just a material shift to post-industrial products; and more, indeed, than the combination of this with the way in which the patriarchal spirit of an older industrialism has itself come under siege. Reinforced by the development of the wired home, it has symptomized, too, a cultural involution, a flight to the private, which has issued from a growing sense of exhaustion with the whole industrial project. Resource limits, external effects, and global poverty have all pressed in. Indeed, together with terrorism, crime, and the threat of war, these difficulties have been woven together into a composite picture of gathering doom by the very entertainment media which consumer audiences turn to for solace and escape.

This, and the very real stress of urban living, whether at its centre or at its commuter edge, has led, in turn, to a curious elevation of the nature-as-escape motif which was only secondary before. Cars in contemporary ads are almost never shown in city streets, and often not on roads at all. Instead, they stand in fields, by the sea or on the surface of the moon. In these and countless similar ads for liquor, tobacco, fashion, and food, tranquillizing pictures of earth, sky, and water have become commonplace signs for Nature as the ultimate balm: the redeeming maternal opposite, in effect, of city, industry, and Man. As a mirage projected from progress gone wrong, and just as we are bashing in her planetary skull, the Great Mother, it seems, is staging an ironic return.

In the end, as a result of all these shifts and reversals, the masculinist complex has not only begun to fade. It has given way to a contradictory melange in which the wider meaning of gender within the advertising cosmos cannot with any consistency be pinned down at all. If male and female are still tied to one another as complementary poles, the assignment of gender values to particular forces, institutions, and product types has become much less fixed. In effect, the whole symbolic system wherein male and female are projected on to the world has become free to float. Ads, in consequence, have begun to take a more circumscribed, and even abstract, approach to gender coding. Some products, like quality watches, are designed from the start to be displayed in matching pairs – a minimalist binary of his and hers that reduces male and female to marks (colour, shape, size, etc) of a purely external difference. In other cases these reduced and free-floating symbols have become a topic for play. A 1985 car stereo ad juxtaposes two images, a sporty red car and the black, powerful tuner and tape-deck itself. The first is named 'beauty', the second 'the beast'. While the ad uses conventional young buck imagery it is also tongue in cheek. The aim is to flatter the consumer not so much sexually as intellectually – as a person smart and contemporary enough to appreciate the semiotic wit.

Male sexuality

The displacement of men in ads from family roles and the wider retreat of masculinity as an ideologically fixed term have been complemented, finally, by a parallel loosening of masculinity as a *sexual* construct. Here, an even more basic aspect of the old patriarchal code has come unstuck, putting in question not just the traditional (or heterosexual, aggressive, dominant, etc) model of male identity, but the very polarity between the sexes which has hitherto defined gender as codeable at all. At the risk of oversimplifying what has evidently been a highly complex and contradictory development, a comparison between two starkly contrasting ads, one from the mid-1950s, one from twenty years later, may serve to illustrate at least the general direction in which the promotional representation of male sexuality has, in consequence, begun to change.

The first, for Kayser stockings, appeared in the May 1959 issue of the *New Yorker*. It is dominated by two vertically separated panels. The smaller one on the left, face-on and in close-up, shows the right-hand side of a man's face. The page's edge bisects it vertically through the nose, and the picture is cropped at the hairline, the edge of the eye, and just below the chin. The man is looking directly to his right, and his features seem to twinkle, with a barely suppressed whoop of amazement, approval, and delight.

As we follow his gaze the object of all this admiration comes immediately into view. In the right-hand panel his eye is drawn towards a magnificent pair of female legs. In a straight line past them, tucked away to the top right, his gaze comes to rest on a small but bright clump of inscriptions. These consist of a floral logo, the word 'Kayser', and in tiny letters, the denotator that finally identifies what is actually for sale: 'hosiery'. The legs themselves, to which his eyes and ours continually return, are like pillars: statuesque, alabaster, and curved. Incongruously, though presumably without meaning to spoil the effect, they are supported from below by the daintiest of spike heels, with one foot raised slightly from the ground.

The awkward shoes and submissive posture ill-suit this woman (for so we take her to be) for fight or flight. She is viewed from behind, and seems to have swivelled round to the left. It is as though she is now leaning against someone, and has tilted her face (which we can only imagine) for a kiss. Equally constricting is the tight skirt whose hem-line is just apparent at the top of the frame. By all these signs she gestures her helplessness in the social jungle, and her correlative need for a protector. At the same time, they are gestures of self-display. To emphasize which, the covetous male eye is shown level with the woman's calves, as if (though this is just a photographic trick) she is standing on a raised platform – a pedestal, no less – expressly to be admired. And so the circle is complete: his gaze and her legs, the passive activity of the one complemented perfectly by the active passivity of the other. Nor, according to the summarizing caption below, is there any other way for desire to flow. As the prescriptive caption at the foot of the page pointedly puts it: 'You' (Kayser wearer; women) 'owe it' (the allure of self-display) 'to your audience' (men).

There is nothing surprising in nylon manufacturers playing on the fetishization of female legs, for that is already the basis of their value as apparel. The ad is remarkable only for the clarity with which this promotional point, and the gender myth to which it is tied, is pushed. The ad's stripped-down structure also makes the myth itself transparently easy to read. The terms at the left and centre, centring on the legs themselves, gather together to provide a meaning for the brand-name posted on the right. The result is a set of identities: Kayser equals hosiery equals

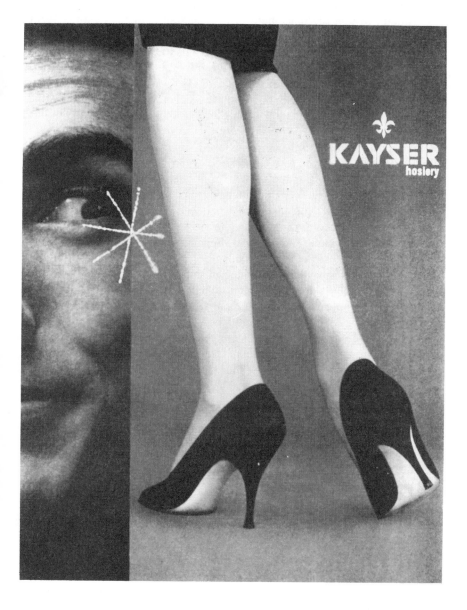

* YOU OWE IT TO YOUR AUDIENCE

women's legs (the kind that attract men); all of which equals the magical essence of femininity itself.

But there is also a reciprocal movement in the other direction. The whole syllogism is emphasized, indeed its logic commanded, by the male gaze which is the ad's principal visual thread. And this connective is further underlined through the placement of a small star at the eye's lower right-hand corner, a theme which is echoed in the logo atop the Y and S of 'Kayser', and again in the asterisk that draws us to the caption underneath. At once a further set of equivalences are implied. Kayser, like stockings, like women's legs, like Woman herself, are all as one with the star, at once desirous and idealizing, which burns in Man's eye. Man himself, moreover, is equated with that same star, but this time as the subject, not the object, of its light. Thus in defining femininity the ad defines masculinity too. If Woman exists sexually only in Man's eye, Man himself only exists in the (Woman-watching) exercise of that same organ.

The second ad, for Braggi after-shave, appeared in the September 1975 issue of *Penthouse*. One scene dominates the page. Awash with yellow and amber light, it shows the inside of a bathroom, cut off on the left and framed by an open folding door on the right. Sitting on the counter top to the right of the vanity – pink and shiny, pipes showing – is an elegant woman wearing a kimono-style bathrobe, slippers, ear-rings, and, we guess, nothing else. Without a flicker of emotion she looks straight into our eyes, her line of sight just a fraction higher than our own. To her left, occupying the whole vertical plane, is a naked man. Tall, lean, muscular, dark-haired, tanned, he stands intently before a mirror, in whose reflection (which he is watching too) we can see that he is shaving. The whiteness of the reflected cream we see on his face – on a line between the couple's actual two heads – is picked up by the whiteness of the bath towel draped around his neck. From the towel itself our eye descends down his back: drawn visually, if not erotically, by the lighter shade of skin on his buttocks (small and neat) which are virtually at eye-level in the middle left quadrant of the page.

At the lower right is a smaller rectangle. In this, against a jet black background, a male right hand is gently holding a bottle of the product. The hand is clean, manicured and wears a gold bracelet around the wrist. The product itself is a transparent elixir within a fist-sized straight-edged glass bottle, whose colour (emphasized by the black cap and black-and-gold label) derives from all the flesh-tones it reflects. And in dazzling white letters, directly above the hand and its prize, is the caption wherein both the brand-name and its freight of meaning are tersely spelled out: 'Braggi: for the man who can take care of himself.'

The sexual codings invoked here are more complex than in the case of the other ad, but they are quite legible and the contrast they present is certainly clear. In the smaller box, Braggi is the aroused penis of the masturbating male. Paralleling this, Braggi in the main picture, a fragrance welded on to the manly act of shaving, is the medium which transforms this daily grooming ritual into one of pleasurable self-indulgence.

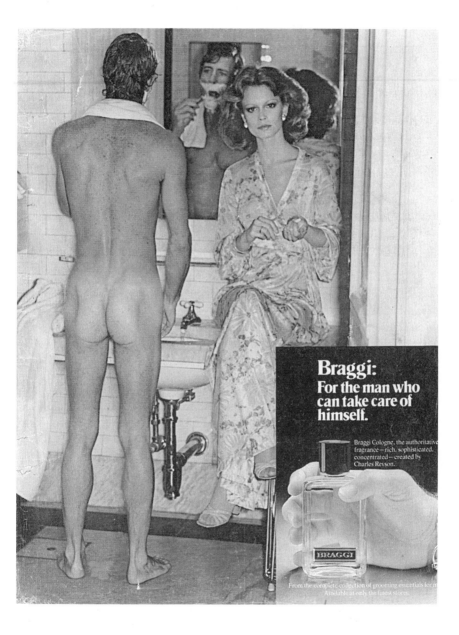

Again, the pitch is unremarkable given the nature of the commodity being promoted. It runs exactly parallel to multitudinous ads for similar (make-up) products aimed at women. But this is exactly what is so striking. For a narcissism which has long been culturally encouraged for women, as the gender defined as the object of a look, runs altogether counter to the heterosexual voyeurism which in the traditional code has been 'natural' to men. In that context, moreover, the ad's treatment of narcissism is especially norm-breaking. The homo-erotic desire which is always implicit in taking oneself as a sexual object, and which conventional masculinity is largely constituted as a reaction against (See Horowitz and Kaufmann, 1987), is here fully exposed. And not only (though they are doubtless one of the target markets) in a way designed to appeal to gays. For as our eye strays to inspect the man's body, it is constantly interrupted by the eyes of the woman who is herself always looking on. Those eyes at once judge and condone. But above all they provide, both for him and for us, a crucial heterosexual cover. What more is happening (this is *Penthouse* after all) than just a man shaving after he and his girl-friend have spent a pleasurable night together in bed?

Between the first ad and the second there is evidently a reversal of terms. If, in the former, Man is defined as the one who gazes at Woman, in the second it is he who is the object of such a look. And in switching roles, like the female nude-with-mirror of classical erotic art (Berger, 1972: 45–64), he himself, as the one admired, becomes redefined as the being whose natural condition it is to be in love with an image of himself.

It would be misleading to suggest that the kind of active, outwardly directed version of male sexuality presented by the Kayser ad has now been replaced, across the board, by the passively narcissistic version presented by the one for Braggi. The latter may symptomize a trend. But, as casual scrutiny of any current women's fashion magazine would show, it is not the only one. At that more general level what we currently have, in fact, is a heterogeneous picture in which both constructions of masculinity have come to coexist. The after-shave example itself, replete with *Penthouse* fantasies of the bachelor pad, at once bespeaks the old gender code and breaks from it. Like the Eves ad it is an ingenious compromise. What the contrast does make clear, though, is that the monopoly of the older code has been broken; and that as one result the iconic conventions of promotion are becoming flexible enough to allow men and women to be positioned at either end of the objectified/objectifying sexual continuum.

At the limit, particularly in ads for brands aimed at both sexes, male/female interchangeability may be emphasized as a feature in itself. In the androgynous imagery which often results, even the sexual orientation of the figures depicted (not to mention the consumer) may then be left in the air. A 1985 Lee jeans ad shows two males and one female draped around a bicycle, all wearing the hip-hugging product, each in physical and visual contact with the other two. Like the demure orgies shown in Calvin Klein's Obsession campaign, the sexual meaning of the scene is completely open.

The reading it permits is male as well as female, gay as well as straight. Beyond which, indeed, can be discerned yet a fifth possibility – bisexual and genderically indeterminate – which synthesizes the others in a polymorphous identity based on the very principle of gender equivalence which keeps all these possibilities in play.

Man in the mirror

The same overall point can thus be made about the promotional depiction of male sexuality as about that of men's familial role and of masculinity as a wider symbolic term. Since the early 1970s, advertising imagery shows evidence of having incorporated, alongside a code of gender difference and hierarchy, a code of sameness and equality. According to the former, while men are active, instrumental, inner-directed, and identified with power, women are passive, expressive, dependent on others, and trophies of war. According to the latter, male and female are to be conceived of as fluid, mobile categories which occupy, in the last analysis, equivalent if not identical places in the world.

In this, it may be said, the dynamics of promotion have been led to echo an actual egalitarian trend. However, the emancipatory content of the shift towards a code of equivalence in the promotional imaging of men is less far-reaching than it might seem. Three qualifying comments should particularly be made.

The first, and most straightforward, is that in gender, as in class, the ascendancy of equality as an approved value, particularly where embedded in descriptive-seeming representations, mystifies the inequities which continue to prevail. It is one thing for men and women to look and behave more nearly the same in the unencumbered leisure situations typically shown in ads; quite another for their economic, cultural, and political power to have actually become equal. In any case, even at the level of ideals, advertising does not simply echo the values it uses. It processes them. Even at its most expansive, the vision of male–female liberation that advertising has begun to project is limited by where it occurs. The new equivalence code is only an abstract equality, premised on the levelling effects of the market.[5] As such, moreover, it is a distorted echo not only of trends towards women's equalization with men as holders of external economic roles; but also of trends towards men's equalization with women as consumers. The softening up of male sexual identity, by playing to men's anxieties about how they look, is a direct concomitant of their more intensive cultivation by advertising precisely in that role.

The second qualification concerns the significance of the kind of gender re-coding represented by the Braggi or Lee jeans ads for the evolution of promotional imagery itself. The de-linking of masculinity from fixed familial, cosmological, and sexual positions has effectively transformed it, along with other sex/gender terms, into a floating signifier, free within any given promotional context to swirl around and substitute for its paired opposite at will. A postmodern sensibility may find in this vortex of signs a new experience of the sublime.[6] The commercial realities which predominate, however, give it a duller and more alienating edge. Like colour, setting, and decor, sex and gender have become arbitrary predicates of the commodities with which they are associated, the choice of any particular set being determined by the marketing context in which they are tactically deployed. In this way, male and female, masculine and feminine, men and women, have joined with other symbolized aspects of life and society to become the mere stuff of cultural coinage, circulating without any organic reference to what such tokens purport to represent and express.[7]

The third qualification is social and concerns the relation of all this traffic in persons-as-signs to corresponding developments on the plane of everyday life. Leaving aside what has happened at work, and the (lagged) implications of this for the distribution of domestic labour, for men to be imaged as women's semiotic equivalents replicates, and also naturalizes, a change which has occurred with respect to the ascribed place of men and women in socio-sexual circulation at large. In effect, as work and leisure sites have become more sexually desegregated, and sexist barriers to meeting and mating have begun to crumble, the primordial asymmetry within the social relations market between males (seeking) and females (sought) has begun to disappear. And with this shift, the culminating phase has been reached in that broader transformation of kinship noted by Lévi-Strauss (1969): from a 'restricted' system, where mate selection is closely prescribed, to an ultra-open one of 'generalized exchange'.

At first sight this dynamic points to a clear social gain. But for all its liberating potential, the expanded circulation which – from the dating/rating days of their youth – men, like women, are now constrained to enter into if they are to find suitable friends, lovers, and mates, is hemmed in, and even deformed, by its socioeconomic setting. Interpersonal exchange may be competitive, but it is certainly not free. Besides the persistence of inequalities between the sexes themselves, class differences and the status hierarchies based on them crucially mediate the search for interpersonal satisfaction and ties so that the whole process becomes (or remains) deeply enmeshed in the more general scramble for wealth, power, and status.

Even if the interpersonal market were perfectly competitive, however, the very fact of its being a market would have problematic implications for the forms of life it mediates. Besides being invidious, the element of interpersonal competition continually introduces an element of extrinsic calculation into the ostensibly authentic transactions and interchanges which move the process of meeting and mating along. In such a competitive context, whether at school, work, prayer or play, who you are is always a function, at least in part, of who you are with; just as – and in an age of equivalence to exactly the same degree – the status of spouse, lover or friend is also a function of yours. Forming attachments has to meet the test of status. At the limit, you don't make friends, you network.

Given the increasing extent to which men's and women's place in this contest has come to converge, it is clear that the recent rise of male-oriented fashion magazines like *Gentleman's Quarterly* and *Face* has responded to a real demand. As with women's magazines, that demand evidently has a dual character. To become an attuned and knowledgable consumer of clothes, entertainment, and 'lifestyle accessories' is not just a matter of attending to products. It means attending to your own construction as a salable package. What every glossy page of these publications impresses, in short, is that the more intensively, on the interpersonal front, men have entered into competitive circulation, the more they have become, like women before them, analogous, even in the act of consumption, to consumer goods themselves.

There is a giddying reflexivity in this. For the quasi-commodified person that circulates on the socio-sexual market is not only a creator of that same product, but a promoter of it; in relation to which, just as with inanimate consumer goods, that product (Here I am! Take me!) is itself constructed as a self-advertising promotional sign. At work, to be sure, at least for salaried employees, men have long been in that situation. The fact of a labour market creates a contest for positions and career advancement which (starting with the job interview) generates the need for self-promotion at every competitive turn. It is not, then, that men are being converted into self-promoting signs of themselves *de novo*; but rather that this condition has been qualitatively intensified through its extension from men's occupational lives to their private ones. Equalization of the sexes, in this respect, involves the converse for men of what it means for women. If men must learn to become more fashion-conscious, women must learn the skills of careerism. The outcome, though, is convergent. The entry of men and women more fully on to the stage of inter-individual competition has intensified the salience of such competition for both sexes; and, just as in the commercial sphere, the opening up of a market has engendered a further extension of promotional practice.

Of course, this new market has a distinctive character. For it arises from the commodification, and quasi-commodification, of individuals them-selves. Not only, then, is the object of production here its own producing subject. In a parody of the inner-directed individualism which this implies, the active, self-investing self is also a promotional subject, while the self it is creating is a promotional construct attuned to the requirements, and prejudices, of the market/audience whose custom that self-producing and self-promoting subject seeks.

It should be added that the constructed side of this self is not just an external veneer, a matter of dress and style. Nor is it only a question of generating, through personal and occupational history, a competitively successful 'profile'. The fleshly emphasis of fashion and clothing ads – for men now, as for women throughout history – shows that the self-construction of the individual as 'an advertisement for myself' extends to the very body on which these products are draped. In which context, these products themselves, finally, have a singular quality. For the function for which they are designed – fashion – is itself, at another level of market competition, a prop for their purchaser's self-promotion.

C.B. McPherson (1964) coined the term possessive individualism to describe the Lockeian individual at the centre of liberal contract theory. Considering that what is owned is not only traded but advertised, we can say that the possessive individual of early capitalism has transmuted today into a more advanced variant: the promotional individual.

It is from just this angle that the body-flashing exhibitionism and narcissism played on so explicitly in ads like the one for Braggi is so revealing. The equalization of gender status which is beginning to occur in the sphere of consumption is not in the least the equality we might dream of: the equality of free and self-determining beings in free and self-determining association with one another. It is the equality, rather, of self-absorbed, and emotionally anxious, personalities for sale. With the make-up mirror dangled invitingly before them, men, like women, are being encouraged to focus their energies not on realizing themselves as self-activating subjects, but on maximizing their value as circulating tokens of exchange. The practical conclusion may be drawn that if gender equality is to mean real freedom – though individual psychology is hardly the place to begin – the mirror which bids fair to hold both sexes in thrall will certainly have to come down from the wall.

Notes

1. For an examination of the persistence of women's 'double day' of labour, see Luxton (1980).

2. The importance of sexual renunciation to the clean-up-the-town-and-move-on hero at the centre of the 'American monomyth' has been explored by Jewett and Lawrence (1977: 12–15 et seq.).

3. The thesis that there is an intrinsic connection between male social and cultural dominance and the rapacious conquest of nature associated with industrialism has been a staple of Frankfurt School critical theory. The classic formulation is Horkheimer and Adorno (1972). Of similar inspiration is Leiss's *Domination of Nature* (1972). The argument has also been taken up by eco-feminists like Dinnerstein (1976).

4. The idea that technological progress in the age of electronics and computers reverses the explosive and expansionary effect of an earlier form of industrialism was forcefully advanced by McLuhan (see especially 1965: 346–59).

5. For a feminist critique of the kind of abstract gender equality promoted in liberal theory and market-driven practice see Mitchell (1976) and Maroney (1985).

6. Berman (1982) develops an experientially oriented analysis of modernism in precisely these terms. For a linking of postmodernist aesthetics to the romantic notion of the sublime see Jameson (1984). A shorter version of this latter paper is to be found with others, similarly searching for a critical-progressive tendency within 'postmodern culture', in Foster (1984).

7. For a nullifying (if ultimately apolitical) critique of modern mass media in terms of the over-production of de-referentialized signs, see Baudrillard (1981), especially the essay 'Requiem for the Media'.

4
(RE-)IMAGING TECHNOLOGY: THE CASE OF CARS

He doesn't design cars, he designs missiles.

Enzo Ferrari, referring to Ferdinand Porsche

The progress of 'progress'

In the early 1980s, IBM ran a remarkable series of ads preparing the way for the coming world of PCs. One of its aims was to reinforce the identity long built up between the name of the company and computers as such. But as a major in the market IBM also had a stake in the pace at which the new technology could be introduced, hence a concern to allay the anxieties of those whose lives, particularly at work, were about to be disrupted by the stresses and displacements computerization would bring.

Reassurance, at any rate, was the theme of the campaign, a message deftly delivered by suggesting that computers would eventually be regarded with the same wistfulness which earlier inventions of commerce had now come to evoke. By this device the shock of the new was put magically into reverse. From the perspective of an imaginary future, computers, like bicycles, cars, and planes, were converted into the romanticized spirits of a simpler, bygone age.

Considering the excitement which has long surrounded technical progress, and the ideological benefits derived from this by the economic power-holders of industrial society, the defensiveness of the pitch is as noteworthy as its sleight of hand. There is, here, no boundless, Nature-conquering enthusiasm for what technical progress might bring. At the same time, the campaign does link computers to earlier icons of technology, principally from the realm of transport, which have been associated with just that kind of science-based Frontier optimism. All of which would suggest, on the one hand, that computers have indeed inherited the mantle of that myth, while, on the other – and perhaps as a result – that the myth itself has changed.

Particularly revealing is the ad in the series which recalls the birth of the car. Along a glorious country road a vintage automobile speeds towards a horse and carriage. The horse has bolted upright and a woman passenger leans forward and points in a gesture of astonishment. In the lower right hand corner (in computer graphic style) we see the logo *IBM*; and across

If computers scare you, just imagine how people felt when they first saw the horseless carriage.

The promise of a new era implies change. And change can be unsettling at first.

That's why we at IBM feel that right now is the time to talk about the computerized office – and your power over it.

Right now, because we are on the threshold of a new era. Technologically and economically. The benefits Canadians will derive from the new office technology will be tremendous.

Just look. Today you can use a desktop com-puter, such as the IBM Personal Computer, to help you see several futures for your business. So you can plan for the right future.

And there are IBM systems that let you com-municate with other computers, across the office or across the country, to bring you the informa-tion you need to get the job done successfully.

Desktop computers that can simplify and improve almost every aspect of your work.

In fact, affordable IBM computers and office systems not only help you stay on top of your job, they help you get ahead of it.

Yesterday, the car pushed transportation into new frontiers and gave us mobility beyond our wildest dreams.

Today, IBM office technology holds the prom-ise of improving productivity and prosperity, even for small companies, by giving us power over time and information.

And there's nothing frightening about that.

IBM

the whole scene, the caption: 'If computers scare you, imagine how people felt when they saw their first horseless carriage.'

The surface meaning is plain. New technologies may upset old ways, but there is no need to worry for computers will become as banally ordinary as cars, their benefits just as self-evident – and all this just through the natural passage of time. When we probe a bit more deeply, however, matters become more complex.

The central image of car-meets-buggy is itself a hoary cliché. But even as a dead metaphor for progress, for 'modern' overtaking 'traditional' society, it implies a whole way of seeing things (history, for example, as an open road) which can easily be made to sustain a host of problematic assumptions about the actual interplay of the developments it depicts. And the same goes for the cars = computers analogy into which the image is drawn. What is it, one is prompted to ask, that the early car and the new computer are supposed to have in common? And what precisely is the relation between the progress from horse to car, and the progress from the latter to the IBM PC? Does the computer, indeed, have a precursor which parallels the horse?

Since transport and information processing are distinct functions we are left, in the end, with only the vaguest of abstractions for an answer: that these artefacts, as a series of ever more advanced forms of applied natural power (animal, engine, electronic), are all instances of 'technology'; that the historical movement from one to the other represents 'progress'; and that in their succession along the highway of history we see modernity itself unfold. What horse-and-carriage, car, and computer all share, in other words, is the capacity of their images to function as equivalent signifiers for 'technology', in a cumulating series which, taken together, also means 'progress'. From this angle, as a kind of cultural language game, the ad's real content is not about cars and computers at all. It is about the relation of these objects to a cluster of symbolized values; and what it tells us is that the car as a symbol (in the misty past) of technology's cutting edge has now been replaced by the computer.

Now, a glance at the real history of symbolized technology will show that the movement depicted in the ad is significantly abridged. The car, as a sign of the eclipsed (that is, pre-computer) version of that myth, is shown only at its moment of arrival, and then only in relation to the horse. Its predecessor, the railway, and its successors, the aeroplane and the spaceship, are not mentioned. And, most importantly, the subsequent history of the car itself – which, despite its technical supersession by mechanized flight, has continued to present itself, through styling and promotion, as the very sign of the progress it no longer materially embodies – is left out of the frame.

What we have, then, is myth about myth. This meta-myth condenses three symbolic events: the supersession of the internal combustion engine by jets and rockets as the up-to-the-minute expression of mechanization and thrill-endowed speed; the much more recent decline of the car, borrowing imagery from other transport forms, as a generalized symbol for progress; and, most recent of all, a shift in the meaning of technology itself, linked to the rise of computers as a differently inflected sign. To decipher the meaning of these developments their erased history must be restored. What, then, has happened – especially since its heyday in the 1950s – to the imaged automobile as the symbol of technological advance? And how has the meaning of that idea, which continues to be manufactured into cars, shifted under the sign of 'high tech'?

Cars as signs

The production of cars as signs is a special case of the way in which, since the industrial revolution of the late eighteenth century, all mass-produced consumer goods have come to intersect with the world of meaning. That is: their visual appearance is designed to be continuous with the advertising through which they are mass marketed. But, as a self-promoting commodity-sign, the modern automobile has two additional distinctive features.

First, besides their function as transport, cars have always had a promotional role for users themselves. Parked at home, like furniture, like the domicile itself, they project a sense of their owner's relative social standing. Out on the road they carry that same sense of class/cultural identification into the wider cultural domain. Cars, in this respect, are similar to clothes, constituting indeed a kind of third skin for ambient industrial man. Like clothes, too, as markers of identity within an anonymously circulating public they readily become subject to the fashion dynamics of competitive display, which manufacturers themselves have naturally encouraged to accelerate obsolescence and sales. Despite there being fewer and fewer corporate players, the proliferation and turnover of styles has thus kept far ahead of strictly engineering innovation. Ford, the first US motor giant, was at first slow to change lines. But declining sales for its Model T brought the lesson of fashion home. Thus the Model A of 1927 was followed by the V8 in 1932 – after which came a complete change of look with the introduction of streamlining, pioneered by Chrysler with its 'Airflow' model in 1934. After the war it was General Motors that took the lead. With the establishment of GM's Art and Color Department, renamed the Styling Division in 1955,[1] the fashion mode became institutionalized, complete with travelling Motoramas and the still surviving ritual of 'this year's new model'. The overall effect has been that car design (especially at the level of feel and look) has become a predominant element of car promotion. Overwhelmingly, from billboards to show-rooms, cars have been advertised by being shown, giving pseudo-auratic texture to that endless parade of vehicles on the actual highway, which itself has served as one vast ad.

Secondly, unlike such products as pottery, furniture, and clothes which were previously hand-made, the automobile was a new invention. It never existed outside the framework of industrialized mass production. The history of its received meaning has always been bound up, then, with that of its manufactured meaning as promotionally designed; so tightly, indeed, that for consumers as well as producers cars have been taken, from the start, as veritable emblems of the techno-economic transformation which had made them possible. By the mid-1920s, mass-produced cars signalled the promise of mass affluence – hence Hoover's 1924 election slogan: 'a chicken in every pot; two cars in every garage' – and Henry Ford had become an international byword for the assembly-line system he had pioneered in his Michigan plant. The American painter Charles Sheeler developed a whole aesthetic on the basis of such industrial landscapes. In *Criss-Crossed Conveyors* and other works Ford's Dearborn factory was itself converted into an icon of the new era.[2] Italian Futurists like Marinetti, Mario de Leone, and Auro d'Alba made a similar fetish of the actual vehicle. In Picabia's precisely rendered pistons, carburettors, and camshafts the focus is more narrowly on the engine: a machine of finely interlocking parts whose efficient, well-oiled motion embodied the spirit of an industrialism which was itself the idealized expression of male sexual power.

Cars themselves, moreover, like other new products (refrigerators, typewriters, phonographs, cameras, radios, etc) came to symbolize that entire new world – and world of the new – which industry and science were sensed as ushering in. And quintessentially: for the spread of cars rapidly transformed the whole ecology of life, creating massive dependent industries, road-systems and transformed cities; while, at the individual level, it accelerated private and occupational mobility, altering our whole sense of time and space. For cars to be promotionally presented, then, as symbols of Modernity, Technology, and Progress, was never entirely arbitrary. The establishment of a land-based transportation system based on the automobile really was a crucial element in the civilizational changes established at the beginning of the twentieth century, and to whose triumphant dynamic these mythicized terms refer.

Up to this point I have spoken only of cars-in-general. But their constructed symbolism has varied: not just through time, but by divisions within their market. Since the earliest Fords and Oldsmobiles, there have, in fact, been three cultural reference points for car imagery, each broadly corresponding to a different market segment for which different kinds of cars have been designed.

First, and closest to the technology complex itself, is the imagistic set associated with roadsters, sports cars, and the Porsches, Trans-Ams, etc which are now their 'muscle-car' equivalent. Inspiring them all, for over eighty years, has been the spectator sport of car racing, a powerful ritual of male competitive prowess which has conveniently enabled companies to promote themselves while testing R&D. From which, not surprisingly, the racing-car – and the road models derived from it – emerged as an almost

perfect symbol for the masculinist technology values racing itself cele-
brates: a male-identified machine, shaped like a bullet, and experienced
from within as an exhilarating rush towards orgasm, the future, and death.
This sense of the car has perhaps never been more passionately expressed
than in Marinetti's 1905 encomium 'To the Automobile' where the car is a
modern Pegasus and the mechanical takes flight.[3]

In complete contrast have been the design characteristics of the luxury
car, a vehicle which has continued to trail associations of the genteel upper-
class carriage which came immediately before. Such archaism, marked
even today by the use of wood and the relative boxiness of limousines, has
served not just as an antidote to future shock, but as a sign of that abstract
Tradition which industrialism itself has converted into a token of status.
Hence, too, the wider diffusion of this complex to other types, whether in
the persistence of 'tonneau' design until the mid-1920s, or in the use of
coachwork language ('Bodies by Fisher') in mainstream ads since then.

Lastly, and occupying a kind of symbolic mid-point, we have the family
sedan. Designed for mixed use by the whole family (at first, one car per
household) its imagery has likewise been mixed. As a commuter/leisure
vehicle for the chief breadwinner, it has invited sportiness; as an index of
social status, indications that the household is up to date, tasteful or rich.
But an element of symbolism has also attached to it as a vehicle for the
family as such.

Generally, as a kind of moving home, it has been built to appear
respectable, functional, and safe. It has also been given design features
which materially represent 'the family' as a particular (yet seemingly
universal) type of group. Thus, in a transposition from the Victorian
landau, the 4–5 seat saloon – throughout this century the family car's
instantly recognizable form – not only assumes that the family is nuclear. It
also sets up a seating grid within which, by custom, the father/husband
drives, the wife sits at his side, and the children form a row at the back.
More latterly, as this hierarchical, role-divided model has softened and car
ownership by youth and women has increased, the mass car has continued
to reflect the prevailing family form, though in a way that is correspondingly more unisex, age-neutral, and varied in size and composition.

This, then, is the matrix within which the history of car imagery has had
to unfold. Evidently, like the matrix itself, that history has been multi-
levelled and does not reduce to any single thread.

To be noted, first, is a dynamic constant: while no type has been
symbolically pure, the family car (still the industry's backbone) has
peculiarly come to serve as a condensation-point for all the image clusters
cars can attract. As a mass vehicle it was, and is, designed to appeal to all
but the wealthiest households, as well as to all in them. For that reason,
too, since artisanal traditionalism, techno-futurism and the values surrounding 'the family' (not to mention their class/ethnic variants), do not
exactly cohere, its imagery has tended towards ambiguity and compromise.
Hence, whatever the idiom of the day, its characteristically average look,

in which potentially clashing elements are softened at the edges or even made to cancel one another out. Within that mix, modernist/masculinist technology values have always been prominently expressed. But by the same token their influence has also been checked; and by considerations no less related to the logic of market appeal.

With respect to the coding of status, secondly, there has been a steady tendency for Quality Street references to horse-and-carriage, despite their anachronistic persistence, to recede gradually from view. A major change came when modernized styling, introduced in the early 1930s in such models as the Ford V8, began to connect engine to cab in one steady line (Heskett, 1980: 72–4). With that step, pre-car imagery migrated from the car's actual body to the once-removed rhetoric contained in its ads. In the 1940s and 1950s, through such devices as depicting cars as paintings, the horse and carriage 'craft' cluster was still further attenuated: blurring into an image of timeless pre-industrialism ('Buick: a classic') wherein, having separated from the car's material form, it lost contact with that form's history as well.

Besides the present-oriented push of fashion, the boom and bust of capitalism have, as a counter-trend, increasingly made stylistic up-to-dateness itself an essential aspect of the car's capacity to convey esteem. For post-1945 working- and middle-class householders, modern-looking cars were a visible way to put the Depression and poverty behind. More generally, in the anxious and dispersed culture of twentieth-century consumerism, being up to date and modern became a crucial badge of social membership. The import of this for the imaged car's incorporation of technology values has again been ambiguous. With mid-market cars, as with fashion, if it became important to be contemporary it also became risky to seem too far in front.

Finally, the element of car imagery which has to do with the encoding of techno-myth has itself significantly changed – not least because the car as a symbol of driven speed, and thence of technological progress, became outmoded by faster forms of transport, especially by ones moving through air. Corresponding to this, the mass-produced car was successively re-designed – from the 'airflows' of the 1930s and the fins-and-tails of post-war Detroit to the 'aero' models of today – with each new style mimicking the transport form currently closest to the speed/progress ideal. On one level, of course, the plane-influenced trend towards streamlining was a practical move, reducing not only wind resistance but the attendant costs of fuel. But it has also had a purely symbolic aspect.[4] In such baroque, rocket-like machines as the 1955 Cadillac 'Eldorado', aerodynamic efficiency was actually sacrificed in the interests of an aerodynamic look. If cars, as a result, became planes, missiles, and spaceships, driving, in fantasy, became a flight: a potent metaphor which, as post-war 'depth' promoters well understood, alluded at once to a technicist (and space age) notion of progress and to the promptings of sexual desire.

In its guise as a machine, the car has also been made to seem alive. This has by no means been merely a matter of consumer transference, though the ease with which popular speech has absorbed the metaphor ('she handles really well') shows how culturally resonant it is. Through promotion and design such animism has been given tangible shape. In a first step, the engine radiator, mounted at the front, was given a grille (mouth). Then were added two separated headlights (eyes), and a pointed bonnet (nose) – compensating, presumably, for the vanished face of the horse. The high-point came with the customizing craze of the 1940s and 1950s, together with the almost equally flamboyant monster-types it inspired in the industry.[5] Figuration in so blatant a form, however, declined after the Ford Edsel – a car whose spectacular marketing failure (in 1958) was perhaps best explained by customer comments that its grille looked like a vagina (replete, we may add, with teeth). Since then, the beast theme has been domesticated and made the stuff of advertising copy and brand-names (Mustangs, Colts, Foxes, Rabbits, etc); while cars, physically, have been contoured more as cyborg-like extensions of their own drivers. On the darker, Frankensteinian, side, this robotic trend has triggered horror film images of riderless vehicles (Stephen King's *Christine*, Stephen Spielberg's *Duel*), out to destroy their human creators for giving them no soul.

The car's imaging as alive has also implied its presentation as sexed. In the first instance, and from the side of the male driver, the car has been projected as Woman: whether as flashy possession, mistress or wife.[6] However, in this (variously nuanced) scene of the male-led couple the car has also figured as rocket, bullet or gun, that is as a sexual extension of the male; while for both sexes, as an enclosed place in which to escape, it has at the same time played the part of a womb. Whence has arisen one of the car's most striking symbolic features: its gender ambiguity. Thus if promotion and use have tied it, like Adam's rib, to the cosmos of phallic technology,[7] they have also given it the character of an androgyne.

Until recently, these intertwined tendencies towards flight and animation have constituted the main line of development. But since the 1960s the story has been complicated by two additional symbological developments.

First, with the rise of space technology (military and civilian), advances in transport have increasingly come to rely on improvements not so much in propulsion as in guidance systems and their finger-tip control. More generally, the rise of computers and informatics has made communications, rather than transport, the exemplary site of technological progress as such. While there are parallels between the accelerated movement of things/people through space, and of information/thought through electric circuits, they are not the same.[8] A shift in attention from one to the other has implied as well, then, a shift in the register of 'technology' as a cultural idea. McLuhan, who was beguiled by this, saw an explosive/atomistic world of mechanization giving way to an implosive/holistic one of electronics (McLuhan, 1965: 346–69). For imaged cars, more narrowly, this change has been reflected in the way that looking modern has come to mean not just looking fast and airborne, but being linked to computers and all that they connote.

Secondly, and cutting across contrived symbolism of any kind, car design and promotion have been affected by the resurgence of functionalism. Until the late 1960s, the Bauhaus maxim of 'form follows function' was more prevalent among European than American manufacturers, both as a creed and as a stick with which to beat their transatlantic rivals. But in the wake of the 1960s cultural upheaval, and in the shape of energy-crisis 'econoboxes', such anti-decorative purism began to exert a strong pull on North American car design too. Like streamlining, the functionalist revanchism has had a partly economic motive – reflecting, during the post-Vietnam downturn, the renewed importance to consumers of efficiency and price. But the pre-eminence of function is also a value; and as such (despite itself) it is always liable to become an explicit element in the rhetoric and styling of artefacts made over in its name. For progressive designers in the 1920s[9] functionalist principles provided a utopian definition of modernity itself. In the North American car market, more prosaically, they have come to provide a salable counter-image to set against the self-congratulatory New Frontierism which, at least in the United States, has been that idea's predominant form.

With all these various forces and tendencies in mind let us now turn directly to our original question: the meaning of the car's post-1950s imagistic shift.

The rise and fall of the rocket

The 1950s-style American car, today an object of veneration, is an instantly recognizable type. From the 1948–9 GM models which initiated it, to the fins-and-tails cult classics which came to epitomize the whole Eisenhower period, its design was marked by a combination of animism and streamlining taken to almost self-parodying heights of excess. In such a form, it served at once as a commuter vehicle for the suburban family and as a freedom-endowing one for the restless young.[10] In this guise, too, it became an international symbol of the post-war boom, indeed of free enterprising America itself. Soaked in Buck Rogers images of space and the future, it signified, above all, that new romance with technology which gave Cold War ideology its heady, expansive edge.[11]

A 1950 ad for Oldsmobile shows clearly the value-complex such a vehicle was designed to evoke. The car itself, shot sideways-on as if streaking across the page, dominates the horizontal plane. Its sleek, forward-thrusting design, emphasized by decorative chrome, seems to rise slightly in the air as our eye follows its body lines from tail to nose. The same motion and the same shape, though this time with a distinct, if gentle, angle of ascent, is replicated in the miniature spaceship jetting away in the top left. In case the point is missed we also get a caption: the car's

Sm-o-o-th!

"ROCKET" ENGINE AND OLDSMOBILE HYDRA-MATIC

*Hydra-Matic Drive optional at extra cost on all Oldsmobile models.

This is the car . . . this is the power team that's completely different from anything else on the road today. The surging power of the high-compression "Rocket" Engine! The silken smoothness of Oldsmobile Hydra-Matic Drive*! Sm-o-o-o-th is the only word for it. Try the "Rocket" Hydra-Matic "88" at your Oldsmobile dealer's soon. Drive it and discover the big difference in automobile performance yourself!

OLDSMOBILE

A General Motors Value

'"rocket" engine' (what else?) gives you 'sm-o-o-o-th' driving. So, via engine and body-shape, the Oldsmobile '88' is identified with a spaceship and, through that figure, with male sexuality itself.

This quintessential triad – car, rocket, penis – is linked in turn with a social idea, represented by the smart and happy young couple whose car this evidently is. In fact they appear twice. Inside the car, clean-cut and be-jacketed, the man sits comfortably at the wheel; while in the passenger seat beside him his brunette companion looks confidently ahead. (In this classic pose, settled and domestic, we read them as married – parents-to-be, perhaps, of the very generation which rejected the road they are culturally motoring along.) Above them, in the Rocket's literal reprise, and with the sloping '88' above the car as a launch pad, the machine's double (to scale) has actually lifted off. And here the couple appear again, this time straddling their pride and joy like bikers, with hubby waving from the front and wifey, side-saddle, clinging lovingly on from behind.

The two signifying clusters, rocket technology and companionate marriage, have a common term in the male dominance which is central to the pictorial representation of both. But there is a processual point as well. At this moment of take-off, we may suppose, the car has become theirs, a dream-come-true of upward mobility, growing affluence and technical progress, all fused together in the happily consummated marriage at the centre of the scene.

There is clearly great discontinuity between this ideological universe and our own. Scarcely eight years later, indeed, the first rumblings of change were already apparent in the marketing catastrophe of the Edsel. The failure of that exaggerated vehicle, as the car industry subsequently learned, not only signalled the end of a design era but foreshadowed a crisis, which had become palpable by the early 1970s, for the whole value complex which such styling bespoke.[12]

First, in the sex-gender upheaval of the late 1960s and 1970s, the technology complex to which the 1950s car had been tied became loosened from its neo-patriarchal frame. Not that masculinist imagery and the cowboy complex were wholly eliminated. Sports cars continued to be styled as toys for boys. But such values did cease to be identified with the family car, and indeed during the 1970s the family itself – whether in model nuclear form or not – was rarely depicted in such ads at all. Increased participation by women in work and public life also coincided with a proportionate increase in the number of women on the road. In market as well as ideological terms, then, the assumption that it was men driving the machines became promotionally untenable.

At the same time, techno-worship itself came increasingly under attack. A succession of international crises (Suez, Berlin, Cuba, Vietnam) made the nightmare of the nuclear arms race frighteningly alive. The very use of a projectile as an image for optimism and human progress became over-shadowed by its military implications. Even as a means of human transport ('a driverless vehicle', as Northrop Frye put it) the rocket became a symbol of negativity: technology as a blind and ungovernable force. Such a re-evaluation was further reinforced by the dampened expectations which set in after the long, and seemingly endless, post-war boom plateaued out and then, in the financial turmoil of the early 1970s, came to an end. The result, whose harbinger was the anti-technocratic side of 1960s counter-culture (Roszak, 1969), was a whole-scale resuscitation of Nature as the repressed Other of all-conquering Industry. If ecologism and health campaigns have been its political expression, this cultural reaction has also had an aesthetic side – in food and decor, a preference for natural materials over plastic – in the consumption style of the new middle class. In keeping with such changed sensibilities car design became less blatantly wasteful; fins and chrome were shed, and cars in ads were depicted in fields, identified with free-ranging animals (especially horses) and tied to leisure-related fantasies of rural escape.

Disenchantment, however, was not only at the level of image. The oil crisis of the mid-1970s, growing traffic congestion, and unease with rampant road construction[13] changed mass attitudes to the car itself. Everyone, of course, still wanted one. Suburbanization and the decline of public transport had made the car more of a necessity than ever. But these developments undermined the car's symbolic identification with individual freedom; while that value itself came into collision with what was practically implied – from the midst of a traffic jam – by the car's master-value as the embodiment of techno-industrial advance. Cars materially, then, became a bad sign of what they had earlier celebrated; and just as cigarette promoters had to exorcise the cancer scare, car promoters found themselves having to deflect the negative associations with which *their* product had become endowed.

Occasionally, the car's dystopian associations were taken head on. A 1979 Datsun ad has a black and red close-up of a glowing dashboard and night-time windscreen. We peer through it as if through a port-hole into space. 'George Orwell', pronounces the caption, 'was wrong.' As the small print indicates, 'Orwell' is to be taken as a general reference to all modern prophets of doom – an elastic category that stretched, it seems, even to Ralph Nader. Indeed, the Orwellian lament is taken to have been about neither totalitarianism, nor the manipulative use of modern media to that end, but about built-in obsolescence. Hence Datsun's riposte: 'Our cars will last to 1984 and beyond.' With less literary licence, a 1986 Toyota campaign also risked naming the negative. Driving the product, we are told, is just the way to fight 'road monotony'.

The commonest tactic, though, was simply to reverse the sign. Rather than portraying cars as the pinnacle of urban civilization, ads placed them in green meadows as the embodiment of countryside. Rather than representing world-conquering technology, they were linked to nature as balm and escape. What the car was represented to be, in short, was not what it overwhelmingly was: a commuter vehicle tail-gating traffic to and from work. It was, instead, a means to get away – a piece of magic, in fact, which could wash away toil and traffic altogether.

Even with such strategies, real promotional difficulties were evidently posed. Just as the North American market was becoming tougher, the symbolic resources available for imaging the product were becoming unstable and difficult to use. To some degree the European-inspired return to functionality plugged this anomic gap. With the dramatic mid-1970s rise in petrol prices, the market in any case was placing greater stress on cars' performative side; whence the decline of the gas-guzzler and increased appeal for more functional (and functional-looking) designs.[14] But in the heartlands of consumerism the appeal of such semantic restraint (which made its appearance with the VW, system-designed European cars, and Detroit compacts) was more safe than exciting – raising the spectre, indeed, of an entropic wind-down in which automotive meaning, and with it the whole romance of the car, might finally collapse. Additional ways had to be found, then, for infusing the duller looking vehicles the functionalist reaction was leading to with new symbolic life.

'High tech'

It is in just this context, from the early 1980s on, that the car's rendering as a symbol for 'technology' began to be revised. After a long hiatus, the car's linkage to the romance of rockets was replaced by a new enthusiasm for the communications revolution centred on the microchip. But what, we may wonder, is the value import of this new sign? Does it connote anything more than just a differently dressed version of the same old myth?

Two ads from *Time* magazine, published (in December 1982) during the initial burst of mass computer excitement, may provide the beginnings of an answer. The first, for Volkswagen Rabbit, is constructed around the caption 'High tech. Who gives a heck?' Each of these phrases heads a differently designed page. Both are text-heavy with various performance-related claims; but the graphics and layout of the 'high tech' panel on the left recall a computer-screen, while the writing on the right is in hard print. Thus the new car is to the old as high tech to low tech; and the former is to the latter as the electric age of video and computers is to the galaxy of Gutenberg.

The performative implication is that with the aid of computers the advertised VW is ultra-intelligently designed. There is, however, a curious subtext. The designer seems to be the computer itself. And the microchips built into the car (to regulate engine performance, to ensure the fastening of seat-belts, and to indicate fuel-efficient speeds) likewise seem to turn it into a being with a mind. Both as creator and creation, then, the computer is ethereally alive, a benign intelligence which can even anticipate what we need.[15] As the closing aphorism says: 'If you thought about Rabbit as much as Rabbit thinks about you you'd think about Rabbit.' Of course, the notion of a machine with a brain has nightmare connotations, too. However, in transferring this personified, user-friendly idea of high tech on to the vehicle itself, the bad associations are obviated by the brand-name

which the car has been given. What could be more innocuous, and more in harmony with the natural world, than this furry, herbivorous, little pet?

The second ad, for Toyota, plays with a similar theme. Again there are two panels, topped by a visually bifurcated phrase: 'The Toyota/Edge'. Foregrounded under each is a front-on picture of the car: on the left, as it actually appears; on the right, in computer graphics, an X-ray-like engineering drawing of its hidden ribs and lines of force. Again the computer is depicted as a sign of embodied intelligence, with that quality similarly relayed on to the car. In both cases, too, the wonders of the computer, personified as a god/man with the professional qualities of medic and bio-engineer, give us magical access to the car's hidden structure. And in both cases, finally, this focus on the car's inside emphasizes the car's fantasy role as a womb, a role which is immediately qualified by its doubling as the manifestation of designer (and driver) control. In the Toyota case, this interiorizing movement is made central to the thematic composition of the ad. And it is given a further – youth-oriented – twist by the campaign slogan which appears at the foot of the computer-signifying panel on the right: 'Oh what a feeling!' This, as contemporaries would know, is not just a subjective exclamation of sensual pleasure, but the title of a hit from the dance-movie *Flashdance*.[16]

There are other respects, as well, in which the car's entry into the world of high tech has been accompanied by a movement of interiorization. In physical design, as the Rabbit ad illustrates, growing attention has been given to such internal features as seating and driver ergonomics, dashboard set-ups (digitalized, and with more engine feedback), and on-board entertainment (quadraphonic speakers, tapedecks, CDs, etc). In ads, whether computer-referenced or not, the car has been projected as a kind of wrap-around experience, or even as a mystical inner trip. A 1987 commerical for Honda shows a woman stealing from her husband/lover's bed. Thence, at dawn, she descends to the garage, slips into her car (the ignition is almost silent), and dreamily drives along a deserted coastal road. 'Have you ever wondered', goes the voice-over, 'where your wife is . . .?'

The introduction of computer-related imagery into the promotion of cars has amounted to more, then, than just an updating of the way technical progress is approvingly portrayed. There has been a profound change in psychological emphasis: from conquest to experience, from outer to inner space.

It is tempting to treat this as intrinsic, reflecting a real technological bias. We might further speculate that the culturally implosive implications of computerization, reinforced by liberalizing pressures on the gender code, have facilitated a de-masculinization of technology's imputed sex. But in a crucial sense this confluence of tendencies is historically contingent. A renewed emphasis on subjectivity, experience, and the person extends beyond advertising and is rooted in the whole socio-cultural development of the past twenty years. In ads, as in movies and popular songs, it registers, at one and the same time, an anomic concern for personal

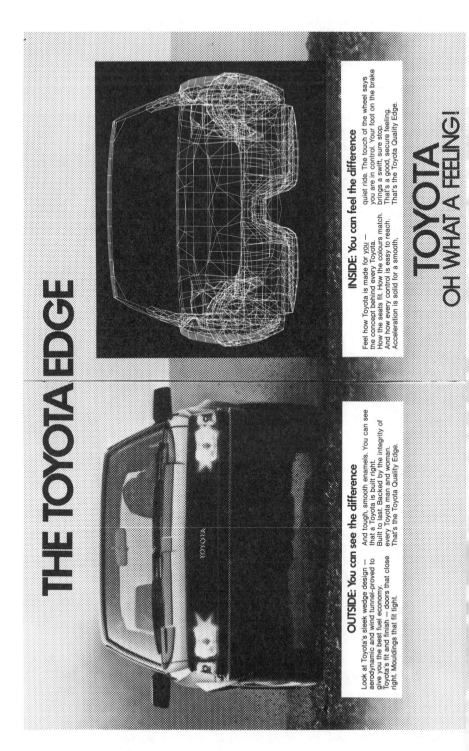

THE TOYOTA EDGE

OUTSIDE: You can see the difference

Look at Toyota's sleek wedge design — aerodynamic and wind tunnel-proved to give you the best fuel economy. Toyota's fit and finish — doors that close right. Mouldings that fit tight.

And tough, smooth enamels. You can see that a Toyota is built right. Built to last. Backed by the integrity of every Toyota man and woman. That's the Toyota Quality Edge.

INSIDE: You can feel the difference

Feel how Toyota is made for you — the concept behind every Toyota. How the seats fit. How the colours match. And how every control is easy to reach. Acceleration is solid for a smooth,

quiet ride. The touch of the wheel says you are in control. Your foot on the brake brings a swift, sure stop. That's a good, secure feeling. That's the Toyota Quality Edge.

TOYOTA
OH WHAT A FEELING!

identity, experience hunger, diffuse anxieties about the human future, and exhaustion with the growth drive of industrial society: a mood which has combined *fin de siècle* pessimism with the ongoing effects of consumerized privatism, and which has not only elevated the importance of how individuals feel, but has deflected attention away from the whole public realm.[17]

The recycled past

For that reason, too, paradoxically, the 1950s car, together with its associated insignia (diners, milkbars, drive-ins, golden age rock and roll), has made something of a nostalgic comeback. Since *American Graffiti* and the mid-1970s rockabilly revival, the whole period it incarnates, re-imaged as an age of innocence, has become a staple of contemporary *recyclage*. There is a striking parallel, here, with the cliched use of the vintage model in the IBM ad. What first made its appearance in clouds of futuristic euphoria has returned, in the context of newer fears, as a symbol of a better past. A straightforward example was a 1979 Ford ad for its remodelled Thunderbird. Beneath a dramatically threatening sky, the new T-bird, glistening red, stands on an empty road beside a lake. Its shimmering surface, which divides the page, seems to reflect the car in the lower panel. But when we look closely (or turn the ad upside down) we can see that the reflected image is actually that of its celebrated prototype. The copy writes itself: 'The thunder's back.'

In itself, there is nothing remarkable in such a move. In the play of fashion, past style has always been as important as novelty as a source for new trends. However, to dress up the post-crisis automobile in the *Happy Days* image of what came before requires some subtle modification. Even in this example, which features an ornamental lady-in-red and is evidently targeted at hustling young males, the vehicle is surrounded by a pastoral landscape, with no hint of the urban drag-strip from which its double has certainly strayed.

A more complicated instance was the autumn 1988 campaign by GM's British subsidiary for the Vauxhall Cavalier. Here the ideological seam between the contemporary and the recycled past is made virtually invisible. Today's Cavalier is yesterday's 'motor car of tomorrow'. Against doubters and pessimists, GM/Vauxhall's newest offering wondrously illustrates that the promised (engineering) utopia of the 1950s has actually arrived: 'Who says tomorrow never comes?'

The ad came in two versions, one for television and one for magazines.

In the video version a little boy, with short hair and wire-frame glasses,[18] sits entranced before a 1950s-style black and white flickering console. On screen, before a 'live' studio audience, a slick master of ceremonies is presenting a mock-up of the car of the future. The boy's eyes grow wider as he learns of its various projected features – self-tuning engine, adjustable

headlamps, automatic windows, non-locking brakes, power steering, and four-wheel distribution. To the swelling strains of Derek and the Dominos' *Layla*, the simulated vehicle on the simulated screen dissolves into a full colour shot of the actual Cavalier. From the outside, streamlined but non-flashy and finless, and seeming to fit its precision-engineered functions like a glove, the Cavalier bears little resemblance to the car which had been fantasized. Yet, in all its mechanical features, it actualizes the dream. Indeed, the efficient unobtrusiveness with which it does so highlights a dimension of design progress (miniaturization of mechanism/ purity of form) which even the futuristic imagination of the 1950s had been too old-fashioned to grasp.

That point visually made, the camera cuts immediately to a close-up of a man's face. With a look of self-satisfaction, he fondly taps his (now expensive-looking) glasses, and strides over to his car. Junior has grown up. Thanks to the escalator of progress, on every level naturalized as the unfolding of nature itself, the successful baby-boomer can now possess for himself what could only be dreamt of in his youth.

In the magazine version, yesterday's enthusiasm for the future is similarly rendered as a flashback of a contemporary consumer. But in place of the TV ad's explicit biographical narrative, told through the changing face of the man-who-was-a-boy, it has room only to contrast two pictorial displays. The first, headed 'The MOTOR-CAR of TOMORROW', covers two pages. These fold back, from the middle, to reveal another, centred on the dazzling gold profile of the 1989 Cavalier. It bears the legend 'WHO SAID TOMORROW NEVER COMES?' On the back of the two flaps, and thus to either side of the second display, the Cavalier's various performance claims are detailed. But this is for those whose curiosity is already piqued. What grabs the attention is the reverberating relation – at once of identity and difference – between the two pictorial tableaux themselves.

The first, as the lower-edge caption tells us, displays 'A motor car of the future shown in cut-away section. In years to come', it goes on to explain, 'motoring will be an effortless pleasure thanks to scientific streamlining and "space age" engineering.' The scene itself is of a Bel Geddes city, all curved concrete and glass. Within it, a well-spaced forest of cleanly contoured towers is interconnected by a multiplicity of advanced transportation forms. In the sky on the right hovers a jet-helicopter, and just beneath that a monorail supporting an underslung three-carriage train. Finally, curving round towards us, is a high-speed roadway, a one-way overpass, along which are cruising, in rapid succession, a snub-nosed boat with wheels, a fin-tailed speedster, and a bus. Heading up the line, and sweeping across the page, is the 'motor-car of tomorrow' itself. Each of its cut away features is keyed by an explanatory bubble; and these stand out, black on white, against the technicolor background of the urban scene.

By many signs we recognize this as not just a picture of the future, but a picture of that future as it might have been depicted by a commercial artist thirty years ago. Stylistically, it is a pastiche of 'fifties-ishness'. This is evident not just in the dated ultra-modernism of its architecture and transport design, but also in the kind of graphics used to represent that idea on the page. The typefaces recall those used in 1950s consumer magazines. More than anything, however, the bubble device for speech and comment, the use of vivid primary colours plus hard-edged outlines and, at the level of what is actually depicted, the futuristic motifs they evoke, remind us of a space-adventure comic book: a genre which, throughout the decade, did most to popularize such imagery among the young. This impression is strengthened by the human figures (the only ones shown) who are riding in the cut-away car. Besides being marked as a 1950s-style family group – with clean-cut husband (at the wheel) and wife in the front, and two doll-like children (one of each) in the back – their space-suit attire would have made them as much at home in a rocket-ship as in a car. The driver might be Buck Rogers or – in Britain – Dan Dare himself, just taking his family out for an Earth-side spin.

If we turn to the margin of the picture we see that we are, indeed, looking at a comic. It is hard-bound – perhaps an annual – and the Motor Car of Tomorrow is on pages 22 and 23. Moreover, judging from the dark-patterned rug the book is resting on, we are reading it, just like the kids we once were, on the middle of the living-room floor. Thus, the same interpellative device is employed here as in the TV version. The comic book substitutes for the black-and-white TV as a nostalgic allusion to the technological fantasia absorbed in childhood by the baby-boomer market targeted by the ad.

Parallel, also, with what happens in the TV version, when the magazine ad moves to the Cavalier itself, it switches from a transparently staged manner of representation to the high realism of colour photography. The settings, though, are quite different. The TV version takes its narrative realism all the way. The car the man is walking towards is parked outside his house. In the magazine ad, the Cavalier is off the road, and no people are to be seen. Glowing from the reflected light of the rising sun, it stands on a grassy knoll at the edge of town, whose indistinguishable buildings are dimly silhouetted under a reddening sky. Behind the vehicle, in the middle-ground to the left, three black spheres with connecting pipes dominate the horizon.

Now, in terms of conventional codings, that scene has meaning in itself. The car is a golden gift, a beauteous intermediary between town and country, the dawning of a glorious new day. But it also has meaning in relation to the other – and preceding – picture to which it is juxtaposed. And so, in the magazine ad, we come to a third level at which 'the fifties' is contrasted with 'now'. The first concerned medium: the impressionistic factory of comic-books vs the precise witness of the photograph. The second concerned the aesthetics of design: the triumphalist mechanism of the early space race vs the restrained functionalism of embodied high tech.

The third concerned the scenic details I have just mentioned. Here, what is contrasted is the two sets of scenic signifiers in which their then-and-now representations of automotive ultra-modernity are expressed.

The second set, in effect, represents a paradigmatic transposition from the first. Thus, the first picture places the car inside a city; the second places it (just) outside. In the first, the car is moving, in traffic, along a road; in the second it is stationary, solitary, and in a field. In the first, the car has a standard, neo-patriarchal nuclear family for driver and passengers, each member strongly defined by familial role; the second has no people, hence no reference to family or gender at all. The cityscape shown in the first picture, finally, consists of skyscrapers, domes, needles, and skyways. Work, residence, and play indistinguishably merge, and, as the immediate setting for the fantasy car, the city itself seems to pulse with future-oriented excitement. In the second, the city is an unappealing Other, covered in shadows. It has, moreover, differentiated out into distinct zones for living and working. On the right, a distant jumble of low rises suggests a residential suburb; looming on the left an ambiguous procession of spheres and girders (an oil refinery? chemical works? nuclear facility?) suggests an automated plant.

Thus a double logic is at work. On the one hand, the Cavalier as a marvel of contemporary technology, is identified with the engineering advances which, from the naive heights of 1950s enthusiasm, were fabulously foretold. On the other, the techno-mythic associations with which the new car is endowed are brought thoroughly into line with the ideological requirements of that myth's contemporary mode. Not only, then, does the second picture in the ad reflect the sense that the actual movement from industrial power to the silicon chip has involved a sweeping technological change. It also takes account of the entire cultural shift – including the revalorization of Nature and the problematization of gender and the family – which has coincided with it, and which has altered both the content and resonance of what 'technology' means.

As with the IBM ad with which I began, then, the Cavalier ad portrays the larger shift in social myth. In doing so, however, it even further obscures the discontinuity it seems to emphasize. For tomorrow's-car-of-the-future-today is presented as fulfilling a technological dream which, in crucial respects, the promotion for it also disavows. The ad achieves this trick not only by taking into itself all the post-1950s technologically related coding devices we have discussed, but by fashioning the 1950s allusion itself in a way that will retrospectively fit such an operation. The ad's comic-book stylization of 'the fifties' is carefully abstract. It comes from no particular year, has no particular author or artist, and was taken from no particular book. What is recalled from the period's iconography is ideologically selective as well. We have a Buck Rogers/Dan Dare cityscape without spaceships, weaponry, military or police. Finally, though this is a minor point, there is an almost risible anachronism in the green consciouness implicit in the ad's highlighting, as if from the very midst of the 1950s dream-world, the future car's ability to use 'lead-free petrol'.

Cars today

Overall, then, it would be one-sided to suppose that car imagery, in its adoption of computer references, has simply moved to install an updated version of progress-based technological myth. This is certainly one trend, but it has been interwoven with others, including the resurgence of functionalism, the unsettling of patriarchy, a personalist withdrawal from the adventures of industrialism, and indications that car imagery is beginning to be caught up in what Frederic Jameson (1984) has called the 'nostalgia mode'. With this latter development, in fact, we see a pseudo-historical reflexivity enveloping the ideological meta-message of car promotion which signals a further change in its character. It is not just that the Cavalier ad uses stylized images of historical 'pastness' as elements of its semiotic construct. These images are themselves stylizations of previous stylizations, as processed, *inter alia*, by previous ads.

This is not to say that in such advertising the ideological dimension has disappeared. The product is still imagistically identified with resonant values calculated to enhance its consumer appeal. But this operation – the direct mythicization of the car – is rendered less central by being linked to a second – history as a succession of styles ('the 50s', 'the 60s', 'the 70s', etc) – within whose terms the sign-values invoked are themselves just an index of the period to which they 'belong'. To that extent, the ideological meanings transferred to the car are relativized. In the Cavalier ad, today's dreams (yuppie high techdom on the edge of town) no less than yesterday's (the 1950s 'world of tomorrow') address the reader playfully, as comp-lementary positions on the fantasy board, and as objects of quotational wit. Similarly, the 'thunder' that 'is back' in the Thunderbird ad has only a weak relation to the techno-phallic enthusiasm to which it was originally linked. In its return, that enthusiasm is reduced to a mention, and what is mentioned is only a past promotional construct, even for those whose memories go back that far.

All of this would suggest that if techno-myth has been partially revamped and restored, it has also ceased to have the same symbolic force. Indeed, an alternative hypothesis can be advanced: that car imagery, like the rest of the manufactured signage of advanced capitalist culture, is reaching the stage where its signifying gestures refer us only, in the end, to the universe of symbols from which they are drawn. How this should be evaluated is a matter for debate. Suffice to say here that, with the public circulation of signs severed from life by commerce, media, and privatism, there are grounds for arguing that it is not our technology but our culture that is imploding, parallel with a further disintegration of society in the old organic sense.[19]

In its cosy, computer-linked, postmodern guise, the contemporary car certainly bears all the marks of such a process. But its witness is blind since, as a promotional construct, its imagery can scarcely acknowledge what has happened, let alone its own – doubly – mystifying role. What the most recent round of car imagery still obscures, that is, is not just the negativity of the product but the relation between that negativity and the kind of gloss it is given. Directly put: that the car's own disruptive dominance as a transport form is part of the disaffected reality from which our culture, as written into the car's very body, has recoiled.

Notes

1. The Director and key player was Harley Earl. For a vivid description of Earl and his pivotal place in the history of post-war car design see Bayley (1986: 9–20).

2. Several of Sheeler's paintings, including *Criss-Crossed Conveyors*, were purchased by the Henry Ford Museum, where they now hang. See Silk et al. (1984: 97–119).

3. The poem climaxes with:

I finally unleash your metallic bridle . . . You launch yourself, intoxicatingly into the liberating Infinite! . . . Hurrah! No longer contact with the impure earth! . . .
Finally, I am unleashed and I supplely fly
on the intoxicating plenitude
of the streaming stars in the great bed of the sky!

Quoted in Silk et al. (1984: 67).

4. The streamlining idea, replete with futurist enthusiasm, was popularized by the publication of Norman Bel Geddes' *Horizons* (1932).

5. A wonderful extension of monster imagery into filmic fantasy is to be seen in the classic Australian underground movie, *The Cars that Ate Paris*. For the interplay between the post-war fashions of Detroit and the informal sub-cultural development of hot-rodding and customizing, see Moorhouse (1986).

6. e.e. cumming's notorious car-as-virgin poem 'XIX' begins:

she being Brand
-new; and you
know consequently a
little stiff i was
careful of her and having
thoroughly oiled the universal
joint tested my gas felt of
her radiator made sure her springs were O.
K . . .

7. This idea is thematically central to McLuhan's *Mechanical Bride*. For which, see especially McLuhan (1967: 82–4, 98–101).

8. The most important representatives of a transport theory of communications are Harold Innis (1953) and Marshall McLuhan. For an exploration of the place of this model in the thinking of Innis see Wernick (1986: 139–42).

9. And also architects. Outside the Bauhaus group, led by Van der Rohe and Gropius, the most influential in this regard was Le Corbusier, both through his actual buildings and through his manifesto, *Vers une architecture*.

10. It was no accident that several of Chuck Berry's rock and roll songs were about or set in cars, and that Jack Kerouac's beat classic was called *On the Road*.

11. This did not pass critical commentators by, and there were masterful dissections of the car's stylistic embodiment of the technological complex on both sides of the Atlantic. See, for example, McLuhan (1967: 82–4) and Roland Barthes' essay in *Mythologies* (1972) on the 1955 Citroën DS.

12. For an account of the growing troubles of the post-1960s American car industry see Rothschild (1974). For the story of the Edsel itself, see Brooks (1969).

13. For the relation between expressway construction and the crisis of modernity see Marshall Berman's account of Robert Moses and the South Bronx expressway in Berman (1982: 290–312).

14. An irony of modern business is that American manufacturers, so attached to their own vision of progress, were slow to adapt; which left a market gap exploited first by the North Europeans and then by the Japanese with the aid of Italian design. See Bayley (1986: 63–7, 101–10).

15. R2d2, in the *Star Wars* saga, is the very acme of such a machine: a service-oriented robot with a built-in desire to please.

16. On another level, Toyota's reference to *Flashdance* was a tactic for Americanizing the image of its product in the face of protectionist (and to a degree xenophobic) resistance to foreign competition. In a later phase of its assimilationist campaign Toyota reached back to Gershwin, with the catch-phrase: 'Who could ask for anything more?' In quite a different context, Brian Mulroney used the same song from *Flashdance* as the theme tune preceding his live appearances during the 1984 Canadian election campaign.

17. Christopher Lasch (1976) has characterized the outcome as a 'culture of narcissism'. Its historical roots have been examined by Richard Sennett (1977).

18. For older British viewers these glasses would recall those which the National Health Service used to give out as standard issue. One implication is that the child is from a family of modest means.

19. For an elaboration of this now familiar neo-Marxist inversion of McLuhan see Baudrillard (1983b).

5
ADVERTISING MEDIA AND
THE VORTEX OF PUBLICITY

Pervasive influence of advertising – writers of one media [sic] place articles in another media and secure advertising for former as well as latter – writing becomes a device for advertising advertising.

Harold Innis (Christian, 1980: 125)

The promotional intertext

We are bombarded with images which convert consumer goods and services into seductive tokens of psychological and social value. But the perception that advertising helps shape our psychic and moral/political map of the world hardly exhausts the cultural significance of the promotional dynamic which industrial (and 'post-industrial') capitalism has put into play. Indeed, even an investigation which limits itself to that question soon runs into a consideration which takes us far beyond it. Namely: that while it is analytically convenient to treat ads (as I have largely done so far) as a succession of separate texts, such a procedure rests on what can only be regarded as a very provisional abstraction. More even than most textual constructs, ads precisely do *not* stand alone. It is not just that the discourse of promotion employs conventions and mobilizes values which are already embedded in the culture at large. In several respects, the meanings of ads are interdependent among themselves.

In the first place, ads for brand-name commodities are usually conceived (and received) as elements of whole campaigns which repeat their messages, use a variety of media and build their product identities over time. Such campaigns are overarching. Under their aegis the meaning of any single message is modified by, and depends on, the ones that came before. The same is true for sub-campaigns, where even the launching of a new product may build on meanings previously achieved. During the 1980s, for example, ads for Marlboro Lights projected a soft focus version of the leathered cowboy which had already become ultra-familiar in previous advertising for its parent brand.

In such cases, the reliance of later ads on meanings achieved in earlier ones is clear and direct. But the linkage can be more subtle. In the Cavalier campaign described earlier, the TV commercial (April–May 1989) which followed up on the one described made no reference at all to the 1950s 'car of tomorrow' which had been so prominent in the first. It featured, instead, a gurgling baby, with which the car itself (child's play to drive, etc) is tenderly identified. Only in the last few seconds is a link made: a music box tinkles out the opening riff of the same rock anthem which (with guitars, and *fortissimo*) had dramatically climaxed the first. This mnemonic immediately places the new message in a larger frame. If the man/boy of the earlier ad had nostalgically flashed back to his childhood, in the follow-up he is given the chance to relive it through the eyes of his own child. Indeed, since the car is the baby, the very act through which he has become a father – by having the car – is the one in which his boyhood dreams have been realized. Yesterday's utopia is today's bright promise for the future, too.

[Advertising is semiotically interdependent, however, even across product lines.] I have already noted that the signs and conventions from which ads build their myriad product images are drawn from a common cultural pool. But this shared repertoire is not just 'out there', circulating pre-promotionally (as it were) in popular speech, school texts, or in the grand traditions of religion and high culture. Its elements – whether in the form of famous personalities, social stereotypes or mythic allusions – are constantly re-circulated and re-worked in the symbolic universe of advertising itself.

The more pervasive advertising has become, indeed, the more important-ance it has been accorded as a point of cultural reference in its own right. During the 1950s and 1960s, pop art made the re-framing of promotional images a key element of its new, ideologically flattened, aesthetic. In architecture, a similar strategy was advanced by the Venturi group (1988) in their call to 'learn from Las Vegas'.[1] In mainstream discourse, however, perhaps nothing ratified the cultural ascendancy of advertising so much as Mondale's rebuff to Gary Hart in the presidential primaries of 1980, when he asked (echoing a Wendy's hamburger commercial) 'Where's the beef?' The point can easily be summarized: the importance of advertising as a quotational source has become a cultural given for all who would communicate in a recognizable idiom with a broad contemporary audi-ence. And among this number is evidently to be included advertisers themselves.

The self-referring quality of whole domains of discourse has given rise, in literary theory, to the notion of intertextuality.[2] In literature itself, its accession as a concept has also been paralleled by a certain self-consciousness about what the concept implies – a reflexive intertextualism which, in the forms of meta-fiction and pastiche, has become a hallmark of postmodern style. A similar trend is discernible in post-war advertising, particularly in the last ten years. Explicit reference both to other ads and to the imagery which they employ has been increasingly incorporated into the promotional pitch. A low-level form of this is in advertising which names the rival – as in Avis's 'We're number two, so we try harder', or in Pepsi's wistful (1986) riposte to the failed launching of new-formula Coke: 'Why did they have to change?' But it is also evident in ads like those for IBM which make sophisticated play with existing or earlier advertising imagery and technique, and with consumers' presumed familiarity with it, either in order to construct a composite new meaning (the future computer as future retro); or even, as in the Cavalier ad, in order to project such cleverness as a personality-defining attribute of the product itself.[3]

The intertextuality of promotional discourse is not confined, finally, just to ads. In so far as the designed commodity itself serves as (self-)promotion, it too is drawn into the intertextual web. In fact, doubly. For not only are imaged objects, like ads themselves, interconnected through a shared cultural vocabulary which can be quoted and relayed from one promotional site to another. They are similarly interconnected, both with one another and with their related ads, as links in the same commercially motivated chain. These two modes of interdependence, the first through the semantic, the second through the performative, value of the promotional sign, evidently interweave. But it is the second, flowing as it does from advertising's first-order function – selling – which makes the intertextual character of such discourse peculiarly what it is.

Within this latter, sales-related, nexus, two features of the referencing back and forth between imaged commodities and the ads which promote them are worth underlining. First, the psycho-ideological associations conjured up by advertising merge into the product, while the product itself serves as an ad. There is thus no simple distinction, nor one-to-one relation of correspondence, between them. Secondly, the promotional chain to which any product and 'its' ad belongs is endless. It has no unique starting-point nor any unique terminus in a specific commodity offered for sale. The intertext of promotion is an indeterminate circle which may be entered anywhere.

Today, the semiological and rhetorical complexity to which the many-sided inter-relatedness of promotional messages can give rise has reached dizzying heights. In basic outline, however, it has been with us for at least two centuries. The 1790 *St James Gazette* notice which announced the opening of Wedgwood's Portland Vase show immediately advertised a paid event. But the exhibition's centrepiece was designed to draw customers to the wider range of ornamental pieces which themselves promoted the sale of his (more profitable) ordinary ware. All items of the latter, in turn, were stamped with the name of the famous potter whose increased celebrity only enhanced that marque's value as a marketing device. Meanwhile, the cumulative publicity surrounding Wedgwood himself enhanced the publicity effect of the original *Gazette* notice; while, overseas, the totality of Wedgwood produce served as a promotional flagship for other Staffordshire potteries and, indeed, for the sales efforts of British exports in general. In 1965, we may recall, it was service to the latter which also brought the Beatles their MBEs.

What capitalist industrialization has brought into being, then, is not just an apparatus for the mass generation and transmission of value-laden meta-messages, but a dense communicative complex which envelops all imaged goods plus whatever symbolic material these draw in. That complex interconnects, and is culturally pervasive, *as* a complex. Beyond the meaning and influence of the specific advertisements of which it is composed, therefore, its overall characteristics are worth examining in themselves.

This would be so even if we looked no further than at the kind of consumer goods promotion considered so far. But almost all the advertisements cited have been taken from communicative vehicles (magazines, TV channels, newspapers, etc) which foreground other contents. These non-advertising contents, too, can be considered promotional, not least in terms of the ads to which they draw attention. Thus, through the ties which have developed between advertising, commercial media, and mass entertainment, the intertext of product promotion has become absorbed into an even wider promotional complex founded on the commodification, and transformation into advertising, of (produced) culture itself.

The yellow kid

The 'yellow press' entered popular speech in the late nineteenth century as a byword for a tabloid style of journalism which systematically sensationalized its material in order to maximize sales. The term came to cover a whole genre. But it originally referred to two specific dailies: Joseph Pulitzer's *New York World*, and William Randolph Hearst's *New York Journal*. The first, carrying stories such as 'Death Rides The Blast', 'The Wall Street Terror', 'A Bride but not a Wife', pioneered 'yellow' journalism's distinctive techniques. The second, in the frenzied circulation wars of the 1890s, made its excesses notorious.[4]

Their now legendary contest began in 1894, when the *World* – at a quarter of a million copies a day, already established as the largest circulating newspaper ever – found itself rudely challenged by Hearst's purchase of the flagging *Journal*. Hearst's first step was to raid Pulitzer's staff, among whom he netted the entire production team responsible for the *World*'s flagship Sunday edition. The latter, swollen to 48 pages, had become less a newspaper than a magazine, a compendium of pictures, sob stories, and special features on sports, popular science and fashion, whose own circulation was double that of the paper's regular editions.

Particularly valuable among Hearst's new hirings was the cartoonist Richard B. Outcault. One of Pulitzer's most successful innovations had been the development of cartoon strips, and Outcault's *Shantytown* (re-named *Hogan's Alley* in 1894), was the most popular the *Sunday World* ran. So much so, indeed, that the strip's central character, the Yellow Kid, had become virtually synonymous with Pulitzer's whole New York operation. Drawings of the Kid, with gap-toothed grin and hallmark yellow smock, were instantly recognizable, and were regularly used by sandwich-men, or on billboards, as a promotional device.

When Hearst poached Outcault, then, he not only seized an important creative asset, but one of the *World*'s most important advertising symbols as well. In 1896, to capitalize further, Hearst sponsored the '*Journal-Examiner* Yellow Fellow Transcontinental Bicycle Relay' – followed by a mammoth Bicycle Carnival in Central Park to honour the participants. Not to be outdone, with Outcault now producing the *Yellow Kid* for his rival, Pulitzer hired a second cartoonist, Richard Buks, to continue the original strip. So by 1895 there were two Yellow Kids, both vying with one another as mascots for the papers in which they appeared.

For contemporaries, the Kid's colour became emblematic of the effects of intensified commercialization on the whole character of the popular press. Yellow, indeed, was not its only hue. When Hearst followed Pulitzer in issuing a full-colour Sunday supplement, the *Journal* hyped it as 'eight pages of irridescent polychromous effulgence that makes the rainbow look like a lead pipe' (Bartow, 1952: 237). Visual appeal was emphasized in other ways, too – from mastheads and banner headlines to celebrity portraits, dramatic news photos and cartoons themselves. The *World* had even experimented with pin-ups. Hence, in 1884, pictures of the Brooklyn Belles: 'Ladies who grace and adorn the social circle.'

All this, combined with the raciness and populism of what the stories and features actually conveyed, indicated recourse to lowest common denominator appeal. The motive was never in doubt, nor the direction in which it tended. In re-launching the *New York Sun* in 1863 Charles Dana had merely promised 'condensation, clearness . . . and to present its daily photograph of the whole world's doings in the most lively and luminous manner' (Bartow, 1952: 230). Twenty years later, Pulitzer's first issue of the *Morning World* upped the ante: 'There is room in this great and growing city for a journal that is not only cheap, but bright, not only bright but large, and not only large but truly democratic' (Bartow: 233). Pulitzer at least tempered his orientation to mass appeal (which dovetailed nicely with his populism) with fastidiousness about 'Accuracy times three'. For Hearst, whose tolerance of embroidery reached an extreme in the *Journal*'s war-mongering coverage of Cuba and US relations with Spain, there were no restraints at all. His home-base *San Francisco Examiner* trumpeted itself as 'Monarch of the Dailies', and this because (to cite a headline from 12 March 1887) it had 'THE MOST ELABORATE LOCAL NEWS, THE FRESHEST SOCIAL NEWS, THE LATEST AND MOST ORIGINAL SENSATIONS' (Swanberg, 1961: 42). In an editorial to celebrate its first year of Hearstian triumph, the *Journal* was equally unabashed. The paper's 'amazing and wholly unmatched success' was to be accounted for by the strictly commercial principles guiding its design. 'It is the *Journal*'s policy to engage brains as well to get the news, for the public is even more fond of entertainment than it is of information.'[5]

All the ballyhoo surrounding the emergence of the yellow press revolved around the same point: that first the *World* and then the *Journal* had converted the sober business of news reportage and public debate into geewhizzery, human interest, and infotainment. But the establishment of mass circulation dailies as a fixture of urban life heralded another epochal innovation in the development of commodified culture as well. Cheap, and therefore mass circulating, newspapers had been made possible in the 1830s through the enhanced productivity of power-driven machines, particularly the (ever-improving) Hoe rotary press. Fifty years later, despite the rising cost of both capital equipment and, with telegraph rates and the need for larger staffs and journalists on assignment, of news-gathering itself, it remained profitable for press barons to keep them cheap. Why? Because, in addition to revenue directly gained from newspaper sales, they were able to increase substantially what they were able to add from another source: advertising.

Since the *corrantos* of the seventeenth century, newspapers had always been hybrids of advertising and 'publick occurrences'. But the former's significance to the economics of publishing increased dramatically in the decades of Pulitzer and Hearst. Total print advertising outlays in the United States rose from $39m in 1880 to $71 million in 1890. By 1900 they had reached $95m, and in 1910 $200m.[6] In 1880, 25 percent of daily newspaper space was given over to advertising, and it contributed a half of aggregate revenue. By 1910, advertising space had increased to 50 percent, and its share of revenues had risen to two thirds. Under the circumstances, and provided they attracted their requisite share of that expanding revenue pool, newspapers could be profitably sold on the streets for considerably less than their unit cost. In order to boost circulation, and therefore advertising revenue, Hearst, in his first year with the *Journal*, halved its price to one cent. To bring the consumer benefit home, pennies were mailed out to potential subscribers (their names drawn from the electoral roll), together with a message that the *Journal* was the best value a penny could buy. Pulitzer was soon obliged to follow suit.

As in the earliest newspapers, much of the late nineteenth-century press's advertising continued to take the form of small classifieds. In 1885 the *World* printed about 24 columns of advertising a day with an average of some 4000 separate ads.[7] The main expansion, however, involved a quite different kind of copy, more large-scale and creative in layout, and oriented to the promotion of more widely distributed wares. The way was paved by patent medicine makers ('Dr Williams Pink Pills for Pale People').[8] But increasingly prominent, also, was a new generation of industrial manufacturers. These included the makers of Ivory Soap ('99 and 44/100 percent pure'), Eastman Kodak, Budweiser and Wrigley's. The city-wide audience offered by newspapers was also attractive to retailers, especially department stores like J.A. Wanamaker in Philadelphia, and Marshall Field's in Chicago. (Reputedly the first was A.T. Stewart of New York. Founded in 1832, by 1852 it was advertising itself as 'the largest in the world'.) According to *Printer's Ink* (the advertising industry's own trade paper, started in 1888), by 1900 the number of regular print-using advertisers had risen to 6000.[9] It was on this tide that Pulitzer and Hearst (not to mention Rothermere, Beaverbrook, and their counterparts in continental Europe) floated to their seigneurial fortunes. Nor was the timing coincidental. The Great Depression of the 1870s was followed by modern capitalism's first major consumer boom. And this brought with it dramatically increased demand for media space in which to advertise both the burgeoning store of nationally branded goods, and the ever-more glitzy retail outlets where they could be obtained.

It was at this juncture, too, that advertising first became established as a separately organized industry. Led by A.J. Ayer and George P. Rowell in the early 1870s, and J. Walter Thompson in 1886, the first agencies hived off from newspapers to become independent space brokers (at 15 percent commission) which also, on their 'creative' side, produced copy for major clients. To counter their power, and to secure a bigger slice of the advertising pie for the publishing industry as a whole, press owners set up their own association (the American Newspaper Publishers' Association)[10] in 1888. Negotiations followed which standardized the rates for advertising space, and eventually – through the founding, in 1913, of the Audit Bureau of Circulations – provided a credible basis for the circulation figures on which these rates could be based.

In this initial phase, there was no back-up survey research, let alone the battery of demographics, psychographics, and lifestyle profiling which give such analysis its precision today. But, in a rough and ready way, space rates did reflect qualitative as well as quantitative considerations. In the 1880s, the up-market *New York Herald* charged 45c a line, while the *World*, with five times the circulation, charged only 5c for personal classifieds and 25c for full commercial displays. The difference was more than made up in the total volume of space made available; but there was an evident risk in steering newspapers so far, and so exclusively, down-market that they would fail to attract the more affluent readership which major advertisers sought to reach.[11] To counter this, the sheer diversity of the *World*'s and *Journal*'s contents gave them a socially mixed audience; which, in turn, ensured their appeal to a similar diversity of advertisers. Above all, they made special efforts to build up readership among women. Hence not only these papers' overall tone – their 'human interest', their gossipiness, their balancing of 'feminine' displays of pity with 'manly' ones of rage – but also their specialized content. Pulitzer's *World* was the first to target women consumers specifically, by printing, daily, a whole 'Woman's Page'.[12]

What the yellow press initiated, in short, was not just circulation-boosting sensationalism, but that integration of mass cultural production with consumer goods promotion which has been paradigmatic in the formation of mass-mediated commercial culture ever since. In each of its successive techno-economic forms, from the popular press of the late nineteenth century to the polyglot audio-visual media of today, the same symbiosis can be found: a system of mutual dependency, at once financial and functional, in which advertising revenue underwrites a proportion of media production and distribution costs in return for the latter's providing a ready-made audience before whom to present the ads.[13]

Thus, to call mass culture commercialized understates the point. The kind of cultural production represented by the Yellow Kids and their electronic successors is mediated by the commodity form not just once, but twice. For the consumer, a newspaper is a terminal good; but for the advertiser it is a vital relay in the marketing of something else. With respect to the latter, moreover, the whole media product is an ad. For besides the paid ads, the 'real' (or non-advertising) content of a newspaper, magazine, or TV show serves as a magnet to draw audiences to the ads in its midst. In the yellow press, startling stories about new scientific discoveries helped sell Beecham's Pills. The Woman's Page in *The World*, full of society gossip and fashion tips, sold women clothes. Considering that the attractor – here, the stories and syndicated columns of a commercial newspaper – is itself a commodity, we can encapsulate the results by saying that in ad-carrying media the commodified sign serves as a promotional sign for a promotional sign for a commodity-sign (see Figure 5.1).

That the organic relation between the advertising and non-advertising material of commercial media feeds back into the selection, tone, ideology, and style of the latter is self-evident. The space between the ads must provide a good selling medium, which entails the same general sheen of consumerism, the same positive/upbeat tone, and the same touting of conventional values which characterizes the ads. The need to address and attract the audiences which advertisers seek leads, as well, to similar psycho-ideological approaches: in the case of the most mass-oriented media, to middle-of-the-roadism; for media products aimed at a narrower niche, to the integration of each segmented medium's tone and mode of address with the presumed cultural characteristics of the market segment being sought.

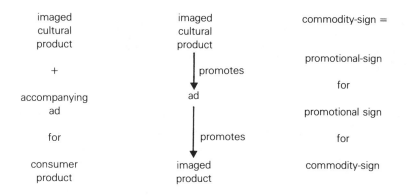

Figure 5.1   *Basic promotional structure of ad-carrying media: alternative formulations*

Advertising also feeds back into programming at the level of style. Hence, the prevalence in commercial media of compressed or rapid-fire forms of delivery, and of ever-higher 'production values'. Hence, too, in a medium which has taken such influence to unprecedented levels, such entertainment programmes as *Miami Vice* in which a continuous parade of fashion ads, car commercials, and video rock sequences is simply given an hour-long narrative thread. Intensifying the integrative effect, the stylistic influence can also go the other way. Ads set in a surround of entertainment themselves seek to entertain, often – as in vignette-style TV commercials which adopt the suspenseful quality of the drama shows into which they are inserted – in the same way. Thus, just as the non-advertising material of ad-based media has become an extension of the ads, advertisements themselves have become part of the show.

Given the varying economic weight of advertising in different branches of the culture industry, the extent of such ideological/aesthetic assimilation is uneven. In general, we can say that the impact of any channel's ad-carrying role on the fashioning of its non-advertising contents is proportional to the extent of its dependence on such revenue. But a calculus of influence cannot be easily drawn up. There is no absolute basis even for distinguishing between those media which carry ads and those which do not. Because of the politics of state subsidy, public broadcasting networks like the BBC are drawn into ratings wars with their commercial rivals, whose ad-revenue-influenced forms they are therefore induced to imitate. Nor are the lines fixed. Any spectacle which attracts an audience can attract sponsors. Almost all forms of commercialized culture, including popular literature and film exhibition, have carried ads in the past; and even those which currently do not are liable to do so in future. Blurring the distinction still further, some kinds of advertising – the paid-for appearance of brand-name colas in movie scenes,[14] or of sportswear and soft drink labels at Wimbledon – are not framed as ads. More diffusely, as McLuhan noted (1965: 254–5), the affluent domestic settings displayed in Hollywood films (or in American night-time soaps) amount to general plugs for the lifestyle package which they glamorously present.

From the pulp press of New York to the film and TV studios of Hollywood, the media businesses making up what Horkheimer and Adorno called the 'culture industry' can thus be construed as one vast promotional vehicle: a functionally interdependent complex within which the line between what is incidental as advertising and what is ostensibly its primary content, as information and entertainment, is reduced at most to a matter of level and degree. To which there is an evident corollary. Promotional discourse, together with its strange intertextual loops, embraces more than the first order practices of advertising and design so far considered. With the transformation of culture into a mass-producing economic sector in its own right, such discourse has come to include the total output of the media which brings it to us.

However, there is one further level of promotion inscribed within the media/advertising ensemble which I have not yet mentioned. This is that the mediatized material which promotes promotion consists not just of commodities, but of industrially mass produced ones. Like all such goods, this material must be massively promoted itself. The implications are not merely additive. In the case of cultural commodities, that is those goods where what is consumed (no more nor less) is the signifying material they contain, the mediatized promotion for the product is delivered by the same means, that is by the same channels of communication, as those which deliver the product itself.

The promotional reflexivity which this implies goes beyond the mere fact that actual ads for newspapers, magazines, films, records, TV shows, etc, are carried – like those for non-cultural goods – in that same range of media. For two reasons, in fact, the use of paid ads for cultural goods is limited. First, there is a commercial asymmetry in that media organs compete, and rivals are reluctant to push one another's wares. Instead – as in the case of the Saturday *Toronto Star* hyping the contents of the Sunday edition, or of a movie house promoting, on screen, the coming month's attractions – mass media companies tend to promote their own. Besides being efficiently targeted, this is evidently cheaper than buying time or space elsewhere. In any case, secondly, the news and entertainment provided by the organs of mass communication are a publicity vehicle in themselves. Why rely on ads explicitly presented, and mentally defended against, *as* ads when a more positive and wide-ranging effect can be achieved by hitching a ride – as 'free media' – on that very vehicle?

Here, too, the Yellow Kids were pioneers. I have already mentioned Hearst's continental bike relay. Even more spectacular were some of the stunts Pulitzer organized to generate publicity for the *World*. Columnist Annie Laurie was sent tearing round the world in an effort to beat Jules Verne's fictional 80 days. Richard Stanley was despatched to Africa to find Dr Livingstone. And, as a grand gesture (presumably not lost on immigrant readers), the *World*, in 1889, organized a vast subscription drive (at a dime a time) to raise money for the installation of the Statue of Liberty (Emery, 1954: 381). The paper's link to the Statue was commemorated ever after through its incorporation into the twin globe logo which had always been printed over the nameplate: Liberty astride the continents of the New and Old Worlds.

A distinctive feature of the media industries' own promotion, then, is that the product which they have to advertise is a privileged site for the advertisement of itself. This has implications, as we shall see, for the organization and texture of mediatized culture as a whole. But it also shapes the form of the individual items of which the media flow consists. As every newspaper editor knows, front-page layout (above the fold) is crucial for sales, since it is here that the reader usually begins. It is also what the prospective reader, passing the news stand, fleetingly sees. This was why the mass circulation dailies of the nineteenth century moved away from an older practice (anachronistically continued by the London *Times* until the 1950s) of placing classified ads there, displaying instead dramatic photographs and banner headlines which sketched out, at a glance, the major story of the day. Hence, too, the image-defining importance of the name-plate and logo, on which, for example, the *World's* well-publicized support for the Statue of Liberty was enshrined.

In the *Sunday World* a drawing of the Yellow Kid himself (see comic inside . . .) was often placed promotionally on the front page. The cartoon-logo which gave its name to a prototypical instance of advertiser-based, circulation-dependent, commercial culture was thus prototypical in another sense as well. In its front-page setting it was part of an ad – as well as itself an ad – for the very commodity to which it integrally belonged.

Varieties of cultural self-promotion

Self-promotion by mass-distributed cultural goods can come in a variety of guises. Indeed, the guises multiply before our eyes once we realize that such self-promotion characterizes not only what occurs within, and at the level of, individual commodities; but also what happens in the aggregate, across the whole surface of the mass cultural flow. Moving, in this way, from the immediate and particular to the mediate and general, the following main forms can be identified.

Hooking

The most elementary is the one just mentioned: illustrated by the attention-grabbing role played by a folded newspaper's exposed front page. The case is similar to that of the circus tent pitched prominently on a village green; though here, as with books, the outside is a cover and not strictly part of the show. More straightforward, with respect to popular performance art, is the street musician whose playing draws an audience towards the performance – and the hat. Sexual soliciting in public places involves the same mechanism. Indeed, in the case of pornography, prostitution's mediatized equivalent, the fact that a magazine cover, like a newspaper's front page, likewise promotes the body of which it is the made-up face, has become the basis of an administrative tactic for restricting its circulation. In many jurisdictions soft-core magazines can only be commercially displayed in corner stores if they are boxed behind the counter, with just the titles visible, and out of children's line of sight.

All these cases exemplify the same general point: that where commodified cultural expressions are inserted into the sweep and flow of public intercourse, their very obtrusiveness enables them to serve as self-advertisements just by being what and where they are. Whether or not the place where this occurs is formally marked as a space for consumer exchange is a secondary matter. Pedestrian traffic is densest at points of retail concentration, and in these places – in the bazaar, the shopping district, the precinct, and the mall – what is outside the stores is equally a space for retail display. Of course, there are great differences between archaic and contemporary forms of commercially occupied streetscape. But as an opportunity space for direct customer solicitation, these amount, in the end, only to how, and by whom, such opportunities are controlled. In the El Khalili bazaar the petty trader is king and the streets belong to Allah. In Newcastle's Metroland or the West Edmonton Mall, a model which the contemporary city has extended to wherever pedestrians go, the walkways are programmed even in their spontaneity, and they belong to the consortium which owns the property as a whole.

The urban concourse within which we encounter self-attracting cultural commodities is not, however, just a physical space. We enter the shopping mall every time we turn on the TV. As we flick from channel to channel (which we can do these days without even having to leave our chair) we similarly negotiate a parade of stores in which a host of sirens (a chase scene, a weather chart, a laughing audience, a couple in bed, the latest video star . . .) compete for our wandering attention. The parallel is more than superficial because, like the pop songs blaring from the audio store or the TV screens flickering in a window next door, each programme which might attract us, at least on a commercial network, is a commodity in itself. To be sure, the fact that the economic relation is the same as in the literal mall is hidden by its form. We do not pay for TV programmes the way we pay for shoes, or indeed for the television set itself. But even if ostensibly 'free', whatever morsel of programming we may alight on has its own exchange value in the ad-based televisual economy, a value which depends, indeed, precisely on the audience it can attract.

Serial promotion

For the itinerant street musician who offers only the performance he or she happens to be giving, that is the end of the matter. But in an industrialized culture the uniqueness and evanescence of such presentations is exceptional. Newspapers, novels, magazines, films, records, and TV shows are not just one-offs. Not only are they mass produced and/or mass distributed. They are serialized in other respects as well, and this serialization is intimately connected to another way in which mass cultural produce self-promotes. By drawing an audience to itself, a record, TV show or film can build a market for the other members of the series, or series of series, to which that item belongs.

The promotionally staged seriality of cultural commodities takes three main forms.

In the first, an integral work (typically a narrative) is split up and released for (paid) consumption, one segment at a time. The principle is exemplified by the old peepshow in which each succeeding glimpse of striptease required the insertion of another coin. Charles Dickens, who first published his early novels in magazines, chapter by chapter, translated the technique into literary form. Marx's *Capital* was also first published in this way. The cliffhanger ending which the nineteenth-century novel perfected has, in turn, become a staple device for weekly or daily serials on radio and TV. The power of the suspense factor was indicated when an audience of 600 million tuned in at the beginning of *Dallas*'s new season in 1985 to find out who shot JR.[15] But suspense is not the only motivator. The soap opera, whose story never ends and which moves at the slow pace of lived time, builds its audience less by tension and release than by the depth to which a more general identification is secured with the characters and their world. Its narrative offers a surrogate community of continuous gossip to which identifying audiences become addicted. And the same can be seen in the ongoing attachment of TV viewers or newspaper readers to the 'real world' soap opera of the daily news.

If the first mode of serialized promotion is through the *serial*, the second is through the *series*. In the case of the former – *Dallas, Heimat, Doonesbury* – what is divided up is a single work, though this may be indeterminate so that the story just serendipitously unfolds. In the case of the *series* – whether as a sitcom, a syndicated column or an episodic cartoon strip like Peanuts (or, indeed, the original Yellow Kid) – the segmentation is more absolute. The segments are not instalments of a single narrative, but self-enclosed. Continuity between them is only in the characters and the format they repeat. What we have, then, is a theme-with-variations, a combinatory whose cosy predictability becomes, in the end, part of its appeal.

This looser form of series lacks an overall temporal thread along which to draw its audience. But, for the same reason, less is at stake in any particular moment of carry-over since nothing is lost by skipping a particular episode. What matters, in terms of holding and building audiences, is the series' more general features: the ideological resonance of its master-situation, the credibility of its central characters, its writing and texture, and the speed and extent to which these can enter the collective imagination before the series as a whole (trapped in a formula it is risky to change) begins to lose ratings, and is scrapped.[16]

Even this may not be the end, for, in television at least, successful series are favourites for syndication. Indeed, it is on re-runs that their profitability to the studio that made them finally depends. Twenty years of *I Love Lucy* turned this show into a nostalgic icon whose appeal far outlasted its original cultural basis. And for this, mere repetition of that which had struck the initial mass chord was enough to sustain long-run consumer demand.

Finally, in every medium and genre are to be found instances of a third form of series which, while often less pre-planned than the ones just considered, manifests exactly the same principle. Stripped to its barest essentials, it consists of a two-stroke dynamic. First, the creation of a new model, marginally differentiated and distinctively imaged. In the music sector this may be a new voice, sound, personality or rhythmic style; in popular literature, television or film, a new hero, sub-genre or idiosyncracy of dialogue or presentation. Then, if a hit is scored, comes the phase of the follow-up – or perhaps a whole string of follow-ups – where the attempt is made to capitalize on the initial audience momentum so as to build, out of its success, a stable market niche.

What distinguishes this more diffuse type of promotional seriality – that of the *sequel* – is its improvised and opportunistic character. This gives it a flexibility which can adapt to a variety of market circumstances. In some cases, a follow-up may be so specifically patterned on its predecessor that it is defined and publicized as precisely that. Hence the practice, initiated by *Airport* and *Airport II*, and taken to still greater lengths with sagas like *Rocky*, *Nightmare on Elm Street* and *Police Academy*, in which blockbuster movies based on an easily duplicable formula spawn numbered successors. At the other end of the spectrum are mere genre follow-ups – early 1970s disaster movies, mid-1980s rap – where continuity is just through theme and form, and where the promotional beneficiaries may include imitators and commercial rivals in addition to those who launched the original. Midway between these is the case of the Elmore Leonard thriller, or the Andrew Lloyd Webber musical, where there is continuity with respect to authorship and style, but no explicit linkage, via plot or characters, of one work with another.

In the most successful cases, the cumulative effect of serial promotion is to create not just a predictable demand, but a body of actual fans who serve, as that term suggests, to amplify the promotional effect. *Star Trek* bred Trekkies, whose organized enthusiasm facilitated the programme's re-launch on film. The apparatus of fandom, indeed, makes visible a further parallel between this and advertising in other fields. Fans are linked to the patented cultural model, and to its imaged set of variants, by ties of loyalty which are only a more excited version of those which tie regular customers to any commodity brand.

Promotion through names

In general: with cultural as with other kinds of mass-marketed goods and services, the marginally distinct identities which products and product-lines are promotionally given condense on the site of a name. The practice applies across the board. There are two respects, though, in which promotional naming in the cultural sphere has a special character of its own.

First, in contrast with the flood of (separately delivered) ads which are typically needed to image the maker (or pretended maker) of ordinary consumer goods, the image built up around the name of a cultural enterprise, be it a publishing house, a TV network or a record label, is primarily self-generated: a cumulating function of whatever is communicated by the cluster (or sub-cluster) of commodities which fly under its flag. And the same applies to any designated product line (or named series) which these enterprises may produce. When Kate Bush recorded *Hammer*

Horror she could assume that her audience would know the kind of films Hammer Studio used to make. And this directly: not just from seeing ads or posters, but from seeing (if only in TV re-runs) the films themselves. For her as well as for them, the residual associations – what 'Hammer' means – may have been no more than just a vague sense of what defined the studio's characteristic style: the grainy gothic of 1940s and 1950s *film noir*. Underlying it, however, was the experience, and memory, of having watched actual films, like the *Hound of the Baskervilles* and *Terror of the Rue Morgue*; or actors, like Peter Cushing and Vincent Price; or performances, like those of Christopher Lee or Boris Karloff in sequel after sequel of Mary Shelley's *Frankenstein* or Bram Stoker's *Dracula*.

A second difference, as this example suggests, is that in the case of cultural commodities a multiplicity of brand names are involved. With other kinds of produce, at most only two are normally singled out for promotional mention: those of the producing organization (with or without reference to the larger conglomerate to which it may belong), and of the specific product or product-line being advertised. In some cases, both names may be promoted, as in Wedgwood's *Queensware* or Vauxhall *Cavalier*. In others, just one, either because the name of the company (Lever Brothers) is effaced before that of its products (*Persil*, *Downy*, etc), or because the names of company and product (*Coca-Cola*) are the same. With cultural commodities, the list is much longer. Besides analogues of the producer/product names just mentioned – such as Touchstone/(Disney)'s *Splash* – any single work, be it a film, TV programme or pop song, will generally highlight, as well, the names of the work's creators, its principal performers and, in some cases (such as James Bond), even its fictional characters.

Thus when the curtain goes up and the credits announce that Hammer Studios are presenting Christopher Lee in Bram Stoker's *Dracula*, no fewer than four levels of naming are brought into play. Five, indeed, if we take into account that *Dracula* is both a character and the title of the film. Two of these, moreover (Lee playing the title role), are sensorily present throughout the film itself. A third, Bram Stoker, is only, here, an empty embellishment; though in the case of a more canonical author – Agatha Christie in relation to *Orient Express* – we can see how the celebrityhood surrounding a movie's (otherwise uninvolved) original inspirer can also be vital to the promotional image it has.

At each of these levels is to be found the same thing: that combination of person with image, of celebrity with profile, which, at the limit, constitutes named individuals, whether actual or fictional, in character or as they 'really are', as *stars*. The star system is culturally pervasive, and certainly extends beyond just those of stage and screen. It has correlates in every field of publicized creation and performance, from video-making to academic writing. A star, in this larger sense, is anyone whose name and fame have been built up to the point where reference to them, via mention, mediatized representation or live appearance, can serve as a promotional booster in itself.

In relation to particular cultural commodities, such stardom, whether of novelist, film director, actor, singer or fictional character, is an intermediary, a link in the chain of serial promotion, of which it represents, as well, a special case. The arena to which stars draw an audience is the one on which their own drawing power has been built. At the same time, the publicity surrounding stars has a dynamic of its own. And for all the evident inter-relation, this dynamic is not reducible to the publicity process surrounding the filmic, literary, musical, etc, vehicles in which they immediately appear. The construction and use of imaged celebrities is thus a promotional practice in itself: a practice which – in the case of the living – actively engages, and confers tangible benefits upon, those whose celebrity it builds up.

The aims and results of star-making are part and parcel of the brand-imaging of the cultural products, and companies, with which stars are creatively associated. Thus capitalists will seek to optimize the promotional value of the celebrified creators or creations they utilize through long-term arrangements which stabilize the link. And the same, in the studio systems of Hollywood, or, today, of publishing or popular music, applies in reverse: performers can only ratify their starring status by securing, with 'majors', a relationship of this kind. The result is a kind of double promo. The Beatlemania which converted the Fab Four into a global signifier boosted not only the immediate sales, but also the promotional value, of the two EMI labels with which they had signed – Capitol for North America, and Parlophone for the UK. In the case of fictional creations, cartoons for example, an even more complete identity may be achieved. Thus both the Yellow Kid and Disney's Mickey Mouse became corporate logos for the capitalists in whose publications and productions they appeared.

Nevertheless, the images constructed around star creators and performers remain distinct from those of the capitalist enterprises which incorporate them into its product. Negatively: fading stars are ditched from the roster; and even when they are not fading, as for example when EMI first signed and then, in horror, dropped the Sex Pistols in 1977, they may still generate associations which are at cross-purposes with the overall promotional interests of their employer. Positively: cultural creators and performers themselves have an interest in promoting their own stardom independently of the profits it contributes to those who employ them, or who contract for their services.

A different way of making the same point is to say that cultural commodities are vehicles for the promotion of more than one producer's serial product. Or, to put it more sharply, that the multiplicity of promotional names on the site of the cultural commodity is not just nominal: it corresponds to the multiplicity of promotional subjects involved. In the simplest case, book publishing, there are just two – the writer (trying to 'make a name') and the publisher. In the performing arts, a third category is introduced, performers, and the publisher is replaced by the company or companies involved in staging and organizing tours. In recording and broadcast media – where the production company may be separate from the distributor, and where studio directors (as an extension of what happens in theatre) can overshadow writers and composers as *auteurs* of the text – the cast of (self-)promotional characters is larger still.

Underlying this multiplication of promotional names is an economic peculiarity of the process wherein capitalism produces culture. At first sight, what has happened through the commodification of culture is the same kind of transformation as has occurred elsewhere: a shift from petty commodity production – mythically incarnated in the early industrial figure of the Artist – to wage labour and mass-producing corporate capital. But this is too simple. The means of communication, from film distribution to newspapers, have certainly been concentrated in ever-fewer hands. Not all cultural workers, however, have been proletarianized as a result. Those who have been able to establish legal title to the products of their creative labour, and with mixed media the number of creators associated with any particular product can evidently become quite large, have retained at least a quasi-independence with regard to the corporate interests on which their access to a mass market depends.

There are parallels, here, with the situation of the traditional independent artisan who preceded the industrialization of culture. But there are two important differences.

First, the immediate market such creators and performers face, in ferocious competition with one another, is not that of the immediate patrons and consumers of their work, but of the highly concentrated production and distribution companies whose backing is indispensable to its circulation. Altogether, in such instances, and however conjoined (through five album contracts and the like), the production process has two distinct moments. On the one hand there is the creation (and sale) of a reproducible model; on the other, its mass production and distribution as a terminal good. Each of these moments, moreover, involves a different set of production relations. The first is in a petty commodity mode, the second (which also sets the market parameters for the first) is fully capitalist. What has come to prevail in the cultural sphere, then – structured, as Althusserians might say, 'in dominance'[17] – is a mixed mode of production constituted as a combination of these two.

This is not unlike the two-tier market structure which has prevailed for most of this century (until trends towards full vertical integration set in) in the field of agriculture. And for much the same reason: it is to the advantage of publishers and media companies that small producers take the risks. In agriculture, these risks have to do with the weather. In cultural production, a sector built on obsolescence and greedy for novelty, they have to do with the vagaries of popular taste. Thus they involve either the start-up costs of developing an innovative line of product (a novelist's first novel, a rock band's three years on the road), or the sorting-out process whereby a new product's commercial viability is test-marketed at the small producer's expense.

A second difference between the contemporary creative producer and the traditional artisan is in the kind of revenue they earn. Where the original product, as with a novel, filmscript or song, is in a form that can be mechanically reproduced, and is copyrighted, income accrues not just on the basis of a single agreed payment, but in the form of an income stream calculated, by contractual agreement, as a percentage of final sales. In the book trade, this takes the form of royalties; in movies and records, 'points'. What the independent mass cultural creator produces, then, is not just a salable commodity, but a property which can generate rent.[18] It is this, indeed, which enables some star turns to capitalize their earnings still further by acquiring the creative properties of others, a famous instance of which was provided by Michael Jackson in his purchase, from Paul McCartney, of the Beatles' music and lyrics owned by Northern Songs.

In whatever form income accrues, though, it is evident that cultural creators have an interest in maximizing the perceived value of their own faces and names. Indeed, not only is that value crucial both for final sales, and for obtaining studio and publishing contracts in the first place: name/face celebrity can also become a tradable item in itself. As a sideline, minor stars open shopping malls and major ones get to host *Saturday Night Live*. Even more lucratively, culture industry celebrities can earn extra revenue by appearing in advertisements for any number of other products. Not just single ads, but whole campaigns are often based on personal endorsements of this kind – ranging from film star Catherine Deneuve's work for Chanel and comedian Bill Cosby's for Jello, to Madonna's video for Coca-Cola in response to Michael Jackson et al.'s for Pepsi.

Not only, then, is the cultivation of celebrity the object of a production process in itself. The stockpiled commodity it produces – an imaged name – represents a banked and transferable store of promotional capital. As such, its results are detachable from the practices and products in whose immediate context they have arisen. It is this feature, as much as its mediatized artificiality, which distinguishes modern stardom from the honour and fame for which the competitive strived in pre-capitalist times. Under conditions of commodity production, such celebrityhood is free-floating. It is a convertible currency in which the registered images of those it elevates can be rented or traded in for cash. The sign-commodities produced by star-making are peculiar, moreover, in another respect. Their use value to those who buy or rent them is not in their consumption, productive or otherwise, but in their associative power to move other merchandise. Thus, within the wider economy of advertising the construction of show business celebrity, indeed celebrity of every kind, serves as a kind of capital goods subsector, supplying inputs both for the (self-)promotional activities of the culture industry itself, and for those of commodity production as a whole.

Promotion as programming: promotional transfer across commodities

The forms of cultural self-promotion considered so far have been both metonymic (in the sense of a figure of speech in which the part stands for the whole) and internal. Metonymic, in that a part of a product, or of a product-flow, has served to promote the larger product or series to which it belongs. Internal, in that such promotion boosts the circulation of that to which it is immediately linked. The build-up and promotional use of stars can be regarded as an extension of the same principles, with regard to both the serial promotion of the 'name' involved, and to that of the show, record, book, film or programme in which he or she appears. In two respects, though, using stars can have promotional effects beyond those attaching to the cultural produce with which they are immediately identified.

First, since the celebrified name associated with the creation of a particular cultural product is itself boosted by that product's circulation, its appearance in that context also helps promote whatever other products it may subsequently – and incidentally – be associated with. Where the owner/publisher/distributor stays the same, for example in the lifelong relationship between T.S. Eliot and Faber & Faber, the carry-over effect remains internal to the marketing operation of the company involved. But the effect may fall elsewhere. Celebrities in one medium can deploy their celebrityhood in another, as when a retired film star (Groucho Marx) hosts a TV game show, or when a soap opera favourite like Kylie Minogue (of *Neighbours*) or Don Johnson (of *Miami Vice*), cuts an album. Also, within their own primary field, stars can transfer from one company to another; and here, again, the carry-over effect (for which the new purchaser/ contractor evidently has to pay) moves beyond the circle of initially associated goods.

Secondly, the media publicity surrounding stars, and which is indispensable to their cultivation as such, is conducted by vehicles and channels external to their own work. Indeed, such publicity, which caters to a desire to get close to the famous, provides the basis for commodifiable cultural material in itself. This material comes in a plethora of forms, from out-and-out fanzines, and industry mouthpieces like *Billboard* and *TV Guide*, to independent consumer reports on who's hot and not in the review and entertainment pages of the papers. Beyond these specialized venues, moreover, a fascination with pop cultural celebrities, especially with their lives and loves behind the scenes, is a ubiquitous element of mass media fare. One of the Western world's largest selling magazines, *People*, is entirely devoted to such material; as too are television programmes like the boosterish *Arts and Entertainment*, or the fawning *Lifestyles of the Rich and Famous*.

Much of this publicity is planted through press releases, leaks, and interviews, or generated by specially staged pseudo-events like charity events and industry-wide award ceremonies. But it is not all sought for, nor, indeed, all adulatory. Not that the negative is necessarily bad. Scandals keep the light shining on the stage. They are also relative in their effects. Ben Johnson's disqualification in the Seoul Olympics for taking steroids may have destroyed his value as a health-symbolizing endorser, but the drug bust of the *Rolling Stones* in 1964 only enhanced their allure. A similar ambiguity surrounds the publicity effect of commentary and reviews. To attract critical attention is to run a risk, but even the most jaundiced critics play the role of consumer connoisseurs; and to pan an actor, novelist or would-be singing idol is only the other side of promoting those more worthy.

Celebrities console themselves, in any case, with the nostrum that bad publicity is better than none at all. Nor is this just consolation. A vicious review can can stir interest through controversy. An incident which temporarily discredits its subject can be recuperated later on. As it played at the time, the televised Tobin enquiry into the Ben Johnson affair was a degradation ritual which publicly ratified the Canadian sprinter's vertiginous fall from grace. It also provided an occasion, however, for Johnson to stage his repentance and renewal; from which (with the Canadian lifting of his ban in 1990, followed by his return debut to indoor track at Hamilton in January 1991) he has already re-emerged as a figure fit for commercial sponsorship – as a promotional signifier, indeed, of enhanced meaning and power.[19]

The point can be generalized. What applies to stars applies to hits. Indeed, from up-scale documentaries about postmodern art to Malcolm McLaren's runaway invention of punk, it applies to large-scale cultural trends as well. At all these levels, the wider publicity that serves, directly or indirectly, to promote cultural commodity A can serve as the informational and entertainment content of (otherwise unrelated) commodity B. Whether to call all such cases of promotional transfer *self-*promotion can be considered moot. In some instances the publicizing vehicle has no commercial stake in the stars, events or products publicized. In others, as when Rupert Murdoch's *Sunday Times* beat the drums for Sky TV, it evidently does. Altogether, given the growth of corporate interlock, and of culture industry conglomerates, the line between what is self and other, commercially speaking, has become increasingly hard to draw. Either way, all the non-advertising publicity surrounding culture industry products is self-promotional in at least an aggregated sense. From the highbrow French television interview show *Apostrophe* to salacious gossip in the British tabloids, entertainment about entertainment serves as self-promotion for the culture and communications sector as a whole.

Promotion as programming: promotional transfer across media

A special case of the primary material of one cultural commodity serving as promotion for another involves the deployment of such a relationship across media. That is: when the rendering of a given model, performance or celebrity in one medium is both a commercial product in itself and an advertisement for another product which is essentially the same work translated into the terms of another medium.

A clear instance is when a best-selling novel is turned into a film script for a blockbuster movie: a happy circumstance whose effect on the original is especially marked when, as with William Blatty's *The Exorcist*, or Peter Bentley's *Jaws*, that was the intention all along. In such cases, indeed, the book-form turns out to have a doubly promotional role vis-a-vis the movie which follows. For the author, its publishing success facilitates the sale of the film rights to it. For the film studio, the initial publicity generated by the book helps boost the film version's own subsequent box-office demand.

A similar relation, but this time involving broadcasting and recording, is to be found in the field of popular music. Playing records on air, which for thirty years has been the staple diet of AM radio, serves to promote their actual sales. Of course, the only technical difference between what we hear on the hi-fi and on the radio is in the manner of playback. But the commercial relation founded on that difference is the same as in the case of a paperback which is also the model for a film. A record played on radio is likewise inserted doubly into the commodity process. To the radio listener, the replayed song presents itself as a terminal good, an entertainment service, in return for whose use the broadcaster pays royalties to the publisher and others having ownership shares in it. But for the record company, and especially when the record is a current release, its broadcast by radio is also an ad – through the lure of on-tap repetition, a promotion for individually bought copies of that very same piece.

From a business standpoint, this second function of the broadcast record, particularly when showcasing new groups and releases, can be more important than the first. As the payola scandals of the late 1950s illustrate, it even gives studios an incentive to bribe stations outright to secure air-time for their product. Of course, commercial broadcasters are not automatically pliant. They have an independent stake in who listens to what, which leads them to gear play-lists to the specific tastes of their own target audiences. But this does not prevent a more general convergence of interests. Flagship radio stations, like CHUM in Toronto, regularly sponsor stadium concerts by the recording artists they play. Since the very beginnings of the recording industry, moreover, broadcasters have joined with the music press to convert the competitive side of record-selling into a form of entertainment in itself. Hence 'Top Forty' radio, album and concert give-aways, and, above all, the combined fashion mart and competitive spectacle represented by the Hit Parade.

Since the early 1980s, with the rise of music video, radio's role as a promoter of records has been increasingly taken over by television. In teen-rock, the music industry's largest market, whole networks (MTV, MuchMusic) have been built round such material, and a similar format has been developed for country and western.

In one respect, the embellishment of a pop song with visual images changes nothing. The record continues to be played on air, and its copy continues to be sold. But it also transforms the record's meaning, both as music and as promotion for its makers, so that the video form of a record constitutes an aesthetic expression in itself. Critics have pointed out that the addition of visual images can be impoverishing in that it closes what is otherwise a more open auditory text.[20] A video also elevates an act's visual image over its sound, making hit-making an even more narcissistic exercise than it was already. At the same time, music-video has more dimensions to communicate with than a sound recording on its own; in which respect, the expressive possibilities of the record's ad can exceed those of the actual product being pushed.

From the point of view of cultural commodification, there is something extraordinary in this development. Music-video originated as a high-grade complement to the demo tape. In the past decade, its function has broadened so that it has come to serve as promotion vis-a-vis the consumer market at large. Records themselves meanwhile (on disc or tape) have remained the principal music commodity. But principal only in terms of profits: for, at the point of reception, what was designed and still functions as pure advertising for this commodity has become an overshadowing mode of entertainment in itself.

For all their differences, these examples illustrate the same tendency. The produce of some media has become systematically drawn into a promotional relation to the same produce as translated into the technical-sensory terms of others. The media dependencies which form on this basis are not arbitrary. McLuhan, who had in mind such progressions as film, theatre, speech, noted that 'the "content" of one medium is always another medium' (1965: 8). His immediate point was technological; but the 'Chinese boxes' relation which caught his eye has an economic dimension, too. Films exhibit to larger audiences than theatres, which are larger again than those for private acts of natural speech. And their commercial significance likewise varies. A similar point is implicit in the earlier schema developed by Benjamin. To move from cave paintings to movable ones in art galleries, and then again to woodcuts, lithography, photography, and moving film, is to ascend in degrees of reproducibility – which is also to ascend in degrees of profitability of display.

The implication for culture industry careers is evident. As with a bar-band that makes it on to disc, or in the progression from *Amadeus* the play to *Amadeus* the movie, the fortunes of an act or work advance as it moves up the scale of reproducibility. And with each step, the market established by gaining an audience in a 'lower' form builds demand for a version of the same product transposed into a more widely distributable medium.

Overall, two summary propositions can be advanced. First, in cultural as in other economic sectors, what is most valorizable is what can be most readily produced in a form which enables it to be individually purchased and mass consumed. Hence, after an initial phase dominated by print, the centrality, in capitalist cultural production, of the aural and visual recording. Secondly, cultural expressions in media forms of lower commodifiability tend to become re-positioned as promotion for the same expressions rendered into a commercially more strategic form. Hence, rather than vice versa, pop music on radio and television pushes record sales, while successful plays and novelettes pave the way for a film.

Live and recorded

The most important manifestation of this logic, however, can be seen in the revised cultural position that the rise of reproduction-based technologies has entailed for the oral: that is, for shows and performances which are presented, as a recording-based culture puts it, 'live'.

In the romantic version of this story, as told in scholarly tones, for example, by Walter Ong (1982), the culprit was technology, the movement is towards orality's eclipse, and the decisive moment was the introduction of print. The mediation of this development by commerce, however, has produced a more complicated outcome. When the story teller was replaced by the writer, and the reading aloud of hand-made books was made redundant by industrial production, mass literacy and silent reading in private, the spoken word lost much of its communicative function. The result, though, was not the complete disappearance of oral performance from the literary scene. In public readings by famous writers – at their zenith, in the latter half of the nineteenth century, in the speaking tours of luminaries like Mark Twain and Oscar Wilde – the oral returned as promotion. Or, to be more precise: it reappeared as a dual function promotional event in which, on the one hand, the star status of authors is capitalized on to create a show which, as far as possible, pays for itself; while, on the other, that same show provides literary lions with an opportunity to enhance the cult of their personality while boosting, more immediately, the sales of their latest book.

A similar promotionalization of the oral is traceable in music. The European music business which grew up in the eighteenth and nineteenth centuries was based on the sales of printed sheets and of the instruments (primarily the piano) with which these could be played back at home. Here, again, the live was not wholly eliminated. It was retained in playback itself, for the reproduction of music via printed sheets still required their human performance.[21] A place for live performance was also retained in the public sphere; though here, as in literature, its role was transformed. The orchestral concert, a society occasion made all the more lustrous through the personal appearance of the composer, or of 'name' orchestras and virtuosi, was an indispensable channel for publicizing what was available in published form. Further down-market, music halls, vaudeville, dance halls, and music cafes represented similar hybrids of ritual, paying spectacle, and advertisement. Hence, in the pre-recording days of Tin Pan Alley, the pressure for a constant supply of new material: a pressure which came not only from patrons seeking novelty, but also from publishers and song-writers anxious for a 'plug'.

This technical–economic configuration, with its promotional subordination of the live, has persisted to this day. To be sure, with the replacement of reproduction-by-performance by reproduction-by-recording – a process which began with player-pianos and piano rolls and has culminated (so far) in digitalization and compact discs – the overall place of the live has been further reduced. Thus electronic equipment has replaced piano-playing, singing, etc, as the principal form of musical entertainment at home; and a similar switch has been evident in public entertainment, where the local dance hall has given way to disc jockeys and discotheques, just as muzak has taken over a role once played by itinerant musicians. Within the sphere of promotion itself, finally, recorded performance on radio and TV has replaced live performance as the primary vehicle for directly publicizing music in its commodity form.

For all these displacements, however, just as in the case of literature, concerts and other forms of live musical presentation have retained at least an ancillary promotional role. The cult of King's College Chapel, globalized through the annual broadcast of its Christmas Eve carol service, underpins a continuing market for whatever the choir records. With less ambivalence, stadium gigs by supergroups are frankly conceived of as a marketing device. Underwritten by record companies, they are usually timed to coincide with the latest release, and may even be billed, as with Michael Jackson's *Bad*, U2's *Rattle and Hum*, or the Rolling Stones' *Steel Wheels*, as named embodiments of the album itself.

In one respect, indeed, the live has become even more significant than it was before. At its most extreme, this heightened importance is manifest in the mass hysteria which, in the audio-visual age above all, has come to attend the personal appearance of the biggest mass-mediatized stars. From the millions who lined the streets and docksides to wish Mary Pickford and Douglas Fairbanks well on their European honeymoon, to the bobby-soxers screaming at the feet of Frank Sinatra, or today's pre-teens clutching at the clothes of *New Kids on the Block*, the live has become a place of magic, an enchanted mirror through which the most publicized celebrities can leap off the celluloid, or out of the record track, into direct sensory range.

The point is even more vividly illustrated by the crowds who turn up to a rock concert to see their heroes playing (often supplemented by actual tapes) note-for-note renditions of what they already know by heart. But here, too, we see the paradoxical character of what has occurred.

The displacement of live performance by recording, of auratic culture by the mechanically reproduced, has led to a countervailing nostalgia for the living, the authentic, and the original. At its most intense, as in Beatlemania, it can even express itself in a primal desire for ritual fusion. At the same time, the way that the live, in an age of mechanical reproduction, is subsumed into promotion profoundly crosses it with the quality of its opposite. Films and records, unlike performed scripts and scores (or read-aloud books) are not interpretatively mediated re-presentations of an original. They are exact reproductions of what was originally taped. Moreover, the commodity here is not itself an abstract model, but a performance. Or, rather: a performed rendition which is edited into a version which, from the moment of release, becomes the authoritative version of what it is.

At the limit, both to promote the record and because the public demands to hear the same as on disc, the live is constrained to imitate the recorded. With the live re-staging of a video this goes even further: the enacted simulation is at the level of the performance as a whole. Of course, the concert performance (*Bruce Springstein Live!*) can provide an alternative to the studio as the source of its own raw material. But this is only an apparent reversal, since the original already anticipates the recording which is simultaneously being made. Either way, in spite of the aura conferred by real presence, the live loses its performative paramountcy. Instead, the studio version rules, and the live performance is either a feeder into it or the mimetic repetition of what the studio has already produced.

Promotion without end

Considering that commercial entertainment, from newspaper columns to live shows to TV soap opera, is self-promotional in all the ways just described, what presents itself to the media consumer as first-order programming is even more densely promotional than the commercialized writing commented upon by Harold Innis. It is not just a 'device for advertising advertising', but advertising to at least the power of three. Thus, (1) the mediatized programming which draws audiences towards the ads in its midst is serially related to (2) the promotion of its own associated names and brands, and thence (3) to the output of commercialized cultural production as a whole. Moreover (4), through the use of celebrities and other allusive devices, the symbolic field which other, paying, advertisers draw upon is continuous with the material in which that advertising is embedded. In short, the compound of news, entertainment, and advertising circulated by ad-carrying media, is promotional both throughout, and in depth. And every promotional point on its multiply promotional surface is connected, multiply, to a multitude of others.

Figure 5.2 depicts the general structure: an interconnected lattice of (self-)promotional triangles in which any single segment of culture industry product may be implicated, immediately or at one remove, in as many as eleven basic promotional moves.

To illustrate the endless convolutions to which such relationships can give rise, I will offer, finally, just one banal instance. This is the 16 October 1988 issue of *Observer Magazine*, the colour supplement of one of Britain's 'serious' Sunday newspapers. I have already examined the multi-page ad for Vauxhall Cavalier to be found on its inside front cover. It is a question of putting under the microscope, then, one of the contexts in which that spectacular advertisement was set.

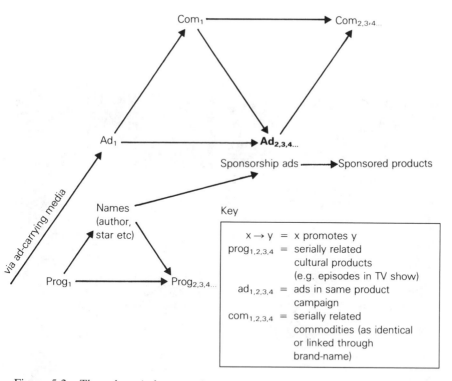

Figure 5.2   *The culture industry and the web of promotion*

The issue in question has 100 pages, of which 70 are taken up with (explicit) advertising. Most of this consists of one or two-page 'glossies' for national brands. In line with the paper's orientation to affluent 'AB' consumers, the vast majority of these are for products and services in the luxury or semi-luxury range. Only four (for Benson and Hedges, Heinz 'new spicy soups', C&A casual wear, and Lever Brothers detergents) promote products consumed by lower income groups as well.

Interspersed through the ads, and just as lavishly illustrated, are seven regular and seven special features. Of the former, one is a cartoon (*Peanuts*) and one a games page (chess, bridge, crossword). The rest are either about celebrities, lifestyle advice, or both. Examples of the first are 'Opening Shots', wherein humorous captions accompany photos of Neil Kinnock, Martina Navratilova, Mick Jagger, and a clutch of Royals, and 'The Expert's Expert', in which famous people reveal the names of their favourite photographers. Representing the second is 'Winebox': 'Paul Levy's wine and cheese party'. And an instance of their combination is 'Room of my own' which this week explores the living-room of designer Edina Ronay. The special features have the same flavour. Thus we have: 'London Shows All' ('Nicola Jeal visits the London Fashion Week and meets the designer of the Year, Rifat Ozbek'); 'A Cosmopolitan Cook' ('Jane Grigson meets Anne Willan, the Yorkshirewoman who started one

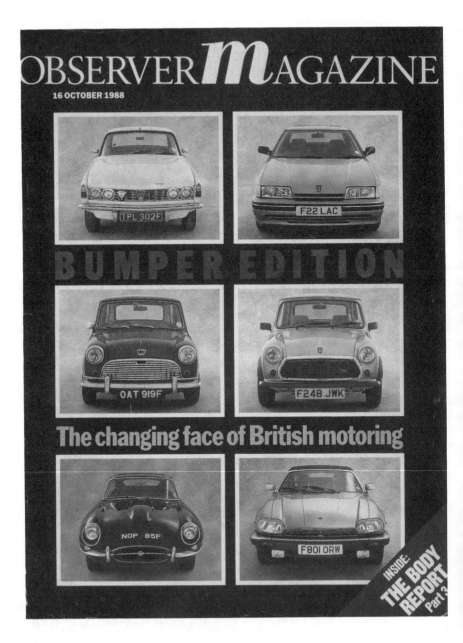

of the most successful cookery schools in Paris'); a 'career review' of Dame Peggy Ashcroft; and a three-page spread on Desert Orchid, the season's most successful race-horse.

What all this amounts to, clearly, is lifestyle fodder for the (moderately) affluent: a mosaic of 'editorial' content and advertisements which merge in a generalized picture of the Good Life, together with its purchasable symbols and accoutrements. Part of this fodder, moreover, is a diet of celebrities – either ones already established, who give *People*-style spice to the dish, or ones on the rise, like Rifat Ozbek, for whom (and also for the fashion industry he works for) the added publicity is a brand-enhancing bonus in itself. Finally, in the continuity of format between this and previous/subsequent issues, a further set of promotional relationships are set in play. The magazine is serially promoting itself; and, through that, the newspaper of which it is a giveaway weekly element.[22]

The promotion conducted at each of these levels has its own complexity, a complexity further compounded by the way in which they are spliced together. But what makes this issue of the *Observer*'s colour supplement especially interesting is that woven into it is yet a fourth promotional circuit, centred on what the front cover trumpets as its special unifying theme. Suitably illustrated with front-end photographs of six new models of (British) cars, that theme provides this week's issue of the magazine, in fact, with its very own title. It is the 'Bumper Edition'; and it has a big story to tell: 'The Changing Face of British Motoring'.

As with most instances of hype-through-labelling, the title promises more than the product delivers. When we turn to the inside we find that the theme is only a sub-theme, pursued by only three of the issue's fourteen articles. More surprisingly, the promised emphasis on cars is not reflected in the focus of the ads. Only two are for cars at all – the four-page spread for Vauxhall Cavalier already examined, and a two-page ad for Volvo. Moreover, though the first of these products is manufactured in Britain, neither company is British owned. These absences, it may be said, give the lie to the hype. For the shortage of advertised British brands of cars reflects the actual decline of the British car industry, while the shortage of car ads as such points to the weakness of the *Observer* itself as a competitor for such advertising. (Its circulation at the time was only one half that of *The Sunday Times*.) Nevertheless, the front cover itself, together with the three special inside features on cars, does constitute a kind of advertising for what Margaret Thatcher has called 'our great car economy' – advertising for which, moreover, no money has had to be paid.

The first of the three thematic features, 'And The Show Goes On . . .' (a baby-boomer allusion to Sonny and Cher's 1960s hit 'And the Beat Goes on'), makes clear why the car theme has been chosen. There is a topical hook. The week of 16 October marks the opening of the annual British Motor Show. The Show itself – an industry-wide trade fair originally held at Earl's Court, and now held in the more spacious facilities of the National Exhibition Centre in Birmingham – is a promotional event. By publicizing it the magazine is promoting a promotion for cars. But the Show's opening also helps circulate the magazine, for it provides the occasion for an audience-drawing retrospective which can at once push the button of nostalgia and provide tips for the fashion-conscious about the direction of contemporary style.

In that vein, after a friendly plug for the Show and its aims ('a grander mixture of show business and motor business than many of its international counterparts' which 'coincides with a buoyant mood in the British motor trade . . .'), the lead article undertakes a number of capsule comparisons. These range from then-and-now facts about the Show itself, to comparative data about car owners, the roads they drive on, and the style and performance features of the cars themselves. A follow-up article by the same author looks at the enduring popularity of convertibles: 'Sue Baker finds more and more motorists have a soft spot for the soft-top. Are you already converted to the convertible?' While a third, by Stephen Bayley, focuses on a quarter century of car design, and how such changes are to be socially and culturally interpreted.

The tone of these articles, underlined by the pictures which illustrate them, is both celebratory and wistful. With an over-the-shoulder glance at the (1950s and 1960s) 'golden age of motor design', progress is shown to be triumphantly marching on. Vauxhall could hardly have chosen a better setting in which to place their own ad for Cavalier, with Bayley's piece on the history of style providing a virtual guide as to how the iconography of this ad is to be read.

The Bayley piece itself, moreover – 'A Nice Line in Cars' – introduces yet a further promotional loop. For the cognoscenti, the author himself is a 'name'. A highly regarded (and telegenic) researcher in the field of industrial design, Bayley had come to public notice through *Sex, Drink and Fast Cars* (1986). Indeed, his piece in the magazine, easily the best written, gives a thumbnail sketch of that book's central ideas. Nor is Bayley's the only commodity, and career interest, incidentally promoted by his article. Under its last line we are informed that the 'Photographs are from "Power behind the Wheel" by Walter J. Boyne, those in colour by Lucinda Lewis, published by Conran Octopus on Thursday, £19.95'. Still, the publicity opportunity was particularly timely in Bayley's case. For, as the same note tells us, he had just become Director of the London Design Museum, which was due to open the next July. There was perhaps no room to add that the Museum's first scheduled show was to be Bayley's own production; nor that this baptismal exhibit was to be entitled, with an appropriateness whch went beyond its mere subject matter, 'Commerce and Culture'.

It is not easy to determine, here, exactly what is promoting what. Bayley's article, crammed with stunning photographs of classic car models from the Silver Arrow and SJ Speedster to the VW Beetle and Ford Brezza, at once helps promote the Motor Show (itself a promotion), provides an iconographic and semiological reference point for the back-to-the-future Cavalier ad, advertises the photographer and the book from which the photography is taken, and publicizes the name and work of Bayley himself. In turn, Bayley's Museum project, for all its serious historiographic intent, provides a showcase for industrial design: a practice which synthesizes the genius of the engineer with that of the publicist, and converts mass-produced commodities into consumable signs. As it is actually printed, moreover, the same article is wedged between advertisements for *Chic'n'Supreme* New World kitchen appliances, and Lever Brothers 'genuine article' soaps and detergents. Readers turning to it, then, are automatically drawn towards an encounter with these ads. In addition, the whole Motor Show sequence which Bayley's piece anchors provides the main story (advertised on the front page of the Sunday paper to which it is attached) for this issue of *Observer Magazine*. This organ is itself, finally, multiply promotional. For its publishers, it is both a means to raise advertising revenue, and a device for raising the circulation of the newspaper into which it is inserted. For its advertisers, it provides a direct marketing outlet. It is even promotional for its readers, since much of its copy offers guidance about how to self-advertise through appropriate lifestyle choice.

It is as if we are in a hall of mirrors. Each promotional message refers us to a commodity which is itself the site of another promotion. And so on, in an endless dance whose only point is to circulate the circulation of something else. To be caught up as a cultural consumer in the vortex of promotional signs is not only to be continually reminded of the myriad things and experiences we lack. It is to be engulfed, semiotically, in a great, swirling stream of signifiers whose only meaning, in the end, is the circulatory process which it anticipates, represents, and impels. Andy Warhol, whose multiple silk-screens of publicity icons have come to be celebrated, and priced, as great art, explained the meaning of his work as 'all surface'. His wisdom consisted in recognizing – apparently without regret – that even those who would illuminate that empty vortex can do no more than launch messages into it: messages whose referential point disappears in the instrumental uses to which these artistic utterances themselves, beginning with their role as self-advertising for their author, are inescapably put.

Notes

1. The self-conscious basing of art on promotion has been taken all the way by the English painter Simon Linke. His canvases replicate, with a photographic realism, the ads which appeared in *Arts Forum*, offering thereby an ironic, but affectless, comment on the promotionalization of art itself.

2. The term was originally developed by Julia Kristeva. Against the vulgarization of 'intertextuality' to mean the way in which many of the elements of (literary) texts are derived from other (textual) sources, she deployed the term as a way of drawing attention to the way in which the semiotic interconnection of texts makes their meaning undecidable and polyvocal. 'The term "intertextuality" denotes [the] transposition of one or several sign system(s) into one another; but since this term has often been understood in the banal sense

of "study of sources" we prefer the term *transposition* because it specifies that the passage of one text sign system into another demands a new articulation of the thetic – of enunciative and denotative positionality. If one grants that every signifying practice is a field of transpositions of various signifying systems (an intertextuality), one then understands that its "place" of enunciation and its denoted "object" are never single, complete, and identical to themselves, but always plural, shattered, incapable of being tabulated.' (Kristeva, 1984: 59–60).

3. A noteworthy example of such a pitch was Guinness's mid-1980s 'Pure Genius' campaign in the UK. In the TV commercials, a puzzling series of apparently disconnected narrative scenes was followed by the thematic slogan, which indicated, most immediately, the 'pure genius' needed to decipher it.

4. Information about the history of these papers, and their celebrated circulation war, is provided in Bartow (1952), and Juergens (1966).

5. Editorial in the *Journal*, 8 November, 1896, cited in Swanberg (1961: 90).

6. These figures, and the others cited in this paragraph, are taken from Emery (1954: 395–402).

7. These figures are calculated on the basis of information provided by Juergens (1966: 336–7).

8. For an account of early patent medicine advertising in the press, see Emery (1954: 400).

9. *Printers' Ink* CXXV, 29 October, 1948: 102. Cited in Emery (1954: 402).

10. For a history of the American Newspaper Publishers' Association, see Emery (1950).

11. A spectacular instance of this down-market trap is provided by the near-bankruptcy of the pro-Labour (London) *Daily Herald* in the early 1920s. The paper's troubles came not so much despite, as because of, its record high circulation. As George Lansbury noted in his memoirs: 'Our success in circulation was our undoing. The more copies we sold, the more money we lost.' Lansbury (1925: 160), cited in Curran (1977: 221).

12. For a discussion of Pulitzer's efforts to win women readers, see Juergens (1966: 132–74).

13. Dallas Smythe coined the term 'free lunch' to describe the free (or subsidized) media fare provided to customers in order to lure them into contributing their 'watching time' to the ads. His analysis of this relationship is set forth in Smythe (1981, Ch. 2, 'The audience commodity and its work'). See also Bagdakian (1984, Part 2, 'The High Cost of the Free Lunch').

14. Such tie-ins can be more direct, as when Coca-Cola took advantage of its ownership of Columbia Pictures, between 1982 and 1989, to insert gratuitous visual mentions of its drink.

15. For an analysis of *Dallas*'s mass appeal, see Ang (1985).

16. For an account of the relation between TV show formulae and cultural shifts in the market, see Gitlin (1985).

17. For the theorization of a social formation as a combination of modes of production 'structured in dominance', see Althusser and Balibar (1977: 182–5 and passim).

18. For a discussion of the artist as 'model-maker' and rentier, see Attali (1980: 78–83).

19. As is happens, Johnson's indifferent performance at the sponsored events in which he subsequently starred undermined this fresh start and his price once more began to plummet.

20. For an illustrative analysis of Madonna's (Monroe-quoting) video of *Material Girl*, see Kaplan (1987: 116–26). It is probably the case that the visual imagery in this, and many other pop videos, are remembered by the audience long after the sonic shape of the piece. Still, the absence of critical attention to the latter, i.e. to the musical side of music video, which is evident in Kaplan's otherwise comprehensive account, bespeaks a visual bias in our culture which the aesthetic binding of music to image in music video only reinforces.

21. Human playback in the music industry provided a mass of local markets, as well, for private music tuition. Hence the rise of a centralized licensing system, through music academies and their grades of exams, and a performance ethos of disciplined and rigorous exactitude to the written text. Turning human performers into record needles spelt the end of a previous latitude for improvisation, whose residue can be seen in the cadenza which traditionally climaxes the first or third movement of an instrumental concerto.

22. The immediate competitors were *The Sunday Times* and *The Sunday Telegraph*, each boasting its own, similarly functioning, colour supplement. The following year, however, the *Observer* faced two new entrants to its market: the *Sunday Correspondent* and the *Independent on Sunday*. One of the competitive ploys of the latter was to offer a new format magazine section which combined the usual lifestyle and celebrity material with semi-serious think-pieces, plus reviews.

6
PROMOTIONAL POLITICS

The social meaning . . . of parliamentary activity is no doubt to turn out legislation and, in part, administrative measures. But in order to understand how democratic politics serve this social end, we must start from the competitive struggle for power and office and realise that the social function is fulfilled, as it were, incidentally – in the same sense as production is incidental to the making of profit.

Joseph A. Schumpeter[1]

A Polish election poster

The Polish election of 4 June 1989 was widely hailed as a turning-point in the dismantling of East European Stalinism, a crucial step on the road, not just in Poland but throughout the region, from one-party rule to Western-style multi-party democracy. The actual form of the election was a compromise. Following the Round Table Agreement, open contests were held for all the seats in the Upper House of the *Sjem*, but only for one third of those in the more powerful Lower House. In the event, Solidarity won all but one of the seats it could legally contest, a result which at once de-legitimized the ruling (Polish Workers') Party and guaranteed for its once banned opponent at least a share in governmental power.

The drama of the campaign was well captured in a poster which Solidarity plastered all over Poland in the final days before the vote. The poster's principal motif was a Wild West sheriff, striding towards us, fingers at the ready over the holsters at his hips. A quintessential pose – one indeed whose precise likeness consumers of American culture will have seen before. For beneath the stetson is the ultra-familiar figure of Gary Cooper in a still taken, moments before the climactic shoot-out, from that classic among Westerns, *High Noon*. As befits the stern-jawed image, the poster's re-framing is achieved with a minimum of words. Just the Solidarity logo (prominently, across the top, and again, in miniature, on a button which has been superimposed on the cowboy's lapel); and, in crisp characters across the bottom, a simple caption, *W Samo Poludie* – High Noon – followed by a date, 4 June 1989.

The basic point, insolent in its ellipsis, is plain enough. The election is a showdown between the good guys and the bad guys: High Noon for Poland. No prizes for guessing which side is which, nor who is destined to win. It is this self-certainty, indeed, which gives the poster its punch. Its appeal for votes doubles as an act of sympathetic magic in which

W SAMO POŁUDNIE
4 CZERWCA 1989

Solidarity's wished-for victory is depicted as inevitable. With the story-line fixed, the only question for the reader/voter is whether the picture presented is a mirror or a window, whether what you see is your enemy or yourself. Which side are you on?

It is no accident that Solidarity appears in this scene as a sheriff. The forces of Good are the forces of Law. Which is to say that the syndicalist movement which cracked the template of People's Democracy is no mere rebel, still less an anarchic force: it is the legitimate embodiment of the Polish state. A minor photographic substitution reinforces this hegemonizing move. Gary Cooper's right hand clutches not a gun but a ballot paper.[2] Correspondingly, runs the subtext, while the old regime could only be maintained through military repression, the new one rests on the power of the vote. Thus the (redemptive) Law which Solidarity brings to the Polish Frontier is not just Law, but Law in its most lawful form: Law based on popular consent.

But there is more to the poster than this. Indeed, the more closely we look at it, the more levels we can see at which it encodes what Solidarity means to mean on the electoral map; and the more levels, as well, at which it assigns a meaning to the wider transition which the election and its signage themselves represent.

Let us stay for a moment with the Wild West. While only one element of that wider myth complex is shown, this element so obviously belongs to it, in a sense even sums it up, that it serves as perfect visual shorthand. The Solidarity sheriff invokes Western-ism in general: a world of clapboard towns, saloons and store-keepers, cowboys and horses, and homesteading families carving out a dream of abundance from the resistant land through the sweat of their individualistic brow. And in so doing, besides offering a little homily about law and legitimacy, the poster cues the voter/reader to Solidarity's general socioeconomic stance. Over Marlboro County hover the ghosts of Locke and Jefferson, of possessive individualism and the ideal of a property-owning democracy. Thus inflected, country-and-western iconography is a figure for free enterprise: in the theme-parked American version of history, a prelapsarian vision, indeed (that is, pre-urban and pre-monopoly), of capitalism's origin and essence. By employing such iconography here, Solidarity signals its impeccably anti-Communist espousal of the market, and its practical intention to privatize the Polish economy.

This is not to say that the Western complex signifies only the values of the market. The sheriff at shoot-out time also implies the primacy of action over words, of life in the raw over citified refinement, and of real men over wimps and women. Through this system of oppositions cowboy imagery in North America has long been linked both to the political right and to the style-culture (especially in music) of the industrial working class. In the contemporary 'post-feminist' conjuncture it also offers a reactive vision of masculinity which calls to mind a once-upon-a-time when men and women were different and both knew their place. The mythos of the Wild West evidently has a different resonance in Poland than it does in the United

States. But if these codings are not deliberately intended, they are not censored out. Nor is this surprising given, on the one hand, the extent of Solidarity's enthusiasm for the market and, on the other, the relative strength in Poland of traditional patterns of male dominance, buttressed by a rural-based, and religiously monopolistic, Catholic Church.

The poster identifies Solidarity, though, not just with the legend of the West, but with this legend as translated into film. Moreover, the sheriff is a star, the movie is a classic, and the genre which it typifies is itself one of Hollywood's most successful and recognizable forms of entertainment. To deck Solidarity out as the hero of *High Noon*, then, has the further effect of identifying the movement with all that such entertainment generically represents. That is: with the leisure ethos projected by commercial spectacles; and, beyond that, with the whole consumer culture whose most banal products cast a galling light on the low wages and drab shop windows of a failed state-socialism.

If, then, through its reference to the *content* of the American Western myth[3] Solidarity expresses its support for capitalism as a mode of production, the poster's reference to that complex *as filmed* also expresses Solidarity's support for capitalism as a mode of consumption. It points enviously to the affluence which capitalist restructuring promises to bring. Not, of course, as an instant reward. The miserable condition of the Polish economy is only exceeded by the misery – starting with unemployment and removed food subsidies – which restructuring would be bound to entail. But, in the end, a reward nonetheless: one which is merited, we may infer, indeed morally merited, by the Polish people's willingness to undergo a period of bracing Frontier toughness: Poland's pot of gold at the end of the transition-to-capitalism austerity rainbow.

The poster's Western motif indicates, finally, Solidarity's partisanship on the international stage. If the Wild West and Hollywood are signifiers for capitalism-in-general (as a toil-based, consumption-oriented way of life) they are also national icons of the United States. Or rather: of that mythicized 'America' which epitomizes free enterprise, is (still) the Leader of the Free World, and which continues to serve as the main reference point for the swelling ranks of those who, from Warsaw to Beijing, now wish to take the capitalist road. Not just ideologically then, but geographically, the poster looks West. With California as the new Mecca, indeed, it looks to the Westernmost edge of the West, to the West of the West of the West: to the West, symbolically speaking, as such.

In that context, the poster's sheriff also strikes a more specific political chord. It was only six months earlier that the eight-year term had come to an end of an American president who himself was not only an ex-movie star, but liked nothing better than to pose, literally and figuratively, as a cowboy. Reagan played this part so well, indeed, that as the curtain came down on his presidential reign he was able to ride off into the sunset, with Vietnam and Watergate forgotten, national pride restored, and America, as promised, once more 'riding tall'. The reviving effects on a flagging capitalism were not only domestic. The Reagan administration's arms build-up also amplified the effect of the unstoppable stirrings of reform which, for other reasons, were kindled during the 1980s in the countries of the ideological East. At this level the poster not only tips its stetson to Reagan, and to the roll-back forces whose mediatized embodiment he was. It also carries a subtextual assertion about the larger significance of the present contest. Namely, that the Polish electoral shoot-out was itself the last battle of the Cold War; and that in this final engagement that larger struggle, too, was about to culminate in the victory of the Good. Leaving aside the simplistically dichotomous (not to say eschatological) register in which all this is pitched, for historians looking back on liberal capitalism's *annus mirabilis* of 1989-90 the poster's implicit world-historical claim will not seem to have been entirely empty.

All the meanings considered so far have been intrinsically connected to the poster's principal rhetorical aim: which is to associate the political cause it is electorally promoting with various kinds of imagistic appeal. In this, of course, the poster is structured just like any commercial advertisement. What makes it especially striking, however, is that through its choice of symbols the poster also, if less overtly, implies a set of reflections on the very fact that its message is structured along such lines.

I have already mentioned one respect in which the poster makes its point through substitution, that is, by replacing a signifying element we expected to see – a gun – with one which we did not expect to see – a ballot paper. But there is another substitution that is more important. It is, indeed, fundamental to the composition of the poster, and without it this first substitution could not even take place. What makes the poster visually startling is that it has replaced conventional political iconography with a Hollywood film star. We might have expected to see a picture of Lech Walesa. What we get is Gary Cooper's sheriff. This must have been especially startling in a country whose political symbolism had been dominated for four decades by photo-portraits of official leaders and by stylized (realistic or romantic) representations of the working class and its heroic deeds.

The joke element aside (and I will return to it in a moment), the substitution of an improper Hollywood image for a proper political one implies an equivalence of some sort between electoral multi-party politics and Hollywood itself. In the midst of people power rhetoric, a curious admission. For it permits the thought that the kind of liberal democratic politics being championed, here, is itself a form of mass entertainment. It is just this similarity, indeed – the fact that commercial movies and electoral politics both provide audiences with a type of staged spectacle – which allows the apparently incommensurable symbolic expressions to which showbiz and even the most serious kind of politics give rise to share the same discursive space.

What makes the poster's implicit analogy more pointed still is that its design incorporates not only an instance of commercial entertainment, but an advertisement for one.[4] The shot of Cooper's sheriff is a publicity photo which initially served to advertise the movie from which it was taken, and which continued, thereafter, to circulate as promotion, both for its star and (via the trade in recyled personality posters) for Hollywood stardom in general. Nor is the incorporated material just an incidental and subordinated quote. It visually dominates the whole poster. With only the slight modification mentioned, in fact, all that the poster does is to re-label an entertainment ad as a political one.[5] Which is to suggest not only that democratic politics, as here both practised and proposed, are formally at one with the wider culture of commodified spectacles; but that free elections are themselves quasi-commercial events, wherein the competition for votes is similarly conducted as a positioning and counter-positioning game of promotional image-making between rival company brands.

To identify the arrival of parliamentary politics with the ethos of Hollywood and the practices of Madison Avenue implies a severe limitation on the benefits such a politics can be presumed to bring. It raises the spectre of media manipulation, of one more respect in which market-based socioeconomic development implies the domination of form over content, of image over truth, of the hyper-real over the original and the unfeigned. But the point is by no means delivered straight. It comes in the form and context of a joke, and this jokiness gives a real ambiguity to the qualification about the virtues of electoral politics which the poster's apparently self-undermining structure implies. Jokes generally involve an incongruity, a disproportion between a signifier and a referent. The tension released deflates symbols into signs. Here, what is comic is that something so serious as Solidarity's grand political project should be signified by something so trivial as a hackneyed snippet from a popular film. This self-deprecating witticism makes the poster's stance towards the ideals of democracy more playful than biting. The effect, indeed, is disarming. For if the poster's campy image of the sheriff and the shoot-out punctures Solidarity's self-seriousness, the values and programme which that image gestures towards are themselves, by being thus cut down to human size, made all the more reasonable as ones to be affirmed.

In the context of an overall message which affirms the re-introduction of market principles as moral and progressive, the poster's stance towards electoral democracy can thus be glossed as an open-eyed choice of the lesser of evils. The absorption of politics into entertainment, showmanship, and promotion are just the price to be paid for what is still a real improvement. So: only two cheers for pluralist democracy – but none at all for a continuation of bureaucratic one-party rule.

But such an interpretation still misses the twinkle in the poster's eye. For does not the poster's very humour show that the diverting superficiality of the new politics involves not just a loss – in seriousness – but also a gain – in fun? The poster's ambivalence towards its master-value of democracy discloses, in any case, a deeper point. By switching to a form of politics based on elections and electioneering the era of a politics based on totalizing world-views, grand narratives, perfect visions, etc, is declared to be over. Indeed, the upheavals of Eastern Europe have spelt the end not only for Marxism–Leninism as a world-redeeming ideology, but also for the new utopianism of the 1960s, and even, in the resolutely disenchanted atmosphere of the 1980s and 1990s, for liberal-democracy itself as a transcendental ideal.

To this (post-)modernizing[6] move is closely related another. To substitute a re-framed Hollywood personality icon for a picture of the People or its leaders is to wave farewell to what David Apter (1965) called the 'collective-sacred', that is the transcendental form of the collective social-political subject. It is to refuse an idolatory of the political which, in modern-secular form, has been with us ever since the French Revolution. Again, the immediate target is Marx and his heirs. Let there be no more talk of the 'revolutionary working class' in whose name so many outrages have been committed. But, again, the point is also reflexive. The dissolution of Stalinism's unitary state, and the introduction of multi-party politics, marks the end of any such unitary myth.

Such a disavowal, which may seem optimistic in the face of resurgent nationalism, is partly necessitated by the vote-gathering exigencies of the campaign itself. Solidarity contests the election as a multi-tendency formation (syndicalist, Thatcherite, social-democratic, nationalist, social catholic) whose supporters are only united in their desire to be rid of the old. To achieve maximal inclusiveness the ad is therefore precluded from invoking – at least univocally, and without qualification – such ethnic, religious, social or ideological totalities as the Nation, the Workers or the Church. Of course, the *Solidarnosc* inscribed (twice) on the poster is the name of a union, as well as of a traditional collectivist virtue; and the Polish flag flies proudly over its 'r' and 'n'.[7] Also, the sheriff-figure itself can be read as a simple stand-in: an equivalent signifier for the People, Solidarity, etc, which performs, even more explicitly, the same mythifying work. But the substituted sign is of a peculiar kind. Not only is it a metaphor, it is the reframed representation of a dramatic enactment. From the point of view of contemporary sensibility, moreover, that enactment (Cooper's cool sheriff, the filmic showdown) is itself exaggerated and melodramatic. Its reappearance in the poster is almost as a cartoon. The poster's tone, in short, is mock-hyperbolic. It asks that Solidarity and its mission, as world-historical as they may be, should not be taken too seriously.

This very quality, of course, is essential to the poster's appeal. It entertains as it promotes. Moreover, like the history-of-cinema references in a Spielberg film, its humour is flattering. The poster addresses the reader from within a knowing 'we' made up of all those clever and literate enough to get the joke – here, virtually everyone. It also appeals through what these qualities connote at the level of style. The poster's pop cultural pastiche identifies the cause of Solidarity with a very contemporary irreverence towards the symbolic. This irreverence, in turn, is confirming.

It validates – by making actual – what the poster's mature embrace of an admittedly imperfect political form already implies as a meta-ideological ideal: the thoroughgoing de-mythologization of Poland's political culture. Thoroughgoing, because it would de-absolutize even the values of liberal democracy. But appealing, too – for it promises an enchanting disenchantment of an over-ideologized symbolic world.

Such a pitch evidently gains both meaning and power from the contrast it implies with the literal-minded and didactic ethos of Solidarity's main political competitor. The poster's very imaginativeness transfers on Solidarity a promotionally constructed imagistic difference. But to say this is to remind ourselves that even in its densest moment of reflexivity the poster remains an advertisement – just as the fact that it is based on one continually threatens to foreground that potentially self-subverting recognition.

The poster, in fact, is a (self-)deconstructive text. On the one hand, it resists the artificial semiosis it instantiates through the way in which its subtext ('this is an advertisement') subverts its surface meaning ('vote for Solidarity'). But at the same time, since that subversion also gives the poster a certain promotional esprit, the text as a whole can never completely break free from its first-order rhetorical function. It refuses, then, to have any stable meaning at all. Like those optical illusions which show stairs going up and going down, the poster perpetually oscillates between its moments of promotion and reflection, of critique (of its other) and meta-critique (of itself). The final meaning is undecidable, because the oscillation is irreducible to either its critical-reflexive or promotional poles.

At first sight, this ambiguity is just a quirk of the poster's design. But it matches so well the condition of the collective subject for which the poster claims to speak that it is tempting to regard it as not only illuminatingly faithful to its provenance, but as positively self-aware. It is as if a spirit larger than electoralism has brushed against the page. Which is not to stray into mysticism, but simply to suggest that in this respect the poster bears a trace of the more than normalized aspirations of those who authored it.[8] But only a trace. For the poster remains an electoral advertisement. By virtue of which, the voice which speaks through it already anticipates Solidarity's transformation into an electoral party, and thus its own death as a movement; already anticipates, that is, the adoption of a political model in which calculated promotion substitutes for the kind of consciousness which is/was generated at the moment of rebellion and rupture: volatile, de-repressed, truth-telling, impudent.

The quality which reconciles these opposites is irony. It softens the first into a 'but yes' and the second into a 'yes but'. Yet it prevents a full reconciliation by keeping both modes in semiological play. From the point of view of post-1960s culturology all this will strike a chord. The poster's meta-message (or rather meta-meta-message) runs along the knife-edge between the playful/stoical pro-market affirmations of postmodern liberalism and the critical (and anti-commodity) utopianism which passed through

Marx and Frankfurt to contemporary critical theory. Issues dividing Rorty from Jameson, Derrida from Adorno, Lyotard from Habermas, dance within the poster's frame. It is this, indeed, which, beyond its brilliance as political art, is the poster's most remarkable feature. The transitional character of the election in whose medium it speaks, and the conjunctural contradictions of Solidarity itself (up from the Underground, bidding for legitimate power), are reflected, if that term be permitted, in a structure of meaning whose paradoxical import (what, today, is progress?) touches on conceptual and ideological dilemmas which have become strategic for contemporary thought. Of course, as good (post-)structuralists, we may well want to reject all imputation of subjectivity, expression, and intent. But even so, the self-subverting, yet undecidable, character of the poster's design still permits us to disengage such a meaning from the text. Still permits us to use it, that is, as a meditation object, the significance of whose significations, for those comfortably outside the zone of combat, lies in the way that the poster's determinate ambiguity visually displays a major fault-line – at once political and philosophical – in contemporary cultural debate.

Not that such matters concerned the Western newspapers that seized on the poster as their own symbol of what the Polish election meant.[9] For them, rather, the poster was reassuring. Through all the blur of unassimilable events, one thing at least was clear. Not only were 'their' politics becoming like 'ours', but also their choice of symbols, and even the humorous uses made of them. Five months before the Wall came down, what the poster attested, for Poland at least, was that what had been a definitive difference was already virtually erased.

The rise of political promotion

As a sign of political convergence the Solidarity poster is, indeed, stunningly apt. Its main device – a reworked film ad – symbolizes with perfect clarity what the importation of free elections, Western-style, is these days bound to bring in train: not just democratic participation and popular power, but all the calculating and media-oriented razzmatazz which go with the modern electoral game. Within such a framework, parties contend for votes the way that movie studios contend for audiences; and elections are fought with the same public relations instruments – and with the aid of the same advertising agencies – which commercial enterprises use to sell commodities. As it is in Europe and North America, so shall it be in Poland. The poster which makes its point by quoting an advertisement heralds the arrival of a politics which has itself increasingly been subsumed by advertising.

It is this wider development that I want to focus on here: not with the aim of documenting it (the task would be enormous), nor with that of denouncing it (the Solidarity poster itself should caution us against adopting too simplistic a stance); but to ponder its significance in terms of the rise to cultural power of promotion itself. For here we have an instance – a prime instance, at the heart of what systems theorists call social steerage – of how promotional practices originally commercial in function and inspiration have made their strangely transformative appearance beyond the commercial zone. How is this extension to be explained? As contagion or parallel development? And how has the rise of political promotion articulated with that of other kinds in the formation of late capitalist culture as a whole?

These questions must be approached with care. It is evident that Saatchi and Saatchi did not invent the manipulative use of political symbolism. The distinction between power and authority is as old as the history of the state; as, too, is the use of resonant images, steeped in the contemporary language of values and beliefs, to clothe actual or would-be rulers in the magic of popular legitimacy. At random, we might think of the temples of Rameses II, the coins of Augustus, the coronation of Charlemagne, the white rose of the House of York, and the Mother India aura projected by Indira Gandhi.

From that angle, the image-making practices in which political parties engage in their quest for votes is only a special case of a much older, and larger, phenomenon. So, indeed, modern political theory has tended to regard it. For Marxists such images, and the ideological configurations they condense, secure the subjective allegiance of collectivities to particular arrangements, or counter-arrangements, of political power. In the language of Gramsci and Althusser: they provide the ideological cement necessary to combine social forces in class alliances ('blocs') able to exercise – or challenge the exercise of – hegemony within a class-based socioeconomic order.[10] This holds true for all state forms, whether electorally based or not. Whence arises, in all of them also, a system of ideological management, more or less stable, more or less a site of struggle, which intersects with other aspects of social domination, and which utilizes all manner of institutions (Althusser's 'state-ideological apparatuses' (1971)), including, in liberal–democratic regimes, parties and elections themselves.

For liberal theorists, the presence or absence of representative democracy is obviously of greater account. Here, too, however, where electoral promotion has not been treated merely empirically or pragmatically ('electoral studies'), the symbolic means used by parties in competition at the polls has tended to be subsumed within a more general theory of communication and power. Typical of such an approach, which had its heyday in the 1950s, was Kenneth Boulding's *The Image*. Political life is a 'process of mutual modification of images through the processes of feedback and communication' (Boulding, 1956: 102). What distinguishes 'democratic' from 'authoritarian' systems, in this view, is simply their mode of combining and modifying images, and their sensitivity to feedback. The conclusion is evident. Modern industrial societies require more democratic institutions than pre-industrial ones because their greater role complexity requires a more open and decentralized method both for decision making and for allocating individuals to political roles. The thesis has hardly dated. Shorn of its cybernetic gloss, an identical argument has recently been made by Peter Berger (1987: 72–89); and inside the Soviet Union itself the rationale for 'glasnost' has been advanced in precisely such terms.

None of this, however, is particularly helpful if we are to grasp what is specific to the way in which political symbolism operates in the functionally modern, or liberal–democratic, case. The relation between electoralism and promotion must be thematized in itself. But here we come to another difficulty. For if it is tempting to swallow the problem up in an overarching theory of ideology and political symbolism, it is also tempting to foreshorten the analysis historically: by identifying the promotionalization of electoral politics with only the most recent, post-1950s, phase of that process.

This is not to deny the evidence of our senses. Over the past thirty years there has certainly been a qualitative shift in the weight of promotion within the mainstream politics of the advanced capitalist democracies. In the United States, which led the way, the point at which it became palpable is indicated by the titles of the books which were among the first to draw it to public attention: Theodore H White's *The Making of the President: 1960* (1961), and Joe McGinniss's *The Selling of the President: 1968* (1969). As illustrated by the American experience, four intertwined developments have been involved.

The first is the one foregrounded by McGinniss: the vastly increased prominence of commercial advertisers and their techniques in the conduct and management of election campaigns. The organizational imprint of this is easy to trace. In 1956, the loosely structured Eisenhower campaign secured the voluntary services of Rosser Reeves from Ted Bates, and hired two ad agencies to prepare radio and TV ads, BBDO for the Republican National Committee, and Young and Rubicam for Citizens for Eisenhower. The more cash-strapped Stevenson team countered with the less high-powered Norman, Craig, and Kummel, and relied on the cheaper format of 30-minute concept pieces. Both used personal speech writers, though Stevenson, who neither understood nor sympathized with what he dismissed as 'merchandising', preferred, in traditional style, to write his own.[11]

In 1960, while Nixon had a full media corps headed by Ted Rogers, he similarly distrusted their advice and ran the advertising campaign himself. In live media appearances he insisted on 'winging it', even in the TV debates for which he stubbornly refused to prepare (Jamieson, 1984: 146–161). Kennedy, practising the craft in a wholly new way, had a tightly structured public relations organization. Pierre Salinger headed up the press corps, Leonard Reinsch handled the broadcast media, and Archibald Cox (Dean of the Harvard Law School) directed a whole speech-writing team that, like the others, reported to Sorenson who was overall director of the campaign. Anticipating Thatcher by twenty years, Kennedy also took speech lessons from a Boston professional, learning, among other tricks of the trade, how to speak from the chest (White, 1961: 251).

How much Nixon learned from his defeat became clear in his second presidential run eight years later. His closest political advisers, Haldemann, Erlichman, and Coulson, all later of Watergate fame, were seconded directly from the California branch of J. Walter Thompson. Headed by Shakespeare and Aisles, his advertising team was given the formidable task of portraying Nixon as a man of peace abroad and reconciliation at home. '1968 was the first time', McGinniss noted, 'an advertising agency was given the task of creating something radically different from what it was with the cooperation of the candidate.'[12]

The effect of advertiser-driven campaigning has been felt in more than just the professionalization of electoral propaganda, though the slickly produced political advertisement is certainly its most visible product. Promotion has been drawn into the heart of the process. Through the 1970s and 1980s it has become normal practice for the managers of campaign advertising to be recruited directly from the highest ranks of the advertising industry.[13] Their role, moreover, sometimes in collision with the official party machine, has been not just to supervise the specifics of advertising, but to map out entire strategies. The scope for involvement is endless. Every public statement or gesture by the campaigners, whether intentional or not, can be considered part of the campaign, and is therefore susceptible to promotional orchestration. The tell-tale signs of such co-ordination are in the sometimes creakily artificial degree (as in the Canadian Liberals' 'the land is strong' campaign of 1974) to which the resulting flows of managed information are integrated; and integrated not just thematically, but – from logo and slogans to speeches, appearances, and spot ads themselves – in every signifying detail. The down-side (as Harriet Woods discovered in her unsuccessful run for the Missouri Senate in 1986 when she summarily, and publicly, fired her media consultant and polling firm (Luntz, 1988: 59)), is that the price of unmanageable conflict between, or with regard to, campaign advertisers can be a fatally incoherent message. In context, a message which signifies fatality itself.

Nor has the entry of advertisers and advertising into the political process halted at the gate marked 'end of election'. Formal campaigns only intensify, by sanctioning as primary, what is always already the case. The vote which marks the end of one campaign marks the unofficial start of the next. The demand for the ongoing ministrations of handlers, press agents, make-up artists, and the like, has grown with that realization, which has itself been strengthened by their normalization as a vital element in the machinery of political life. With technicization, political promotion has become prosthetic. Staff and media extend the very bodies of the permanent candidates to which, like Freud's jaw, they have become permanently strapped. Today, every major office-holder communicates through an official mouthpiece – Sheverdnadze has his Gerasimov and Gorbachev his Shishlin, just as Nixon had Ziegler – who, in channelling and deflecting high level exposure can become celebrities themelves. For the most powerful players, a small army of spin doctors are constantly on hand to manage, as well, even the media interpretation given to their latest, direct or indirect, communicative act.

Complementing the rise, at all these levels, of political advertising has been the increasing application to the analysis of voter preference and intentions of techniques developed in the field of market research.[14] Survey research based on random sampling was first used to predict Federal election results in the 1930s. By 1956 its techniques had become refined enough for their predictive power to be taken seriously. Early predictive failures – especially that of 1948[15] – also led to more frequent surveys, particularly in the final weeks of a campaign.

Behind the scenes, the scientific analysis of voter preferences has formed the research base for front-stage promotional strategy. But on the mediatized proscenium, the publication of polls has also turned them into a crucial site of struggle in itself. The extent to which such information feeds back into actual voter preference (via the 'bandwagon effect') has long been a matter of controversy;[16] as too has the uneasy sense that elections themselves – the holy sacrament of Western democracy – are thereby downgraded into just another poll. Hence, in the UK and elsewhere, the efforts made, when public polling first became a regular feature of the process, to restrict their publication, especially in the crucial closing moments of a campaign.

The rise of published polls, however, was only the tip of an informational iceberg. Katz and Lazarsfeld's path-breaking *Personal Influence* (1955), which examined the interaction of opinion leaders and media coverage in changing voter preferences during the 1952 presidential campaign, inaugurated the study of voter behaviour as a full-scale academic speciality. Such work in the public domain has also been supplemented by private studies commissioned by governments and parties themselves.[17] In contemporary campaigns, commissioned soundings are taken virtually every day. The principal actors are thus provided with up-to-the-minute information on every facet of voter opinion, which enables them to gauge with statistical precision popular attitudes (as broken down by class, age, sex, ethnicity, region etc) towards the policies and candidacies currently on offer.

The more accurately that parties, pressure groups, and governments have been able to monitor the tides of public opinion, the more such information has short-circuited the active side of the process in which opinion is formed. The gallery's responses to policy proposals and the like can be anticipated by the players before the curtain goes up, indeed before the script is even written. The effect, defenders will point out, is plebiscitary. As in the commercial marketplace, rule by opinion poll simply gives people the policy outcomes they want. But the feedback is not as democratic as it seems. There are tricky questions about the origin and status of the 'opinions' actually measured. Moreover, public polling affects the way that policy alternatives, and the agenda of issues on which they rest, are themselves formulated. The simplistic and disconnected way that issues are presented in questionnaires (on a scale of one to five how would you rate the government's performance on peace? crime? the economy? inflation? the family? defence?) is doubled by the way such issues are treated in the actual policy process – starting with the very fact that they are defined as 'issues'. The Bush administration's War on Drugs, with its military/jingoistic language, and stupefying disconnection from a previous president's equally sloganistic War on Poverty, is a sufficient illustration of the chimerical forms that problem solving can take when social problems are conceived, and operationalized, in such terms.

A third change – for a generation brought up on McLuhan and TV dinners it may seem the most decisive – has been at the level of media. From the moment of its rise as a mass consumer product in the early 1950s, and in pace with what has happened to popular culture more generally, there has been a shift in the strategic focus of mass political communication from print and radio to television.[18]

It is by no means clear that the four famous television debates between Nixon and Kennedy were as crucial as political folklore subsequently made them.[19] But they did mark a watershed. Thereafter, such staged confrontations, wrapped around with manoeuvres and negotiations about format and timing, became a regular and climactic fixture of the election calendar. It need hardly be said that a television debate, preceded by hours of coaching, even rote learning of answers, perorations, and quips, only simulates what the term debate used to denote. The televising of party conventions, press conferences, rallies, and mainstreeting has had a similar effect. Even meeting the voters, publicly discussing the issues, going, as they used to say, on the hustings, has become reduced in this way: a feel-good invocation of a mode of electioneering to which these camera-oriented flourishes no longer remotely belong. In all these cases, the genius of modern media advisers and performers is to make what has become a conventional sign seem indexical. Not merely to dissimulate, but to ensure the high production values on which, *inter alia*, the candidate's or party's own reputation for competence depends.[20]

Corresponding to television's stress on visual imagery the tradition of merely verbal rhetoric has declined. From an entertainment point of view, the effects, for example in the televising of legislative proceedings, have been paradoxical. Mediatization has led legislators to develop safe self-presentational strategies which, if they make the show tidy, also make it boring. Stage-managed performances obviate the spontaneity and unpredictability which make for good television. On the other hand, when television began, politicians attuned to press and radio were hotter in their self-presentation and, in their very incongruity, made excellent viewing. To such an extent, indeed, that the tele-spectaculars of the Kefauver enquiry into organized crime[21] (in 1952) and the Senate Sub-committee hearings which pitted McCarthy against the army (in 1954) won mass audiences that helped market the new medium. These political shows also revealed the power of television to create a celebrityhood which could circulate beyond politics itself. The Kefauver Committee enquiry, with its parade of mafiosi, paved the way for *On the Waterfront*. It also helped the Senator himself gain a vice-presidential berth on the Stevenson ticket in 1956. The McCarthy hearings made a celebrity of the Army's attorney, Robert Welch, leading to his starring as a fictional judge in *Witness for the Prosecution*. Of course, they destroyed McCarthy himself, which graphically illustrates how TV can function as an anti-ad for the unwary.

As these examples suggest, the introduction of television has had the effect not only of displacing and transforming the live dimension of electoral politics, but of personalizing it. Not in the intrinsic sense that greater scope has opened up for real individuals to make an actual imprint on events, but semiotically. The person foregrounded is only the specular image of a person: a figure which, in television advertising has become the privileged intermediary for imaging everything.[22] Persons in this multiply imagistic sense – as personalities, as product presenters, as flickering phantoms on the screen – have come to serve as key media signifiers for the parties, ideological positions, and social forces which they represent. The latter have retreated to the shadows. Correlatively, in the inter-individual contest for power which has moved to the centre of spectatorial attention, the capacity of individuals to serve as promotional signifiers for wider aggregations of office-seekers is cultivated as their most important political asset.

While this exalting of the imaged person resembles the 1930s style cult of personality probed, for the links it revealed between Hollywood stardom and fuehrer-worship, by Horkheimer and Adorno (1972: 154–6), there is an important difference. The small screen domesticates those whom it makes famous. It is not just that the images of people we see on a domestic set (unlike in the movies) are literally smaller than life size. Their repeated appearance in the family hearth also destroys their rarity value by making them, precisely, familiar. At the same time, this familiarity is circum-scribed by the sensory form in which politicians appear. The focus is on a two-dimensional moving picture. Television has turned the attention of both participants and commentators to such previously insignificant matters as facial expression, hairstyle, dress, and body language. In consequence, a vital qualification for high office has become the capacity of individuals, above all in the detail of their visual self-presentation, to appear credible in the roles to which they aspire. Their literal image (particularly of head and shoulders) has become crucial to their metaphori-cal one. The *reductio ad absurdam* of this tendency was the selection of Dan Quayle as vice-presidential running-mate in the Republican campaign of 1988. One motive, no doubt, was to appease the Republican right wing by choosing an Indiana conservative to balance off the Eastern brahmin heading the ticket. But handlers let it be known that Quayle was also picked to provide appeal to youth and women, the latter on the grounds that the gender-gap might be closed as a result of his Robert Redford-style good looks.

The intensified attention to individuals and to what their immediate being-in-the-world bespeaks which television has engendered, has also opened up their personal lives to closer media scrutiny. Office holders and aspirants have always been liable to discredit through scandal.[23] But even in the era of a relatively free press – in the United States, in fact, right up until Watergate – deference was paid to the distinction between public and private, and between law-breaking and immorality. And a certain discretion was exercised in the reporting, and investigating, of the peculiarities of politicians' behind-the-scenes personal lives. Today, the powerful, and even those who just aspire to power, are enclosed in a panopticon of publicity. Under its unavoidable gaze the wall between private and public has disappeared. When Gary Hart challenged reporters to prove their charge of philandering, a news team secretly staked out his Washington apartment and video-taped his lover coming out.

While this incident played in the media as a matter of ethics – Hart's and theirs – it revealed a systemic truth: that the personalization of politics, that is, the swallowing up of the concrete-historical individual into the role of promotional signifier, has totalistic implications for the politically ambitious. In the American case, the anticipatory media screening has reached the point where previous presidents of stature would have been screened out. Under the circumstances, only those whose own image is beyond reproach are in a position to moderate the severity of the rules – as when George Bush, no doubt in pursuit of a gentler, kinder America, pronounced that having smoked dope in the 1960s should not, in the 1990s, be treated as a bar to office.

There is finally a fourth development, which, if less discussed, and indeed less tangible, has had implications at least as profound. As a result of the way electoral politics has been made over in the light of the developing techniques and imperatives of mediatized promotion, there has been a change in the way such politics is politically defined and discussed.

The discontinuity has not been absolute. Some aspects of the media's meta-language for politics have remained the same throughout this century. Elections themselves are still sacraments which affirm the institutional order and through which the people speak. Moreover, the trend, which television (and before that radio) accentuated, away from partisanship towards the spectacular as the main mode of reportage, was already implicit in the rise of the commercial press. The electoral contest continues to be glossed, moreover, as a form of spectator sport, with horse-racing, baseball, and football as the most common metaphorical frame. But to all this has been added another discursive level. Pundits in the very media which have become crucial to the new politics of impression-management have come to describe each move of the game in precisely these terms.

A first stage in this discursive shift was already noted by Boorstin (1961) at the end of the 1950s: the rise of a political language which confounded the distinction between the 'reality' of candidates, platforms, etc, and their constructed and perceived appearance in the form of the 'image'. In a further stage, not only has this confounding been accepted as fact by players and spectators alike (hence the cliché that in politics perception is what counts), but also its corollary: that in the constructing and deconstructing of rival images lies the core of the voting game (and of its anticipatory shadow via poll ratings) which itself sets the ground rules for the political process as such.

Elections in North America and Western Europe have come to be commented upon almost exclusively in these terms: as a battle between rival advertising campaigns. Indeed, as a battle in which what is tactically at stake, before the final showdown itself, is not just current standings in the polls but how these have moved, and how they stack up against previous expectations. Dissecting the process in this way opens up the rival campaigns to judgements about their promotional competence, which becomes a game of promotional construction in itself. This emphasis obscures the sense of elections as genuine occasions for choice. But it does not, thereby, wholly mystify the process. Not only has the *transformismo* of 'mature' electoral politics – the chase for the floating voter and the middle ground – reduced the normally articulated policy differences between the leading parties and candidates to a matter of nuance and emphasis. The more that the successful exercise of political leadership, from the military-ideological manoeuvrings of the Cold War to domestic fiscal management, has actually come to depend on public relations, the more rational it is for voters to make their selection on the basis of who can manage their public relations best. This updated version of *ideonitas* – the medieval principle of suitability for office – was succinctly illustrated by the well-heeled New Yorker who, after Gorbachev's impromptu 1987 walk-about at Times Square, gushed into the camera: 'He's a PR genius!'

In the face of such perceptions, there is no necessary critical edge even to the point I am elaborating here. That there has come to be a close parallel between campaigning and advertising, between voting and purchasing, between the electorate and consumers, in short between the economic and the political marketplace, escapes the attention of no-one. To the contrary, the parallel has been explicitly incorporated into not only the language of political commentary, but into the very substance of what it comments upon. It is not just that campaigns have become promotionally self-conscious, and that their ongoing conduct is conditioned by the promotional strategy of opponents as well as themselves. The manner in which strategy is conducted can itself become an issue, so that promotion itself becomes a topic for promotional politics. In the closing moments of the Bush–Dukakis campaign, the Republicans' notorious Willie Houghton spot[24] was seized on by the Dukakis team in an attempt to turn the advertisement back against those who had run it.

At issue in the ensuing debate, which carried over into the 1990

Congressional campaign, was not so much the ad's racism as the question of negative advertising as such. Ostensibly the question was normative: what are the limits of electoral advertising? to what extent does mud-slinging sully the entire process? But the point of attacking negative advertising was also promotional – aiming at once to deflect attention from the charge that Dukakis was soft on crime (read: blacks) and to recode the negativity of the ad as an essential attribute both of its immediate author (Roger Aisles) and of those in whose name it spoke. In the 1989 British Euro-elections, a Conservative campaign which attacked moves to European integration (over an unappetising bowl of sprouts, the slogan: 'Do you want a diet of Brussels?') was similarly repositioned by those against whom it was aimed. Pro-Europeans, inside and outside the Conservative Party, touted the poster, indeed, not just as a sign of negativity but of poor tactical judgement – for it seemed to suggest that pro-government opponents of bureaucratic Euro-rule would best make their point by abstaining from the vote.

At first sight, this concatenation of changes is self-explanatory. Can we not simply say that Western politics, indeed the political process everywhere, has now moved into the television age? Even the cursory account just given, however, should make clear that matters are not so straightforward.

It is important, in the first place, not to fixate on the role of television itself. No doubt, in its visual emphasis, in its implications for the design and presentation of live political events, and in its domestic function as an organ for commercial entertainment, the rise of TV as the principal medium for mass political communication has qualitatively heightened the promotional character of the electoral process. It is also plausible to argue that the rapidity with which the new medium was introduced[25] created an instant demand for new forms of promotional expertise which had to be imported direct from the world of commercial advertising; and that this infusion accelerated the shift to promotionalism at the conscious, organizational level as well.

But that is not the whole story. The modernization of political promotion through better market research and more calculated media usage which the introduction of television did much to stimulate must also be regarded as an independent development. Its roots can certainly be traced further back. Statistical methods for the analysis of electoral opinion were first devised by Gallup and Roper in the late 1920s. Technical advances since then (from improved sampling, to multi-factor analysis, psychographics, and pannelling) have simply kept pace with those in commercial market research. It was in the 1920s, too, that the first tentative steps were taken towards paid political broadcasting.[26] And need we remind ourselves that in this, as in virtually every other aspect of its programming, the groundwork for what was later done with television was laid by radio: a medium whose vote-getting potential was well understood not only by Goebbels and Hitler, but also – via special broadcasts of national importance, interviews, and fireside chats – by Roosevelt and Chamberlain?

From the outset, electoral politics has adapted to, and been shaped by[27] whatever mass media lay to hand. To which end, those with the relevant communications skills have always been employed to provide expert advice, where they have not directly entered the lists as candidates for office and power. Before broadcasting, the key to publicity – in conjunction with mass meetings, street parades, and door-to-door canvassing – was the press. Thus, if in the late twentieth century we have become accustomed to the idea that experienced talk show performers like Trudeau, or film actors like Reagan, could aspire to become heads of state, it is hardly surprising that, in the age of newspapers, editors and journalists should have been prominent not just as backroom managers but, like Benjamin Franklin, William Lyon Mackenzie, and William Randolph Hearst, as political frontmen too.

Since the very beginnings of the mass franchise, in fact, electoral politics has exhibited a dual character. On the one hand, elections have provided the occasion for issue-oriented clashes between rival coalitions of social forces – such as for what social democrats, at the turn of the century, called 'the peaceful translation of the class struggle'. But on the other hand, mass political parties, just to play the electoral game, have also had to serve as election machines. To gain majorities, moreover, especially in the complexly stratified situation of advanced capitalism, parties must not only maximize the vote of natural class-cultural supporters. They must also seek support outside their immediate social base: both from particular social categories, as defined by cross-cutting dimensions of class, ethnicity, and age and gender, as well as from uncommitted and cross-pressured voters.

Parties tied to big capital and a programme of continuity have found the ideological accommodations this requires easier to accept than parties of the left. Among the latter, it has produced a running tension between the desire of activists to keep their platform ideologically pure, and the pragmatic desire of leaderships to broaden, and tone down, the basis of their appeal. Even here, though, while the occasional period of sharp social polarization has tipped the balance towards the activists, the overall trend has been clear. The radicalization, respectively, of the French Socialist and the British Labour Parties in the late 1970s was followed by the transmogrifying of Mitterrand into father of the nation and by Kinnock's new-look party, replete with red rose and the most calculatedly vacuous of slogans: 'People who can. Not people who con.'

In sum, the transformation of electoral politics into a public relations game is a long-term process which has had structural causes. Not only has this process been propelled, at key moments, by the whole-scale borrowing of techniques from the sphere of commercial marketing. It has also responded to long-term changes in the socio-cultural character and composition of the electorate.[28] In both these respects, moreover, what has ultimately pushed it along is the competitive logic of electoralism itself.

Completing the economic theory of democracy

This brings us, indeed, to the most fundamental point of all. The changes of the past thirty years, and the longer arc of change to which they belong, have themselves only expanded, rationalized, institutionalized, and made more fully self-conscious a characteristic of the electoral process which has always been intrinsic to it. Casting a ballot is like buying goods at a store, where what is purchased, as Anthony Downs (1957: 38–45) puts it, is the anticipated 'stream of income utility' deriving from the basket of expected government policies indexed to each available electoral choice. Like a money-mediated market for commodities, then, electoral politics is a system of competitive exchange. And the corollary for the political marketplace is the same as for the commercial one. Any system of competitive exchange involves a contest not only with respect to price and quality, but also with respect to information.

Thus, from the billboards, torchlight parades, and face-to-face hype by which the Whigs sold Palmerston, and the Republicans General Harrison (Jamieson, 1984: 8–11), to the mediatized soft sell which now delivers us Bush, Thatcher, and Kohl, the history of promotion which can be traced in the history of liberal democracy registers not just an external, commercially derived, influence, but the logic of the electoral system's own development as a market.

This is not to deny that as a market the liberal polity has its own distinctive features. In contrast with the exchange process surrounding ordinary consumer goods, consumer incomes and expenditures in the political arena are identical and indivisible. Voters vote once, or not at all. Also, while votes are individual, the products voters purchase are collective. Indeed, and leaving to one side the further complications that come with various systems of proportional representation, a political product is only actually delivered if the aggregate demand for it exceeds that which is registered for rival brands. In addition, though the outcome of a ballot may be oppressive (as is suggested by Lord Hailsham's famous warning about 'elective dictatorship'), and state enterprises may be capitalist, in elections themselves there is no equivalent to surplus value and its exploitative extraction. Votes are used up in their expenditure and cannot be accumulated.

Furthermore, while an ordinary consumer transaction involves a single exchange, of goods for money, the political marketplace is mediated by a double process of exchange. Voters buy policies by voting for parties and candidates while the latter supply, or promise to supply, these policies in return for the benefits of office. As this formulation suggests, moreover, there is an added dimension of competition in that the electoral equivalent of the firm – the policy provider – is both an individual candidate and a political party. (There may even be a third equivalent, where intra-party factions and tendencies identify themselves to voters as such.) Though these may seem to merge, particularly in the cases of the party leader and the presidential candidate, there are thus (at least) two levels at which the competition for votes generates a promotional practice. The precise relationship between candidates and parties, including the degree of autonomy they have from one another, depends on the local rules of the game. Constitutional monarchies with majority party rule have stronger party systems than elective presidencies, and proportional representation with a list system decouples the vote, as such, from individual party representatives. But whatever the constitutional form, the party and the candidate (epecially for government leader) are each entered into the lists. Each, then, is the site of a distinct promotional operation. This duality, indeed, is compounded by another. On their active side, as deliverers of vision, programme, policy options, administrative capacities, etc, both candidates and parties are presented to voters as a kind of product. But from a marketing perspective, each also serves as a signifying device which helps shape the promotional image of the other.

None of these differences, however, negates the central point: that candidates, parties, and policies (roughly tied together in aggregated bundles) circulate in a process of competitive exchange; wherein, as elsewhere, the exchange of information between buyers and sellers is the basis for promotional (as well as price and product) competition between the sellers. In advanced capitalism there has also come to be a more particular parallel between the political marketplace and the one for ordinary consumer goods. In both cases, whether as corporations/ conglomerates, or as established political parties, large-scale organizations confront a disorganized mass of consumer/buyers. Of course, this situation has been reached by contrasting historical routes. In the economic sphere, large-scale production and finance has gradually ousted smaller-scale operations, while market concentration has increased. The political market, on the other hand, has been oligopolistic since the earliest days of Whigs and Tories. Within that framework, what has happened is not the displacement of smaller parties, but a shift in the character of party organization itself. The movement has been from parties as class fractions managing a cross-class alliance, to parties as publicity machines, a tendency which has reduced the reliance on voluntary activists and led to a more attenuated relation between parties and their electoral base.

With regard to the ascendant place of promotion, however, and to the forms it has come to assume, the same effects can be seen. Thus, as with commercial mass producers, the quasi-monopolistic position held by major political parties has come to be buttressed by brand-images which, through design, packaging, and advertising, are similarly manufactured into the very policies, personalities, and leadership teams which they promote. Hence, as resistance to this logic within the political sphere has crumbled, there has come to be the same emphasis on research-based and mediatized mass marketing, the same ascendancy of circulation within the production and exchange process as a whole, and the same incorporation of marketing itself (when you vote for Bush/Quayle or Dukakis/Bensen what are you buying?) into the imagistically designed character of what is actually for sale.

Of course, to insist that there is a deep homology between parliamentary elections and competitive economic exchange is hardly an original point. It has long been a mainstay of democratic theory. In Victorian Britain, where a free market in manufactured goods was established long before property (and gender) restrictions were removed from the franchise, liberal utilitarians argued for democratic reform in precisely these terms. Yet it is remarkable, in a tradition which stretches from Mandeville and Bentham to contemporary analysts of 'social choice', how little theoretical attention has been paid by those who have otherwise insisted on the importance of the parallel between a free market and a liberal polity, to its promotional corollary.

This is not because of an excess of ideological piety. The utilitarian argument for (electoral) democracy is as hard-headed as the analogous one for free trade. In contrast with the more civic, radical, and collectivist, versions of democratic theory which descend from Kant and Rousseau, and which either deify the vox populi or posit a fundamental link between morality and self-government, what Bentham, Smith, and their contemporary followers stress is the 'hidden hand': that is, the unintentionally benign effects on social welfare of allowing each citizen's egotistical calculations a maximal range of free play. But despite that, here, in the promotional aspect of market competition, is an important dimension of egotistical calculation which is systematically overlooked.

In terms of earlier thinkers, one might excuse this oversight in terms of the rudimentary state of marketing itself. With a restricted franchise, promotional practices in the political marketplace evidently lagged behind those in the commercial one; and as for the latter, expenditures on advertising were relatively insignificant, so that contemporaries did not criticize the founders of classical economy for lack of realism in leaving such practices out of account.[29]

But the inattention to promotion in the much more recent, and analytically advanced, work of Downs (1957), Breton (1974), and Riley (1988) is more puzzling. Their updated 'economic theory of democracy' dispenses with simplifying assumptions like perfect competition, and the absence of 'external effects'. More importantly, they acknowledge the existence of (cost-incurring) information flows between parties/candidates and voters; and they even allow that the former's ideological profile, and stance on the issues, is subject to the same logic of brand-imaging as in the case of mass-marketed consumer goods. Nevertheless, the promotional side of policy/ideology is glossed over. As the expectations generated by party platforms it slides into the gap between promises and delivery, and so becomes just a risk factor in the formation of electoral demand. Political advertising itself, meanwhile, is subsumed under 'information' – as if the function of posters, photo-opportunities, spot ads, press releases, news conferences and the like were purely cognitive, and could be disentangled from the constitution of the political product such information purports to inform voters about.

In his moralistic way, John Stuart Mill gave the game away in his attack on the abuses of contemporary electioneering. For him, other than through reasoned argument, direct attempts to influence electoral choice were always a distorting interference. On these grounds he objected not just to direct and indirect forms of electoral bribery. Following the 1832 Reform Bill he worried that: 'If recent legislation has rendered direct bribery hazardous, success belongs to him who expends most money in opening the publichouses, or in hiring agents, canvassers, printers and committee rooms.' Not only, he insisted, should the candidate 'not be required, he should not be permitted, to incur any but a trifling expense for his election' (Mill, 1948: 240). He put his own precept into practice when he accepted nomination to a parliamentary seat (for Westminster) in 1865, but only on condition that he would do no electioneering. 'I thought a candidate', he noted in his *Autobiography* (G. Williams, 1976), 'ought neither to canvass nor incur any expense.'

Transferred to a theoretical plane, this is exactly the same anti-rational disturbance which Downs et al. are keeping at bay. To accept that information images the product, and that this impinges directly on taste formation would be to accept both that voter preferences depend on electoral imaging, and that the parties and candidates for whom voters vote are ungraspable as entities outside the way in which they are marketed.[30] And this is not to mention the indeterminacy which would be introduced into the model if we allowed a space in it for the interdependent gaming through which promotional strategies are competitively deployed.

In other words, for all its icy emphasis on individual self-interest, the economic theory of democracy has a normative as well as a scientific intent. What it claims to be able to construct on the basis of a market model is a paradigm for political rationality itself. But to acknowledge promotion as a basic ingredient of the market would be to acknowledge something which disturbs this paradigm from within.

However, just because completing the economic theory of democracy in this way would undermine its justificatory role does not mean that the whole approach should be ditched. To the contrary, its central premise about the homology between electoral democracy and the economic market is worth retaining, even building on. For if we accept that the liberal–democratic polity is indeed a kind of market, and that its parallel with the economic market has become more marked as the latter itself has developed, then a further line of argument can be advanced: a line of argument which at once goes beyond traditional Marxism and which makes it possible to appropriate a core element of utilitarianism to the more critical forms of social theorizing against which its own face is set. That argument can be summarized in the following propositions.

First, considered abstractly, as any system of competitive exchange, whether money-mediated or not, the market is indeed, and just as Adam

Smith hypothesized, a fundamental social form. That is to say: it can serve as a principle for organizing – and understanding – more spheres of social life than just the commercial economy.

Secondly, the rise of capitalism has been accompanied by the all-round development of the market in just this universal sense. From the money-economy, to the liberal polity, to status competition in careers and 'lifestyles', to the private contest for friends, lovers, and mates, what late capitalism has brought into being, in effect, is a society of 'generalized exchange'.[31]

Thirdly, as a cultural rider (and crucial to understanding what Frederic Jameson (1984) has called 'the cultural logic of late capitalism'), the generalization of exchange has implied the generalization of promotion itself as a communicative mode.

These theses evidently run counter to Durkheim's, Weber's, and more latterly Habermas's, notion that capitalist modernization has entailed a growing differentiation between the institutional spheres of economy, polity, and culture. For electoral politics and the commercial economy have not only de-differentiated in the formal terms I have been discussing. Regarded as sites for the manufacture of signs, their communicative products have also flowed together in the most promiscuous of ways. Whence proposition number four: that the generalization of promotion has led not only to a paralleling of promotional forms between those which have developed in the money economy and those which have developed (for example) in electoral politics; it has also led to their actual conjunction in the same, grand, discursive space.

In the Solidarity poster's use of an old ad for *High Noon* we have already glimpsed the higher-order complexity to which such a conjunction can lead. But that was in the nostalgia mode, and there was no ambiguity about whose promotion the poster actually was. A better illustration is provided by an incident from the 1988 American Presidential campaign, because this time all the promotional symbols joined together in the message are current and alive.

George Bush in Disneyland

After an early lead in the polls, coming out of the Conventions, the Dukakis campaign had stalled. Then came a one-two media punch, after which the Republican forces recovered the initiative and never looked back. The first blow was a foray into the Duke's own backyard where, in an inspired publicity coup, Bush's team had arranged to have him shown pulling a dead fish out of the notoriously polluted Boston harbour. The second was the Labor Day[32] photo-opportunity with which George Bush kicked off the 'official' start to his campaign. It is this that I want to examine here.

The chosen occasion – specially devised, in fact – was the American government's ceremonial send-off to its Olympic athletes in their quest for gold in Seoul. Personally conveying the nation's good wishes was George Bush himself; not, formally, as Republican candidate, but as actually serving Vice-President, and dignified by all the trappings of that role. The location, in sunny California, was Disneyland. And following the handshakes, godspeeds and inevitable quips ('I too am a competitor . . .') Mickey Mouse and friends sang, danced, and clapped before a cut-out of Cinderella's castle, while George hugged his family, and red-white-and-blue balloons and streamers festooned around.

Of course, the pageant was staged for the media. The result: 20-second soundbites for the evening news, and three to six inches of front-page copy, plus pictures, for the papers next day. All in all, to use Daniel Boorstin's phrase, a classic case of the 'pseudo-event'.[33] Nor, whatever the power of the image, was anyone fooled. The media reported it *as* a pseudo-event, and the ratings boost that Bush received had as much to with the much commented upon perception that his performance was relaxed and confident, and that he had not fluffed his lines, as with the symbolic meaning of the scene in which he was placed.

That Bush in Disneyland – life imitating parody – somehow expressed the real truth of American politics was not lost on commentators. Abroad, it was a story in itself. 'At the risk of caricaturing the modern electioneering process', wrote Michael White in the *Guardian*,[34] 'Vice-President Bush staged his major photo-opportunity at the one place in the country that outdoes Ronald Reagan for optimism. In the Town Square at Disneyland there are no muggers, no Soviet missiles, no budget deficits . . . and Disney staff are trained to pounce upon the slightest sign of litter or social deviation . . . It was the perfect opportunity for some hard-hitting, no-nonsense escapism.' In *Amusing Ourselves to Death*, Neil Postman makes the point more generally: '[In the United States] all public discourse increasingly takes the form of entertainment. Our politics, religion, news, athletics, education and commerce have been transformed into congenial adjuncts of show business' (Postman, 1987: 4). From the fun-filled setting to the carnivalesque incongruity of linking Disney to Bush, entertainment value was certainly built right into the piece. But this was not just show business. Amusement, both as symbol and effect, is subordinated here to something else: to the fact that, in political context, the whole message is meant and constructed as an ad.[35]

Not just in its general aim, in fact, but in many details of its construction, Bush's staged Disneyland appearance is remarkably similar to any number of contemporary magazine or TV commercials. Like cola, cars, perfume or burgers Bush is imaged in relation to a target market (Middle America, the Reagan Democrats; in British terms, the C1s and C2s) through an array of totemically inclusive cultural signs. Also similar is the use of ultra-familiar, connotatively saturated, cultural institutions to build up such an affirmatively emblematic meaning. Just as Pepsi, through its mid-1980s parade of video pop stars invoked the spirit and values of (de-fanged) rock ('The Pepsi Generation'), the Bush campaign, through Olympic athletes and

Disneyland, invoked those of Athletics and Entertainment. Given the product, an unsurprising choice. The Olympics, cross-cutting class-cultural lines, trails associations of individualism, deferred gratification, competitiveness, health, and technicized professionalism. While Disneyland means family fun, childhood enchantment, and the story of America as Freedom and Progress, itself written as the story of the world.

In the Bush/Disneyland/Olympics tableau, indeed, patriotism, emphasized by all the fluttering flags, served as a linking theme. Coupled with which, and as a related Middle American ideal, both of the institutions invoked to sell Bush also encoded the values, and untransgressable normality, of the Family. In the US, the Disney studio's reputation for child-centred wholesomeness has been built up as securely as that of Enid Blyton's in the UK. The park itself, through all the upheavals of the 1960s and 1970s, gave discounts to families, discouraged the openly gay, and screened out unsupervised groups of youth. With its archaic Greek associations the Olympics constitutes a more ambiguous sex-gender sign. Still, traditional regularities of behaviour and self-presentation are strongly emphasized both in the surrounding pageantry and in the actual events which, like those of spectator sport in general, are overwhelmingly organized on gender-segregated lines. In sum, by these associations, and reinforced by the decorous but affectionate presence of his own happy brood, the candidate-sign is firmly associated both with 'America' and with the conventional middle-class family, all its parts in harmony and intact.

The point of this transfer of meaning[36] is not difficult to see. On the most general plane, the values invoked are generic. They are idols of the American (political) marketplace. As such, if conservatively inflected (in the post-Vietnam period it became hard, as Democrats discovered, to inflect the Family/Nation cult even slightly towards the left), they have long been essential aspects of American state legitimacy, manifest identification with which is indispensable for those who would become the nation's civil and military chief.

Some aspects of this ideological theatre, however, are more specific to the candidate and his campaign. To counter dimensions on which the Bush image was perceived to be vulnerable, the candidate is counter-coded as rugged, healthy, competitive – not a wimp; able to relate to ordinary folk – not hopelessly upper-class; and his own man, convincingly able to look like a president – not just Reagan's pliant number two. On a broader canvas, the ad also takes its place as an element of a campaign which aimed to build on the success of 1984, with its triumphalist theme of 'It's morning in America'. The maintained emphasis is on thinking positively. It is the campaign, after all, of an incumbent regime. Some of the Reagan glow may have gone with scandals, mounting deficits, aggravated social disparities, and embarrassing foul-ups in Central America; but Bush's America, unlike that of dour, negative Dukakis, or of crisis-ridden Carter, continues to be all smiles. With Bush at the helm, Americans can still feel good about themselves. Why switch brands?

But the Bush photo-opportunity was an ad for more than just himself.

The occasion which framed it, the American people's ceremonial send-off to its national Olympic team, was itself a promotion for the Games. The presence of the Vice-President confirmed the team's status as officially and symbolically representing the nation: an athletic cause which, like the shuttle programme, it was a patriotic duty to support. Nor, though it was that too, was this just a case of boosting an ideological emblem. For the Olympics themselves are a commercial event. They have come to be financed in large measure from the sale of television rights to the American networks: that is, from the increases in advertising revenue which the Games' multi-million dollar broadcast is calculated to produce. And this is not to mention the Olympics' flagship role for the health and sportswear industries, nor the promotional contracts to be won by athletes, no less than by other professional celebrities (including political ones), if they strike gold.[37]

The same promotional point applies to where the Bush send-off ceremony was held. The presence in Fantasyland of Bush and cameras, reinforced by the additional magic of America's stars of the track, was a plug for the Disney theme park as well. Besides generally reinforcing its profile, the theme park's starring role as backdrop for this important political moment confirmed, indeed naturalized, its status as approved Americana. Nor did the Disney-related promotion stop there. For as important as Disneyland, and its sister complex in Florida, is to the profitability of the whole Disney Empire, the theme park itself – the home of Mickey Mouse – is also a publicity flagship. Its fame anchors the Disney corporate image, thus helping to promote all the lines of produce, from T-shirts to movies, to which that mark is affixed.

In effect, then, the Labor Day photo-opportunity is a triple ad. As such, it relies on a triple equivalence of essences – Bush = Disneyland = the American Olympics team – each term of which is identified with whatever is signified, and mythologically embodied, by the other two. From each point of this triangle, moreover, the Bush photo-opportunity serves a multiple promotional role, unleashing a chain of significations which ripple out to promote a whole panoply of other, more and more distantly related, goods. This is true even of Bush himself, for political personalities are no less media-usable as advertising signs than other celebrities. Immediately upon retirement, Ronald Reagan netted two million dollars for a personal appearance at a week-long launch of a new electronics corporation in Japan. Earlier, during the campaign itself, it was reported that Jesse Jackson had issued a writ to prevent a video company from distributing copies of his barnstorming concession speech at the Democratic Convention; and this on the grounds that he personally held the copyright, and was planning himself to raise funds in this way. Nor, finally, should we forget that the success of all this mutual promotion depends on the participation of yet a fourth promotional player, the commercial media, for whom the whole Bush-in-Disneyland event was an attention-getting element of a programming operation which was itself designed to sell audiences to advertisers.

What the George Bush photo-opportunity represented, then, was not just promotional politics but an instance of how this transformed sector of public communication had itself become integrated, both through the advertising props it employs, and as an occasion for advertising by others, into the wider, and infinitely recursive, discourse constituted by promotional culture as a whole.

Notes

1. Schumpeter (1950: 282), cited in Downs (1957: 29).

2. The ballot paper in the sheriff's right hand is inscribed with the word *wybory*, which means election.

3. For a discussion of the American Western myth, which links it to a larger mythology underlying American culture, see Jewett and Lawrence (1977).

4. The reframing of an advertisement so as to convert it into a political message has been a stock-in-trade of the post-war Western left. For example, in 1968 the West German SDS substituted the busts of Marx, Engels, and Lenin for a train on a state railway poster, leaving the slogan the same: '*Alle reden von wetter: wir nicht*' (Others talk about the weather: we don't). In similar vein, English–Canadian nationalists circulated a button in the early 1970s which read: 'Nixon Drinks Canada Dry'.

5. According to Tadek Jarski, the London chairman of Solidarity for Solidarity, the idea for the poster had come to its authors, Jan Andrez Gorny and Pawel Zazac, when they saw a copy of the 'original' Gary Cooper poster in the lobby of the American Embassy in Warsaw where they were applying for a visa.

6. There is a notorious imprecision to the distinction to be drawn between the terms modernism and postmodernism, which is further confused by the different meanings they have received in political and artistic–literary contexts. For helpful attempts to clarify the terminological and related issues see Williams (1989: 31–6) and Featherstone (1988).

7. The designer, in 1979, of the famous Solidarity logo was Jerzy Janiszewski. Its letters were intended, and taken, to resemble a crowd of joyful marchers, diverse and non-military in their arrangement and appearance. The dot over the 'i' is a hat being thrown in the air, while the Polish flag beside is also borne jubilantly aloft. The original, which predates Solidarity as a named movement, was devised as a poster. Its slogan – *Solidarnosc* – together with Janiszewski's figurative rendering of its letters, was subsequently taken up – both as a name and a logo – by the organization which emerged from the 1979 mobilization.

8. That such an interpretation is not far-fetched is indicated by precisely who did author it. Gorny and Zazac were no public relations professionals, but veteran activists. Gorny himself, based in Lublin and credited as the poster's main inspirer, was an Underground leader of Solidarity from 1981 until his arrest in November 1987. He was released, and became active in Solidarity's now semi-legalized operations in April 1988. I am, again, indebted to Tadek Jarski for this information.

9. Among other places, the poster was reproduced in the *Guardian* on Friday 9 June 1989, and in the *Observer* two days later.

10. Gramsci's conception of the relation between ideology (in the organic, i.e. non-voluntaristic, sense) is abstractly sketched out in 'State and Civil Society', and used as the basis of an analysis of the *risorgimento* and the establishment of the modern Italian state in 'Notes on Italian History'. Both are to be found in Gramsci (1971). For a structuralist formalization of Gramsci's framework, see Poulantzas (1969); and for a refinement which seeks to correct its lingering class reductionism, see Laclau (1977).

11. Stevenson's obsession with editing and re-editing his words moments before their live delivery on television had disastrous results. He frequently over-ran his time and was unable to get in the final punchlines. That he lacked a professional media staff is also evident from the incident in which the cameras picked out a hole in his shoe. See Jamieson (1984: 80 et seq.).

12. Cited in Jamieson (1984: 264). Jamieson criticizes McGinniss, however, for being selective in his reportage of the 1968 campaign, and for overstating his thesis about the power of Nixon's advertising both in transforming public perception about the candidate, and in actually swinging the election.

13. For an account of the shift in recruiting patterns, see Luntz (1988: 42–71).

14. A history of the early development of polling techniques and their application to elections is to be found in Bone (1955, Ch. 24).

15. Gallup's and Roper's celebrated misforecast of 1948 was not the earliest example of such a failure. 'In 1936 the *Literary Digest*, using mail ballots, predicted a Landon landslide over Roosevelt, with the latter obtaining only 41% of the popular vote. Roosevelt received 60.7% of the vote and the magazine was liquidated' (Bone, 1955: 571).

16. An example was Lindsay Rogers' *The Pollsters* (1949), which attacked the increasing prominence of opinion polls as mechanistic and manipulative.

17. The first American government department to use private polls as an aid to policy formation was the US Department of Agriculture in 1952 (Bone, 1955: 580).

18. The first presidential campaign to use paid advertising time was 1948. 1952 was the last one in which more was spent on radio advertising than television ($3.1 million to $2.9 million). See Jamieson (1984: 44).

19. For a description of the debates, and of the backstage manoeuvrings associated with them, see White (1961: 279–95) and Jamieson (1984: 158–61). McGinniss reproduces a list of excerpts from McLuhan's *Understanding Media* which were distributed among Nixon's media staff, and evidently influenced their approach to television. In one of the excerpts, McLuhan scorns White's account of the 1960 TV debates: 'White considers the "content" of the debates and the deportment of the debaters, but it never occurs to him to ask why TV would inevitably be a disaster for a sharp intensity image like Nixon's and a boon for the blurry, shaggy texture of Kennedy' (McLuhan, 1965: 287; cited in McGinniss, 1969: 185).

20. This idea, which was first cogently stated by Boorstin (1961), has more recently been cornered by Baudrillard. For a clear statement of his notion that social reality has been absorbed into the 'order of the simulacrum' see Baudrillard (1976 and 1983a). For an elaboration which focuses specifically on television see Kroker and Cook (1986: 267–80).

21. The formal name of the committee Kefauver chaired was the Senate Crime Investigating Committee.

22. The tendency in twentieth-century magazine advertising for such ads to switch from words to pictures, and from pictures of the product to ones of its consumer/presenters, has been well documented and analysed in Leiss et al. (1986: 123–5, 189–214).

23. The libidinal roots of popular resentment against corrupt leaders is explored by Freud in the opening pages of *Future of an Illusion* (1964).

24. This showed a revolving door of prisoners going in and out of jail, followed by a picture of Willie Houghton, a convicted black rapist, who committed a murder while out on weekend leave, all couched as an implicitly racist attack on Dukakis's liberal position on crime.

25. For the explosive diffusion of television set ownership in the USA after WWII see Head (1956: 159). Virtual saturation was achieved within a decade of organized network programming. 200,000 households owned sets in 1948, more than 20 million in 1955. The spread of radio was much slower. Thus, according to Tunstall's (1977: 286) figures, by 1930 in the USA there were only 87 sets per 1000 people, after which the numbers steadily grew, reaching 566 per 1000 in 1948. In part this was because during the 1920s the availability of programming lagged behind that of sets, whereas the TV networks, which were extensions of the organizations already established for radio, were ready to go as soon as they could be received.

26. In the 1924 Presidential campaign, the Republicans, outspending the Democrats 3:1, purchased $120,000 of broadcast time, at $4,000 an hour (Jamieson, 1984: 24).

27. For an analysis of the pre-broadcasting relationship between the newspaper press, public opinion, and political ideology, in the discursive-rationalist sense, see Gouldner (1976: 91–117).

28. For a theoretical analysis of the relation between changes in class structure, in the

distribution of class-based ideology and the policy profiling of mass left-wing parties see Downs (1957: 114–41).

29. There is, for example, no reference to advertising, or any of its synomyms, in Adam Smith's *Wealth of Nations*.

30. In a commercial context, the arguments for and against the informational value of advertising to consumers in a 'high intensity market setting' are set out in Leiss et al. (1986: 36–9).

31. See Baudrillard (1972, 1976). Baudrillard's own formulation extends the concept of generalized exchange developed by Lévi-Strauss (1969) in his discussion of modern kinship.

32. The first Monday in September. A civic holiday which marks the end of summer with the reopening of the schools, Labor Day was inaugurated by the Knights of Labor in New York in 1882. It was made nationwide in the United States in 1909 as an anti-socialist alternative to May Day. The latter, which was proclaimed as an annual international workers' holiday by the Second International in 1889, itself commemorated an American event: the repression, three years earlier, of a Chicago strike for the eight-hour day.

33. The following quotes will give an outline of Boorstin's use of this term: 'While a pseudo-event is an ambiguous truth, propaganda is an appealing falsehood (Boorstin, 1961: 29)'. 'Propaganda oversimplifies experience, pseudo-events complicate it' (36). 'Information about the staging of a pseudo-event simply adds to its fascination' (38). It is evident that Boorstin's notion of the pseudo-event, and more generally of the rise of 'the image', is very close to Baudrillard's own (and later) concept of 'simulation' and the 'hyper-real'. It is presumably because the latter are, precisely, concepts, in the Parisian grand style, that Boorstin is forgotten while Baudrillard has been able virtually to patent this line of analysis as his own.

34. *The Guardian*, 6 September 1988.

35. It may be added that Disney-style entertainment – Debord's *spectacle* – is, in any case, amusement cast, intrinsically, in self-advertising form. What better exemplifies its self-promotional core, indeed, than a film studio's theme park, stuffed with walking replicas of its lovable characters from the screen?

36. The phrase is Judith Williamson's. See Williamson (1978: 21–39).

37. The power of publicity is such that the endorsements may flow even to those who come last. The 'plucky loser' figure cut by British ski-jumper Eddy Edwards in the Calgary Olympics struck a media chord which advertisers were quick to seize on.

7

THE PROMOTIONAL UNIVERSITY

A University is the high protecting power of all knowledge and science, of fact and principle, of inquiry and discovery, of experiment and speculation; it maps out the territory of the intellect, and sees that . . . there is neither encroachment nor surrender on any side.

Cardinal Newman, *The Idea of a University* (1947)[1]

A multiversity is a name. The name of the institution stands for a certain standard of performance, a certain degree of respect, a certain historical legacy, a characteristic quality of spirit. This is of utmost importance to faculty and to students, to the government agencies and the industries with which the institution deals. Protection and enhancement of the name are central to a multiversity.

Clark Kerr, *The Uses of the University* (1966)

Fund raising

When Oxford University launched a massive fund-raising campaign in 1989 there was an almost audible gasp. It was well known that British universities had been badly squeezed by many years of reduced government funding. But Oxford – with a begging bowl? Harder pressed institutions like Salford and Aston had faced major faculty lay-offs. Oxford, with its brain drain, unfilled positions, and unmet capital needs, had only to fret about losing its world-class standing. But this was pressure, nonetheless; and the fact that Oxford was obliged (not without Senior Common Room mutterings) to take its show on the road indicated that even an elite university with vast endowments and glittering ruling class connections was not immune to troubles which, for the past two decades, have come to overtake the academic institution everywhere.

Nor have these troubles been just a British phenomenon. The same pattern is discernible across the advanced capitalist world. After the massive state-funded expansion of the 1950s and 1960s came a long period of retrenchment. The turn reflected both the growing fiscal crisis of the capitalist state (O'Connor, 1973, 1984) and a change in spending priorities associated with the post-baby-boom demographic shift. Thus, while health budgets (serving the old) have soared, education budgets (serving the young) have had to make do with less.[2]

Except when dramatized by protest, a peculiarity of the cuts is that they have been more noticeable inside universities than outside. Accessibility pressures, especially from women, have ensured that the number of student places has been maintained, and even gradually increased. What the 'new reality' has meant for most universities, then, is not so much lay-offs and closures (though these have occurred) as a deterioration in physical and research infrastructure and, on the teaching side, an ever-tightening screw. The aim of government policy – in the immortal words of an Ontario Education Minister (Harry Parrot) – has been 'more scholar for dollar'. Hence a constant search for measures to improve cost-effectiveness, whether by increasing the student/faculty ratio, raising student fees, introducing user-pay schemes, or fund raising. In the same productivity-oriented spirit, universities have also been directed to set their research and curricular objectives more in line with the investment and training requirements of what is euphemistically called 'private industry'.

From a governmental point of view, such rationalization has indeed been rational. But for universities and those who work in them it has meant speed-up, educational dilution, a shifting of costs on to students (and indirectly on to faculty and staff through worsened work conditions), and a growing concern about the university's prostitution to the economic and the short term. It has also required, in everything from teaching methods to university governance, a shift in organizational form. Time-honoured traditions, privileges, and hierarchies have become vestigial elements in a world of contracts and professional management. Of course, if the dissolution of the old faculty guild has led to a decline in academic autonomy, there have been compensatory gains in procedural equity and openness to the demands of the university's various clientele. But none can doubt the qualitative nature of the change. In North America, where it was well under way before the fiscal tide turned,[3] its effects have been so total there is little living memory of anything else. In the British case, the transformation is still incomplete, both because of a resistant traditionalism (most Oxbridge colleges only began to admit women in the 1970s), and because the expansion, and accompanying modernization, of post-secondary education during the 1960s and 1970s was not as rapid as elsewhere. Indeed, while being pushed to revamp their style and methods, British universities are now under pressure to raise their enrolments by the mid-1990s by a further 50 percent.

Oxford expressed its own irritation at the deteriorating course of events when a vote at Congregation in 1988 denied Margaret Thatcher an Honorary Degree. It was, as commentators pointed out, the first time such a snub had been administered to a serving prime minister, let alone to one who headed the Conservative Party and was herself an old Oxonian. There was, indeed, a whiff of noblesse oblige. Not only is Oxford one of the happy few whose disfavour actually matters. It is also one of the even fewer secure enough in its own standing to be able to get away with such nose-thumbing in the lead-up to a major fund-raising campaign. No doubt there was damage behind the scenes. But if Oxford forfeited the good will of the First Lord of the Treasury, it retained access to the superior promotional magic of the Royal Family, who donated (as was well publicized) £25 million to help launch the appeal.

The campaign and the deficit which made it urgent excited comment, however, not only as an economic symptom. There was also something symbolically incongruous about it. For here was the very epitome of the community of scholars, its dreaming spires whispering enchantments from the Middle Ages, self-promoting like a huckster.

This is not to say that Oxford had never raised private funds before. It would never have existed without them. All of its ancient colleges were founded, and for centuries maintained, by benefactors whose highest reward was the commemorative plaque or statue they might gain in return. Alumni, too, have always been called upon to play their part. But although the new campaign built on these traditional forms of solicitation it also marked a break. Whereas the old forms of fund raising were conducted by and on behalf of individual colleges, this campaign was to be conducted centrally, with a focus on the University as a whole. Whereas previous approaches had been discreet, and had drawn on the University's organic ties with the wealthy and powerful, this was precisely a campaign, run by a custom-made organizational machine. And whereas previous appeals had drawn on the University's 'natural' reputation, which had been slowly built up, and which spoke for itself, that reputation was now delineated and emphasized as a deliberate aspect of the campaign.

Altogether, in fact, through glossy brochures, catch-phrases, and public relations events, Oxford has come to be imaged and packaged just like any other marketed product. And not surprisingly. For as a corporate player in the charity market, that is just what it has become. The days of discreetly passing the hat are over. With the multiplication of universities, and with governments insisting that they go to the private sector for a greater proportion of their financial support, university fund raising, whether targeted at corporations, alumni or the public at large, has become a highly competitive business. The various supplicant universities must compete, moreover, not only with one another, but also with all those other agencies, from Oxfam to art galleries, that are similarly hustling for donors.

In the British context, the professionalization of university fund raising is an innovation. Viewed through North American eyes, all that is surprising is that such a development should have occasioned any surprise. Those attached to American or Canadian universities – even State or Provincial ones – have long been used to their institutions being entrepeneurial, public relations oriented, and engrossed in the search for funds. For them, fund raising is no longer an occasional, emergency event. It has become a permanent feature of academic life. The regular purchase of books and equipment, not to mention new buildings, departments and endowed chairs, has come to depend on the ongoing success of whatever is the current campaign. University presidents are chosen on the basis of their fund-raising capacities, while special administrative departments ('Development', 'External Relations', and the like) have been set up to mobilize every campus constituency to contribute time and money to that end. Time: both as backroom volunteers, and by serving directly in promotion, through guest lectures, special dinners, open houses, and alumni events. Money: because, even though students, faculty, administrators, and support staff are not the main target, a university's capacity to enlist their financial support is an indication of good morale which helps hook the bigger fish.

The only coin that universities can offer in return is recognition. To induce donations, then, the university must produce as much of the stuff as it can. As a prize for the most generous, the names of buildings, squares, lecture theatres, and laboratories are all placed on the block; and this within an ever-more finely tuned system of honorifics which calibrates the scale of public mention to the scale of gift. The value of the honorific is itself, of course, only proportional to the symbolic value of the university dispensing it. Hence tendencies to institutional boosterism, which can be frantic in the case of the non-Ivy League and non-Big Science institutions which have relatively little promotional capital and must shout to be heard. For these, particularly, everything which can be construed as an achievement is pressed to the fore, from prowess on the football field to the faculty books which are listed and placed on display. The rhythms of the academic calendar are themselves not exempt. Anniversaries are only celebrated to launch new campaigns. And among students, from Freshers' Week and Homecoming to the crowning rite of Graduation itself, the corporatist and infantilizing love of Alma Mater is (once more) tolerated, even fostered, as a basis for future alumni appeals.

From a fund-raising perspective the ceremonial side of the university is the mere setting for an ad. When the gowns go on, the parents are assembled, and the honorary graduands line up for their hoods, vice-presidents (finance) hear the tinkle of cash. The same goes for charter statements about the 'university ideal' which are regularly trotted out on such occasions. Of course, such vague image-making is not enough. The universities must differentiate their profiles if they are to achieve an identity on the market. Hence that great product of the 1980s' academic planning mind: the 'mission statement', usually produced by presidential subcomittees after a year or two of judicious deliberation. Besides helping governments in their search for differentiation schemes, such statements, if apposite and well-designed, provide the script for the slogans and pictures which focalize each university's particular campaign. It is as if the university has gone through the looking glass. Rather than just evolving, each university's collective identity becomes a matter of obsessive definition, becoming in the end a wholly artificial construct; and the fund raising which had once been regarded as a peripheral chore has become a central consideration in how universities project themselves to the world.

The point can be generalized. Rising competition between universities for private funds is only the most obvious aspect of a broader trend. At virtually all levels of its practice the university has been more and more assimilated to the modalities of the market. At all these levels, correspondingly, it has become deeply implicated in the promotional dynamic which always accompanies competitive exchange. Beyond the issues raised in the

protests of the 1960s, then – state/corporate control, technocratic rationalization, ideological bias, and (socially skewed) accessibility – others have
arisen, no less troubling though harder to frame, stemming from the way in
which the late capitalist university has been (for want of a better term)
promotionalized. Beyond fund raising, there are at least four distinct areas
of academic activity in which such a process can be said to have occurred:
student recruitment, accreditation, faculty career competition, and academic
publishing. But before turning to these, it is necessary to make two things
clear.

First, the developments of which I speak are partly to be understood as
effects of commodification in a more or less direct sense – of the process,
that is, wherein universities have been induced through public under-
funding to privatize their costs and adopt a more businesslike and
entrepreneurial approach. But the conversion of the now idealized elite
bourgeois university into a market-oriented agency for the delivery of
educational and research services (a long-term conversion which the
Reagan–Thatcher reforms have, in any case, only accelerated)[4] is only part
of the picture. For universities, as for late capitalist society as a whole,
penetration by the price-system has been accompanied (and anticipated)
by the extension of competitive exchange in general. As the example of
fund raising attests, the markets in which the university has become
involved are not only those mediated by money. Like promotional politics,
the promotionalized university is a site which brings together the market
for commodities in the ordinary sense with other forms of competition (for
status, for example) of a more purely symbolic kind. For that reason, too,
the forms of promotion and exchange which have come to characterize the
institution are not just pervasive, but multiple and condensed: as complex
in their articulation as they are profound in their organizational and
subjective effects.

Secondly, while aiming to characterize a global tendency, my primary
reference-point is the multiversities and liberal arts boutiques of North
America.[5] This runs the risk of ethnocentrism. However, many aspects of
contemporary North American university development are transnational
while others, though regionally specific, can be considered to have a
teleological typicality precisely because they are North American. Marx
showed Germany its future through nineteenth-century England. Today,
in matters of culturo-economic evolution (or so it is plausible to argue),
Europe must look across the Atlantic. So, if my examples are immediately
Canadian and American (whose differences, too, I shall overlook) there is
no need for denizens of even the most august academies of the Old World
to feel excluded: *de te fabula narratur*.

The competition for students

Trent University, a twenty-five-year-old, college-based, liberal arts and
science school in the picturesque Kawartha Lakes region of Central

Trent University

Ontario (1970s slogan: 'The Personal Touch', 1980s slogan: 'Canada's Outstanding Small University') is justly proud of its publicity materials, for which its communications office has won several national awards.

A simple but striking example is a poster based on a photograph taken at a mid-1980s summer convocation. In the foreground, on a verdant lawn (green is the Trent colour), a cluster of 100 or so professors, in the varied hues of their own graduation robes, smile up at the camera. Behind them, nestled among trees, we see a perpendicular hint of academic building (modernist neo-gothic); to the right, a hint of river; and overhead, silhouetted by the foliage, a wash of cloudless sky. The iconography is easy to read: the medieval quotations mythicized as Tradition (and thence as Quality); these crossed with signs for (True North) Nature; and all these framing the faculty itself (traditional but up-to-date, professional but informal, solidary but composed of distinct individuals), who personify the University as a caring and welcoming community. A single caption – 'Trent University' – links image to institution, and converts the third-order sign they constitute together into the desired selling pitch. Come, says the poster, to our high-grade, friendly U.[6]

Here we have another instance of institutional self-promotion. But while this poster, and thousands like it, has been used as an adjunct to fund raising, its address is clearly elsewhere. The pitch is to students, more particularly to graduating high school seniors; and its aim is to entice them, at the point at which they are filling in their application forms, to choose Trent over its rivals in the Provincial (and, to a lesser extent national) university system.

That such advertising, which virtually all North American universities engage in, addresses prospective students as consumers, and that such an identification is at variance with more ideal definitions, and even practices, of higher education, is too obvious to dwell on. More interesting is that students have a double significance for university promotion, and that recruitment strategy necessarily relates to both.

Through their fees, in the first place, students are indeed consumers, just as courses, both as one-offs and in full-year (or degree-long) packages, are commodities. Of course, such fees are not the university's only source of income. Higher education is also subsidized through the grants governments transfer – on a weighted per capita basis – to the institutions students attend. Both the ratio of fees to grants, and the formula which relates the latter to enrolment, are policy matters which vary from jurisdiction to jurisdiction, and also over time. During the 1980s, as a general trend, institutional grants have been made less enrolment-sensitive so as to discourage growth, while the fee portion has risen so as to further privatize university costs.[7] But whatever the variations, for over three decades the basic logic has remained the same. Directly, in the case of fees, and indirectly, through the tying (more or less) of state grants to enrolments, students constitute a pool of income-bearing units, for whose custom universities are required to compete. Hence, using everything from personal high school visits to media advertising, a constant need for campaigns of student recruitment. And the stakes are high. The worst nightmare for a university is falling enrolment, while rising student numbers can lead to the expansion of a university's whole resource base.

The competition, however, is not just over numbers. It has a qualitative dimension also, which has become all the more intense with post-1960s efforts by governments to restrain university growth. Raising the quality of the student body can even provide a direct financial benefit – as in Ontario, where honours students (defined as undergraduates with a 65 percent plus average or better) earn a 50 percent higher per capita grant. Always and primordially, though, it is a matter of institutional status. Universities always want the best. Devising recruitment strategies which maximize the quality of the student intake, for which the standard (North American) measure is high school averages at the point of admission, becomes a competitive aim in itself.

At this secondary level, students are not merely customers to be wooed. To the extent of their performative potential, they are property to be acquired. As such, indeed, their aggregated profile can serve as a promotional signifier in its own right, both in student recruitment itself[8] and in other arenas of inter-university competition, like government lobbying, where the threshold and average grade-levels of student intake can be used as general indices of institutional quality.

The more applicants, the choosier a school can be. But who applies in the first place matters as well. So universities must also find ways to appeal to the particular quality of students they aspire to attract. In this respect the Trent poster is quite subtle. Not only does it tacitly signal academic seriousness by foregrounding its teachers and by invoking the originary myth of the academy as a community of scholars. By eschewing obvious gimmicks, and by displaying (as buildings, landscape, and teachers) the actual goods, the very aesthetics of the poster's design also turns it into a symbol of the naturalness and flair the school is promoted as offering. Not that all universities go for the same niche. A sister university of similar size, whose own strategy hinged on expanding its (cheap to operate) business administration programme, had earlier used a quite different approach. The poster it used, headed 'A Touch of Class', featured its league-topping football team, decoratively draped over a gleaming, antique Silver Cloud.

The more sophisticated and knowledgable, however, are hardly likely to attend a university (or have their offspring attend) solely on the strength of its ads. What really matters is all the accumulated promotional capital that has gone into constructing a school's perceived academic reputation.

Here, the old and established have a considerable advantage. Inherited status can ensure a maintenance of the student and professorial quality on which that status is perceived to rest. Even real decline can be masked by the recognition value of a well-known name – which, for the credentials-conscious student, may be more important as a recruitment draw than the educational experience which promises to go with it. Conversely, a high reputation cannot be created overnight. At best, it can be striven for as a medium-term goal. It is to this, then, that the go-ahead university will bend its efforts: at the faculty level, by forcing the pace of publication and research, and by buying academic stars; at the student level – where this can be done without scaring away the customers – by imposing tighter academic standards. Either way, and whatever the rhetoric about 'excellence', the point is equally promotional: to protect and if possible raise the comparative worth of the university's credits and degrees. And all of this feeds back. For any university, being known for high standards improves the career exchange-value of the credentials it awards. This, in turn, becomes a key element in recruiting 'good' students, which itself both improves the career potential of graduands and generally redounds to the glory of the school.

The promotionally mediated competition for students between universities is mirrored by what happens within. Here again North American universities are closer than their British cousins to an open market model. Rather than offering specialized degree-courses to which students are committed from entry to graduation, the North American system requires students to assemble their own package of courses in which (for general BAs and BScs) the disciplinary major which accounts for less than half the credits needed for a degree, is chosen after admission, and can then be easily changed. It is this model which makes the university seem (as they say) like a cafeteria, although with departments and interdisciplinary pro-grammes offering their own menus it resembles more the restaurant area in a mall. With course choices limited by aggregation and requirement rules, the curricular market has never, then, been wholly open. Indeed, recent moves by educational nutritionists to improve the protein and fibre content of the dishes, and even (Harvard's 'core curriculum') to create a *table d'hôte*, have reintroduced further elements of regulation whose erosion conservatives like Alan Bloom (1987) have lamented as a cause of post-sixties cultural decline. But however modified, the course-credit system has remained the overarching framework: a framework which encourages the teaching units of the university to compete vigorously with one another for the student custom to which their professional and resource-related fortunes are at least partially tied.

The contest takes place at two levels. There is, first, competition between whole academic departments. In the first instance this is for market share. But from the standpoint of long-term resource allocation (especially permanent faculty complement) going for enrolment growth alone can bring a risk. A department defined as a 'service operation' – and the same aplies to part-time studies, language centres, and mass business and commerce programmes – will be expected to run cheaply in order to subsidize the rest. Hence the importance, beyond raw numbers, of distributional indices like a department's relative share of majors, and the relative size of its upper years. Such a focus dovetails as well with interdepartmental rivalry over the quality of the students they draw.

Again, as with recruitment competition between universities, attracting a more than average proportion of the bright and industrious confers a double advantage. Besides being a market prize in itself, better students, and better precisely in the measurable and performative sense, means a better academic profile; and this, in terms of student recruitment as well as in the battle for departmental resources, means more promotional capital in the bank. At the summit of student attainment, prizes and scholarships bring further reflected glory, both as a general badge of merit, and by providing, together with other data about the academic performance of its students, a productivity-related index of a department's excellence as a teaching machine.

Teaching itself, in this scenario, becomes influenced by questions of corporate self-presentation. There is pressure on courses not just to be good (which means, as a market norm, relevant but challenging, tough but well-structured and fair) but to look good, and in ways which make the department which offers them look good as well. This also entails, whether the impetus is inner or imposed, special attention by teachers to even the physical details of classroom presentation, from dress, deportment, communicative style, and organizational competence, to the outlines, reference material, and assignment sheets handed out in class.

The same promotional interest plays, indeed, into all aspects of a department's interchange with its institutional and professional environment, whether at the level of informal ethos, through its curriculum, or through its record of publication and research. And the same interest is also served by the para-activities departments organize to foster their esprit de corps and, where real ambition reigns, their actual intellectual life. Hence the speaker series, cocktail parties, and special events which even the most unenterprising academic units feel constrained to organize; hence, too, the more nakedly entrepreneurial practice of issuing an annual departmental handbook, which, in the very act of providing useful factual information, touts the technical amenities, faculty qualifications, disciplinary ideals, and general cultural flavour which, it is hoped, will impress colleagues and draw the desired student base.

The course-credit system, finally, also encourages competition for students between individual faculty. While departments also gain, the success of a course establishes the success of its instructor, and the more so the more that departments confer virtual property rights on those who launch courses and/or regularly staff them from year to year. For individual instructors then, just as much as for departments, impressing students through signs and pseudo-signs of academic professionalism will be competitively important; as, too, their need to meet the standards for lecturing and seminaring which students bring with them from the outside: from the high gloss, short attention span, entertainment media which, from infancy, have fashioned and informed their sense of what a performance is. As on TV, many contemporary teachers have discovered that good graphics and a button-down style are a sure bet for boosting the ratings.

Written material is important as well, particularly the course outline (containing course aims, reading lists, lecture schedule, and grading schema) which, circulated beforehand, sometimes in great numbers, can be a crucial promotional device. Those attentive to marketing will also worry about a course's short-form description in the calendar, and even its title. A retired biologist of my acquaintance once told me that he had tripled the enrolment of a flagging second-year offering simply by changing its name from 'Introduction to Basic Entomology' to 'Man's War against the Insects'.

Of course, there is no advantage in attracting numbers if this just means extra work. But where numbers are fixed, or where there are equity rules governing the allocation of teaching loads, having the proven power to draw an audience raises an individual's bargaining power in the process of allocation itself. In any case, the contest is also for quality, wherein, besides the halo effect, there is also an experiential reward. Teaching the intelligent and dedicated is less alienating than ministering to the cynical, stupid, and bored.

In large universities undergraduate teaching as such tends to be devalued in these terms. Both for departments and for their individual members, graduate students are more highly prized, with the biggest status rewards going to those who draw the cream of the incoming doctoral crop. This does not mean, though, that the lower year teaching regularly assigned to junior and untenured faculty is deprived of all promotional point. Teaching is a public activity through which an individual's general sense of scholarly merit can be conveyed to career-relevant colleagues. Besides direct feedback via students, every piece of instructor-authored material contains a subtext about the instructor which is available for all to read. Preparing a mock course outline is frequently a requirement of the hiring process, and the extrinsic promotional significance of actual ones is not lost on those who submit them as supportive evidence in their applications for promotion, merit increments or tenure.

Grades and credits

Students, however, are not just inanimate tokens of income and status. Nor, indeed, are they merely passive consumers. University admission normally depends on an applicant's previous academic record. Thereafter, what students buy with their fees (and foregone earnings) is not so much a quantum of education as access to an opportunity structure whose benefit to themselves depends on the use they actively make of it. Students are players, then, in their own game, for which the most tangible stakes are the credentials which their academic and other kinds of labour can earn.

This is not to say that it is only a game. The fact that full-time students are in a moratorium[9] from fixed identities and roles makes possible a process of self-discovery and re-thinking which can be enriched even by the formal side of university study. As well – granted that the canon is selective, and that the transmission process is filtered, and sometimes stultified, by faculty efforts to reproduce their own disciplinary subcultures – an acquaintance with the currently defined store of great books, ideas, historical developments, etc, enlarges the repertoire of thinkable thoughts and amounts to a form of self-improvement in itself. But even in these respects higher education is more than its own reward. By helping people become culturally attuned, psychologically flexible, and skilled in communications, it confers real social advantage – and in a most tangible sense. Even the most exalted, and apparently useless, aspects of university education join with the most explicitly instrumental in having a career-training role. Considering that occupational rewards are unequal and their attainment a competitive result, what that means is that higher education has not only a use-value for students, but an exchange-value. To be better prepared, and therefore better suited, for a particular line of work is to be more salable, and so in a position to command a higher price.

Just having completed university at all confers an occupationally relevant status value – to an extent which further depends on the prestige of the institution attended. This value-by-association is objectified in the degree certificate which entitles its recipient to place the magic letters, and the university where they were earned, officially after their name. Of course, the degree does more than just testify to attendance. It testifies to the fact that the graduating student has achieved at least the minimal level of attainment set. Even this, though, has a meaning for an employer beyond what it ostensibly measures; indicating, for a start, that he or she is the kind of person who is capable, not just intellectually, but psychologically, of meeting institutionally imposed norms of work.

But formal qualifications go beyond the mere possession of a degree. Whatever the method of evaluation, all the work which counts towards a degree is itself graded; as too the class, or grade-point average, of each degree taken as a whole. Where there is relatively low social mobility (for example, Britain before the 1960s), or the differential prestige of going to an institution balances off any internal distinctions it makes, the recorded calibrations need only be rough. (To this day, Oxford and Cambridge rely on an exam system in which the marks given to individual papers are not officially disclosed.) In more open and mobile societies, and also where mass university education has depreciated the tradable value of the degree itself (especially the general BA), such distinctions become more important, as does a student's more detailed grading profile. The North American model, which eschews the stress and artificiality of a one-shot evaluation (through exams) in favour of continuous assessment (through course assignments), fits this exigency well. For it provides a multiplicity of opportunities to rank and scale the students who pass through.

For both giver and receiver – and the more graded assignments there are, the more this is so – the function of grades is quite ambiguous. On one level, they are just a pedagogical device which, by providing an indicator (more or less artificial) of what, in various subjects, has been learnt, supplies feedback, cognitive structure, and an incentive system which encourages students to work and learn. But grades also have teeth. Bad ones lead to failed courses, even to rustication and debarment. Good ones open doors to careers. Not only, in fact, do marks for individual assignments cumulate into course-credits, and these into degrees. The grade for each course, including failures and abandoned attempts, is recorded on a transcript which is a student's for life.

Grades, then, are more than just a system of academic/behavioural incentives (like the gold and black stars which British primary schools used to post as signs of good or bad behaviour on classroom walls). Together with the larger denomination notes of which degrees are made, they serve as a kind of currency, shuttling back and forth between education, for whose level of attainment they provide a convenient measure, and the labour market, for which they provide an equally handy indicator of a job applicant's relative qualification. For students to fetishize them, then, is not just false consciousness. In the Benthamite sense, it is rational behaviour: an extension of the way that career competition at the upper end of the labour market more generally mediates students' relation to the university. At this level, indeed – though as part of a larger credentialist package, and not therefore at a fixed rate of exchange – grades are commutable into cash.[10]

The hypostasis of grades as a credentialist currency has an important further effect. And I will add: an effect which undermines the essentialist assumptions on which their credibility as a currency ideologically rests. Whether based on written, oral or practical work, a grade always represents the evaluation of a performance. But between the judged performance and the inner compound of knowledge and ability of which it is supposedly the external sign there is always a slippage, a gap, through which all manner of promotional practices can be inserted in order to sell the performance to the critics sitting in judgement.

This is so even in an evaluation model which screens out the live, and ensures anonymity, through reliance on written exams. It is not just that students may underperform because of stage fright. Precisely because direct communication is ruled out, all that an examiner has to go on is how good a candidate looks on paper. Beyond substantive desiderata like logic, factual correctness, depth, and originality (all virtues which themselves have to be enacted), this looking good involves all manner of verbal performances from citations and sentence structure, to making (as I was once assured before taking an exam in economic history) 'the right noises'. And it goes without saying that in addition to right allusions the right noises include the right attitudes, especially in terms of the methodological paradigm(s) currently dominating the examining discipline. Even multiple choice, which eliminates individual bias, can involve second-guessing what the corporate examiner wants to hear.

In a system of continuous evaluation student life is a veritable procession of such graded performances. As well, considering all the variant kinds of exercise which course assignments may entail, the range of presentational skills required is greatly expanded. With papers done at home, even the minutiae of footnoting style and document presentation is a grade factor at the margin. In the case of seminar presentations, and even more where a mark is given for 'class participation', still more such qualities are brought into play. Besides those of orality itself (being coherent, articulate, dialogical, etc), which are themselves shot through with the classroom power dynamics of who gets to speak, and on what terms, they blend, finally, into that multitude of gestural and informal micro-practices which students bring with them from high school, and through which they have learnt to present themselves, on cue, as keen, bright, punctual, conscientious, and really motivated.

And that is just the point. Where everything is graded, everything is a competitive performance; which means not only that the work presented is promotionally constructed so as to provide a convincing display of the qualities required to turn it into a bankable grade, but that being a 'good student' – like Sartre's waiter-being-a-waiter (in *La Nausée*) – is itself a matter of constructed appearance, albeit one which is haunted, in the best as well as the worst of cases, by the anxiety of being revealed as a fraud.

Formal scholastic work, however, is not the only site of career-relevant competition between students. Promotional self-interest extends also to extracurricular activities. Campus film clubs, theatre and music groups, political associations, the student union, athletics, all have their own achievers, cliques, and competitive hierarchies. Through being mentioned on a resume or CV, positions held in such areas become themselves convertible into a form of promotional credit. In fact, as students quickly learn, developing a good resume is a central aspect of career preparation, both in terms of acquiring matter to record and in terms of the document's actual composition at job-hunting time. Here, as in company advertising, the need to promote begets its own distinct semiotic practices and products. No-one on the job market is unaware of dress, deportment, and other such self-presentational skills. But to get to the stage of an actual interview applicants have to be short-listed, for which what is crucial is the bundle of material sent to support an application. The resume, backed by a transcript, is the most important of these, although in an audio-visual age it is not the only way that autobiography can be turned into an ad. In recent years, Ivy League admissions officers have increasingly had to wade through the videos which the most enterprising (and affluent) high school applicants have submitted to the most hotly contested schools.

Further up the educational scale, such blatant hype would backfire. For graduating students, besides the resume and the transcript, the most important supplementary material to be culled from their university career is the faculty-authored letter of recommendation. Here, too, in ensuring that there is a story to tell, the extent of student success reflects the success with which their total performance has been managed. Nor is it enough that such letters be glowing. As with consumer advertising, the promotional value of the endorsement is a function of the endorser's own. The more eminent the recommender the more their word, as well as their name, is worth to the student able to adduce it in support.

The relation of universities to the labour market, then, is not simply as the co-producers (with students themselves) of various high-grade skills and abilities. Universities also produce, and distribute, various kinds of tokens which promotionally stand in for them. It is these tokens, correspondingly, and not just enhanced knowledge, understanding, etc, which a student takes away from a university, as indeed from any educational establishment. Whether consciously sought or not, and however well strategized, what students acquire from their pre-career career is their very own store of promotional capital. Promotional, indeed, in a double sense: for not only are grades, credits, transcripts, degrees, resumes, and recommendations promotional in the credentialist uses to which they are put. What they also represent is the promotional work which, in a multi-dimensional game of competitive performance, has gone into their accumulation.

The professorial CV

The same kind of promotionally mediated contest for career credits as occurs among students also goes on within the faculty. Indeed, in purer form: because if students are cross-pressured, subject to contradictory expectations, and often uncertain about what (if any) projects to pursue, for faculty the rules and reward structure are unambiguously set. Here, moreover, unlike among students (who cannot give credentials to themselves), the main field of play is the peer-group, whose esteem is itself a vital stake in the game.

The academic profession is based on, and divided into, a myriad expert knowledges and idiolects. In the first instance, then, the relevant other for collegial judgements is not the faculty peer-group as a whole but the interpretive community constituted by the academic speciality to which each member belongs. So important is this grouping ('the discipline'), that even in a period when the old division of academic labour is crumbling, and the whole notion of disciplinary boundary has lost its grip, new associations are springing up all the time to encadre new specialist areas, crossovers, and regroupments.[11] And not surprisingly: for it is through these disciplines, sub-disciplines, proto-disiplines, and trans-disciplines, each with their own formal associations and informal networks, their conferences and flagship journals, that the professional status of academics is conferred, whether through the refereeing system (of anonymous readers and reviewers) which serves as the gateway to publication and research grants, or more intangibly, through the accretion of an individual's wider academic repute. It is also upon the judgement of these sub-collectivities, as filtered by local academic departments, that a faculty member's home university must rely when making its own (appointment, tenure, promotion, etc) assessments of merit.

As with students, what sweetens the honorific pot is that such status is commutable into advancement of a more material kind. Appointments, starting salaries, special increments, promotions and transfers to a higher status (or paying) institution, all rely on the professional points individual faculty have been able to pile up. An elaborate calculus has evolved for measuring and comparing them in order to facilitate and regulate such exchange. This calculus is not just informal. As part of a wider formalizing trend, it has increasingly been codified in departmental regulations and faculty union contracts. The rationale, against a background of growing litigiousness, and pushed from below as much as from above, has been to ensure procedural equity and regulate disputes. An effect has been to eliminate from explicit consideration all but the most external and documentable marks of quality – banishing to the shadows such difficult questions as how to evaluate orally transmitted influence, the interdependence of one person's thoughts and achievements with another's, and what professional visibility is itself intellectually worth.

Not surprisingly, then, beyond the basic credentialist ticket provided by degrees and previous positions held, what matters most in the competitive achievement of academic status is tangible output, particularly in the form of published professional work. The productivist scramble to which this leads is more complex than the 'publish or perish' tag might suggest. The assignment of professional credit requires that quality, as well as quantity, be assessed. The latter is easy to measure – just count the titles and pages – but questions of quality are more fraught, especially in a postmodern liberal culture whose master-value is relativism and which privileges the right to hold opinions over the right to make judgements about them. There is, besides, a practical problem. To keep up with the literature, even in a single specialized field, has become physically impossible. And this effect of the 'knowledge explosion' is exacerbated by the fact that the dynamic underlying it has as much to do with careerist pressures to publish as with external factors like the global multiplication of universities, electronic communication, and the progress of various forms of science. Competitive publishing engenders surplus publishing, particularly where profitability for the author is not of primary concern. Journals float on producer demand for vehicles to carry self-promotional articles. There is, then, a built-in tendency for the flow of writing to outstrip the time available for reading it, which leads all but the most strenuous to develop a protective disinclination to do any but skim reading outside their most immediate area of work.

The qualitative assessment of an individual's publications record has therefore had to be operationalized. Page for page, wholly authored books count more for more than collaborations or anthologies, these more than book chapters or journal articles, and these more than book reviews and other occasional pieces. Further discriminations are made on the basis of the relative professional standing of the publishing organ. Refereed journals, which have their own pecking order, carry more weight than unrefereed ones. Books published by a serious academic press are worth more than those by a trade or textbook publisher, with vanity productions having an almost negative value at the bottom of the list. Additional criteria are provided by published reviews of the published work itself; and even by the number and provenance of citations which the American Modern Languages Association, for example, has now begun to collect in data banks. For young high-fliers these latter are especially useful, for they document the extent to which the cited academic author has actually been incorporated into the professionally sanctioned intertext.

After written publications come oral presentations. Here, too, there are further status gradations which depend on the prestige of the venue, the status of associated others, and the extent of star billing. Such performances are creditworthy in themselves, but their main career value is indirect. A live presentation provides an opportunity to plug the presenter's most recent writings, as well as serving, in concordance with the latter, as an arena within which to impress colleagues and make contacts so as to secure more invitations to speak, and publish. At the lowliest level, mainstream disciplinary annual conferences are stocked with hopeful graduate students looking for jobs. At the other end of the scale, celebrity fests like the fortnightly Derrida seminar currently (1989–90) held in Paris attract crowds of travelling academics who just want to rub shoulders with the mighty and increase their store of tradable anecdotes.

The promotional benefits of live performances can flow in more than one direction. Speakers, to the extent they are well known, help promote the event they attend. In print, where a conference or series has been organized with this in mind, they also promote the subsequent book – not to mention the name of the editor/organizer who will appear on its cover. The opportunity to publish, at the same time, is usually a more important inducement to participate in a live event than the mere honour of being asked to do so; and certainly more than the honorarium (if any) which, for all but real superstars, rarely covers even the basic costs of attendance.

Next, after papers written and spoken, come various other professional activities from which career points can be earned. These range from winning research grants, to serving as an external referee (vis-a-vis publications, dissertations, grants or personnel decisions), to being an officer of a learned society or a member of an editorial board. These, in turn, can serve as the basis for more straightforwardly entrepreneurial efforts, with the biggest prizes, for the workaholics who enjoy them, going to those who swim in research money, commute between teaching or research positions on either side of the Atlantic, establish international institutes or specialize in organizing glitzy events. Such activities again serve both as citable achievements in themselves and as the means to secure further opportunities in future. Where a review process is involved (for example in appointments or in the awarding of grants), administrative reason justifies this in terms of track records. However, a snowballing academic success comes not only from actual achievements but from their promotionally amplified effects. So, in every field of academic endeavour from publishing to grantsmanship, the same rule applies to the amassing of professional credits as to money: to those who have shall more be given.

I am describing a kind of calculus. But for it to become operational, that is, to create career credits which can be drawn on for actual advancement, professional activities in the categories mentioned must be not only enacted but recorded and rendered into documentary form. It is only thus that achievements can be counted and compared. Whence the importance of the professorial curriculum vitae. An apparently self-generated appurtenance, the fruit of one's labours, an authority stick with which to beat the less well-endowed, the CV can play a comically unconscious role. In the confidentiality of personnel committees, they are reviewed for size like penises or breasts, with sniggers all round for those found to have been artificially padded.

Selective and nuanced for promotional effect, the professorial CV hovers between fact and fiction, a literary construct, though not without its moment of autobiographical truth. As with the student resume which is its anticipatory prototype, it involves, in fact, a double writing: the story as written down, and the original *fabula*. Penalties against outright fabrication mean that while there is room in editing and design for creative enhancement, optimizing the career-value of the 'real' story is a necessary condition for optimizing that of the typed version actually handed in. The logic this imposes can only be avoided by those who, for reasons of eminence, wealth, eccentricity or rebelliousness, are effectively outside the competitive fray: namely, that in every recordable detail academic life must be conducted as a performance for the sake of the credit marks its subsequent self-recording produces.

Careers structured in this way progress through three phases. In the first, the main task is to gain acceptance for, and then actually produce, printed and oral performances which will gain enough notice and credit to make possible entry into phase two. Here, acceptance is more assured and invitations start to come in, so the issue becomes one of deciding which of the self-promotional opportunities on offer are most worth taking up. In the final phase, for those who reach it, the issue becomes one of expenditure. Given the importance of not cheapening one's name, what is the best way to deploy it? Who should be permitted to benefit when, through conferences, anthologies, recommendation letters, and the like, that name and its lustre are promotionally used by others? At this rarefied level, the promotional game becomes reversed. In academia, as in the culture industry more generally, the celebrities at the top have accumulated so much bankable status that their principal culturo-economic worth, even to themselves, is as promotional signifiers with a rentable value of their own.

I have so far left teaching out of account. This is not an oversight. While there is a clear continuity between the credentials game played by faculty and students, it nevertheless pits them against one another, particularly at the undergraduate level. This goes beyond mutual cynicism: there is a real conflict of interests. Whereas for students the educational side of the university is primary, for faculty what matters most is 'scholarly productivity'. Teaching itself, residual, invisible, and hard to assess, has little credit value in the development of an academic career. Besides an entry for 'courses taught' teaching is rarely mentioned on the CV; and even in tenure and promotion decisions the standards to be met, unlike those for 'published research', are satisficing only. The faculty activity which matters most to students is, for faculty themselves, just work which gets in the way of work.

A counterweight of sorts has been established in the use of centrally administered 'faculty course evaluations', which makes it possible not only to assess but to publicize the quality of formal instruction students receive. Without denying the behavioural effects, the adoption, under (student and administrative) pressure, of such an opinion poll corrective is, however, entirely continuous with the alienated pedagogical condition to which it only superficially responds: both in its blend of consumerism and managerial disciplinarity, and in the way it offers a promotional solution to a promotional contradiction.

Commodity promotion

The forms of promotion considered so far have all been bound up with various ways in which the contemporary university's teaching and research functions have become mediated by forms of competitive exchange which, while being connected to the commodity system through the labour market, or the market for fees and funds, are only quasi-commercial in themselves. But with its multi-million dollar budget, its mass of individual consumers and producers, and its perpetual need for cash, the university has also become multiply connected to the commodity system proper.

To begin at the periphery, stretched budgets and the need to enhance revenues have, first, led to outright commercialization of some of the universities' ancillary operations. Among these, a notable money-spinner has been the intensified use of facilities for residential conferences. This development has responded, in part, to internal demand, wherein growing pressure by faculty, and even graduate students, to provide for academic events has reflected the evolution of career dynamics within the profession. Spurred on, however, by the need to maximize income from residences and food facilities, especially during the idle summer months, there has also been rising competition among universities for the general conference trade.

Publicity aimed at this (highly miscellaneous) market rides largely on the back of other institutional promotion. But it also requires its own separate advertising. Besides the additional flow of material this entails, the promotional effect rebounds back into the university itself. To project the university as a conference centre is to adopt, and diffuse throughout the institution, a viewpoint which reverses the official definition of what is going on. In its terms, the university's educational and scholarly activities are a competitor for space, even a logistical nuisance. At best, like everyday life in Venice, they provide a colourful backdrop to the academic image being sold to customers as part of the package. It is the oldest and most auratic universities, paradoxically, which are most susceptible to being thus transformed into an object of the tourist gaze. For them the tourist industry leaves no escape. Even when, in self-protection, Cambridge colleges close their gates to visitors in high summer they incidentally provide a consumer benefit (look! no tourists) to the paying ones in the conferences within.[12]

Besides becoming an agency for its own self-marketing, the university also provides a ready-made distribution system for circulating other people's goods. Through such organs as the student newspaper and the in-house telephone directory, a diversity of commercial interests, ranging from pizza parlours and record stores to banks, copy services and corporate recruiters, have been able to insert their messages directly into the university's internal communication system – a trend which has only been accelerated by the way these information services have been forced to turn to advertising to cover costs. The biggest-ticket items, however, for which the university provides a market, are in an area which bridges its role as the site for individual purchases and its equally important one as corporate buyer. This is technical equipment, of which the most prominent element currently is computers. Here, special deals have led to contracts which exchange 'educational discounts' for permission to use whole universities as giant retail outlets. The advantage to manufacturers is long range. Like accounts opened at the campus bank, the magic boxes sold to departments and to individual faculty and students are designed to create brand loyalty and gain further business down the road.

A further form of commercial promotion to which universities have become receptive, if more gingerly, is corporate sponsorships. These range from named academic chairs (linked to fund raising), to beer companies subsidizing student bashes during freshers' week. No doubt, in years to come, the same self-interested favours will be bestowed by condom manufacturers.[13] Student culture, indeed, has become deeply entangled in such commercialism. Nowhere is this clearer than in its forms of entertainment. At student dances, advertised bands (or discos) move the booze whose point-of-sale profits dispense patronage to those able to hustle themselves on to the payroll. For the record industry, that same milieu provides a fan base and test market for new acts. The 'alternative' culture which forms at its Bohemian margins provides a fertile source of stylistic innovation for the youth market as a whole. The ambiguity of such alternativeness, which typically combines outrageous stylistic difference with incorporable ideas for product promotion, is anally expressed in running campus battles with campus authorities over the untidy proliferation of student posters. However wild the visual and ideational mix, and however insurgently placed, freedom of speech is exercised here as the freedom to promote. And in a quite straightforward sense: for whether such posters concern political causes, special interest clubs, dances and bands, or even straight academic events, their immediate aim is to maximize attendance at the paying or non-paying events they advertise.

The book trade

As secondary as these instances might seem, they all shape the general atmosphere. But there is one commodity market which impinges on the university's core functions directly. This is the book trade, in which, indeed, the university is multiply implicated. Not only is the university a place where books are bought. It is also a site of authorship. And at both levels it further serves as a crucial – and generative – medium for the promotion which greases the wheels of this whole circular motion.

Consider the situation, first, from the consumption side. While the most visible book buyer in the university is the library, the most important source of intra-university demand for books, both in money terms and because it involves multiple copies, is private purchase, of which the lion's share is students buying required texts for courses.[14] The marketing implications are self-evident. The key to sales success for academic books is getting them included on course lists. The more popular the course, moreover, and the larger the student constituency served by that area in the curriculum, the larger the market at which a text can aim. In these terms, the teaching curriculum itself, with its supermarket of competing course choices, serves as a giant distribution device for publishing companies. It is a two-step process. Through visits and direct mailing, publishers' own efforts are focused on pinpointing faculty specializations and securing adoption of their latest texts. Final sales, though, depend on enrolments; wherein, among other demand factors, instructors themselves, in promoting their own courses, incidentally promote the books which go with them.

If the course-credit system serves as a selling structure, that structure also shapes the end market, determining the kind of product which must be produced to match. Academic text publishers face a market which is pre-organized into well-defined niches, organized, like the range of regularly given courses to which they correspond, both by level (introductory, senior undergraduate, graduate-and-faculty) and by subject area. The arrangement helps publishers standardize their production. It also has industrializing effects on the teaching process itself – particularly at the lucrative, lower-year end of the market, where the high-school practice of teaching through introductory textbooks has become well established in such areas as sociology, economics and mass communications.[15]

But the book trade impinges on the university not only at the point of sale. It also impinges at the point of production, through the intersection of the faculty career contest with the actual authoring of books.

Here, in an intermediate market for talent, commissioning editors scan the academic scene for likely writers, while the same network of publishers' agents which attempts to sell faculty other books is engaged, face to face, in a similar search. The contracts angled for on both sides swap agreed amounts of commercially viable authorial product for a share in the profits. This, though, is only the formal side of the agreement. Contractors and contractees both know that, except for the biggest sellers, royalty earnings are meagre, and that even in material terms the more significant reward for academic authors is the professional credit to be earned, regardless of sales, just by being respectably published. In short, each party uses the validating power of the other for their own promotional purposes. If publishers, with their own refereeing system, manage a terrain which yields career credits to faculty, they in turn utilize the fruits of intra-faculty career competition through the way that the professional standing of authors gives promotional value to the names affixed to a company's stream of university-bound product.

For academics browsing through catalogues, for instructors deciding what books to put on a course, or for students looking through required lists in course outlines to see what they would have to read, it is the well-known and credible author, as much as a book's title and table of contents, which attracts attention. Those who become defined as 'leading expert in the field', and still more those who enter the canon (and so become required reading for all), are automatic entrants into their market segment's list of best-sellers. The situation is the same as in other sectors of commodified cultural production. Familiar and prestigious names help move the merchandise with which they are creatively associated. In this setting, too, the authorial moniker, like any brand-name, serves as a transfer device for giving a commodity symbolic appeal; which it does both as a testimonial mark of personally guaranteed quality and as a way to provide a differential identity for the book by linking it to the culturo-ideological associations which define a writer's own image.

As with other cultural commodities, moreover, imaging books through the authorial name helps both publisher and royalty-earning writer through the seriality of promotional effect. Favourable reception for one book generates promotional value for the name which links it to the sequel. Thus sales can build from book to book enhanced by the way that the publicity flow enhances the selling power of the authorial name. The publishing spin-offs can transcend mortality. 'Classics' by the greats are always good for reprints, and long after their authors are dead can yield continuing additional dividends through a cottage industry of secondary literature. The biggest names, indeed, like celebrities in other fields, become free-floating promotional signifiers; in which capacity they serve to publicize not just their own books, but those of others. For publishers, such use has become systematic. Celebrity endorsement is employed in every aspect of a book's promotion, from the reviewers' comments excerpted in publishers' notices, to the list of mentors, colleagues, and friends gratefully cited in the preface – with a special bonus if a star (Foucault prefacing Lyotard's *Postmodern Condition*) has also been persuaded to write a special introduction which can be highlighted as a feature in itself.

The interests of publishers and publishing academics converge, then, in the importance of cultivating the latter's promotional value. The name that sells a book advances a career, and vice versa.

Of course, this mutual dependency contains an asymmetry. While a publisher's market is all who will buy, for academics the university itself, together with the professional organs, organizations and events based there, remains the primary arena in which the struggle for reputation must be conducted. Within the bounds of the professionally proper, it offers two principal modes of communication in which to shine: writing and talking. With respect to the former, the supreme prize is to become an authority to whom professional specialists must refer. The height of oral success is marked by the crowd-pulling attention accorded, on the Paris/Oxbridge/California lecture circuit, to an academic rock star. Not that these two routes to recognition exclude one another. For the academic, live presentations and written work are complementary forms of performance, just as, in the music business, recorded albums promote, and are in turn promoted by, showcase live gigs.

This though is to speak of homologies. It is only on rare occasions that academia can serve as the launch-pad for a more general fame. In the 1960s, a period which thirsted for gurus, a spectacular instance was the career leap of Marshall McLuhan, a Joyce scholar who turned to media and became a mediatized emblem of the global village he was drawing to global attention. However, as his case suggests (that of Timothy Leary is even clearer), the price of such an amplified celebrityhood can be the loss of purely professional esteem.[16] Publishing itself, even 'in one's area', perennially presents this danger through the ambiguous seductions of popularization. A similar risk faces academics who split their writings into the serious and the popular, for example by writing detective stories on the side. The conventional solution is to split identities by using a pseudonym,[17] which is not a matter of deception but of separating CVs and the performance profiles to which they pertain. It is only in the most exceptional cases that such a duality can be sustained without the need for such an expedient, and only with the most prodigious communicative skills that the transition from academic to popular celebrity be managed in a way that preserves, and even enhances, stardom in both domains.

How can one not, then, admire Umberto Eco? Firmly established by mid-career as one of the master semioticians of our age, he became even more celebrated as the multi-million selling author of *The Name of the Rose*. In launching his novelistic career, Eco's intellectual reputation preceded him, serving even to enhance the mystique of this book's dense, esoteric lore. Nor, conversely, did Eco's promiscuously enlarged audience dim his intellectual star. While his medieval whodunnit was tailor-made for the mass market, and even turned into a Hollywood hit (with Sean Connery in the starring role), literary theorists have hailed it as a significant postmodern novel. Among the ironic charms of Eco's tale is that it terminates in the burning of the Aedificium, in which is lost forever the hidden – written – Truth, the quest for which had narratively drawn all its characters along.

Critique and reform

The burden of the foregoing remarks has been to suggest that the contemporary university's assimilation to its socioeconomic environment, a process that the term 'modernization' is inadequate to express, presents problems with which an older critique, couched in terms of the hegemonic influence of positivism within, and of technocratic control from without, can hardly get to grips. Radical reformers in the 1960s attacked the university's bureaucratization, and its services to the military-industrial elite. An earlier generation criticized industrialism, and the narrowing of knowledge production to the useful, the measurable, and the short term. But these are not the only snakes which have entered the garden. From corporate self-packaging to the accreditation games of students and faculty (however 'critical'), the institution has also come to be pervaded by forms of competitive self-promotion which are themselves intermixed, most notably through the labour market on the one hand, and the publishing industry on the other, with the promotion of commodities in a fully commercial sense.

This is not just a matter of motives, though those who work and study in universities can judge for themselves how much bad faith is involved in the intellectual, pedagogic, administrative, and professional practices with which they are familiar. Both individually and collectively, the adoption of a promotional mode has become indispensable to academic survival. Through meritocratically legitimated forms of evaluation the need to (self-)promote is entered even into the formal rules of the academic game. No-one is to blame yet everyone is implicated, even those who lament what has happened in terms of a higher integrity. Resistance to the marketing practices of academia in the name of traditional humanism provides evidence of the vitality of packageable myths. On the other side, liberal pressure for fair competition – in tandem with efforts to defend 'standards' – simply helps to guarantee the value of the various currencies in play. As for the party of reform, if one existed, before even dreaming of a counter-strategy it would have to take account of the extent to which the pervasiveness of promotional language and activity leaves no discourse and project immune, and has anyway made universities impervious to non-interest politics by hollowing them out as lived institutional space.

It is easy to be gloomy. In calling for a 'completion of the modern project', even the relatively optimistic Habermas was moved (in 1980) to doubt the emancipatory prospects:

> The life world has to become able to develop the institutions out of itself which set limits to the internal dynamics and the imperatives of an almost autonomous economic system and its administrative complements. If I am not mistaken, the chances for this today are not very good. (Foster, 1984: 13)

Nonetheless the fact that this and other critiques can be articulated should caution against too undialectical a view. If academia were not contradictory, and not experienced as such, objection to what has occurred could not arise. The impulses of intellectual life are thwarted but not eliminated by the institutional channels in which they are constrained to run. The hyperproductivity of a career-competitive professoriat heightens that tension, which is further exacerbated by the way in which the expansion of higher education has, despite austerities, extended both the numbers of those playing the professional game and the scale of the student mass touched by the troubled intellectual inheritance academia has come to monopolize. Despite everything, then, there are many sites, in the interstices and at the margins, at which the displaced and dis-authenticated ideals of higher learning – moral–intellectual formation, the creation/ transmission of 'long-term cultural use-values' – can break through and animate a practice.

It needs hardly be said that the scene which such a development would present, if fostered and extended, has nothing to do with curricular tinkering ('back to basics', 'core curriculum', etc) nor with the community of scholars' rhetoric associated with academia's tired ritual round. The bourgeois spiritualism with which Humboldt and Arnold invested the nineteenth-century university has become promotional kitsch whose tattered remnants should be put aside. The challenge – if the ideal aspect of the academic/intellectual project is to have a real future – is to reformulate that project (what, today, is enlightenment?), both in spirit and in line with the actual problems which we have historically been given to think.

None of which is to suggest that a dialectical rabbit can simply be pulled out of the hat. Efforts to reconstruct academia from its margins, though continually arising, face immense difficulties, not least in terms of the culturo-economic mediation I have ventured to trace out. To speak of challenges is to adopt the language of recruitment posters; while if hope is indeed placed in the margins of academia, in the extra-curricular spaces it permits, it should not be forgotten that even here – in the commercially fertile effervescence of university culture, in the informal reading circle that becomes a conference committee, in the informal ferment of ideas that takes wing in print – the multi-levelled dynamics of competitive exchange remain ever in play, and with them all the seductive deflections of discourse towards promotion (of oneself and of other circulating goods) which these dynamics supplementally engender.

Notes

1. Newman (1947: 129) cited in Kerr (1966: 2).

2. For a discussion of the policy issues and fallout from university cutbacks in the US, UK, and Canada, see Mingle (1981), Morris and Sizer (1982), and Skolnick (1984).

3. The organizational modernization of the university was cautiously welcomed by Clark Kerr in *The Uses of the University*. Originally delivered in 1963 as a lecture series at Harvard, Kerr's liberal and economistic vision came back to haunt him in the context of the controversies that broke over his head as President of Berkeley a year later.

4. An ingenious combination of (partial) public funding and the market mechanism is the so-called 'voucher system' which right-wing think-tanks have proposed on both sides of the Atlantic. The effect would be to tie university funding much more precisely to the movement of enrolments between universities and their faculties, thus instituting it (from above) as a complete analogue of market demand in other fields.

5. For similar reasons, I have not referred to developments within the university outside the humanities and social sciences, by which I similarly do not mean to imply that professional schools and science disciplines are not affected by the same dynamic.

6. It should be noted, as well, that the photogenic architecture (designed by the late Ron Thom), and the equally self-conscious choice of a river-bank site, was conceived from the start with an image of a modernized Oxbridge in mind. No accident, then, that their photographic reproduction features prominently in many aspects of Trent's external publicity. The place was a picture postcard before it physically existed. Perhaps this solves the causal mystery of what Baudrillard (1983a) has referred to as the 'precession of simulacra'. The hyper-reality of Trent's built environment (and this can be generalized) is grounded in a design dynamic, in which the image of the projected market-desired product provides the model for the constructed appearance of the 'real'. Hence a category we can call promotional simulacra, here in the form of promotional architecture and promotional landscape.

7. In the UK this has been reflected in the tentative first steps (in 1989) towards introducing (means-tested) loans. Funnelled through the commercial banks, these are thought of as 'topping up' student grants, which are themselves to be gradually reduced. Such a system has been in existence for thirty years in Canada although, as is the long-term intent in the UK, the grants are special supplements to the loans, and many students do not receive either.

8. One of Trent's most striking recruitment posters was a league table of Canada Council MAs which showed Trent graduates, on a per capita basis, to be outperforming every other university in Canada. It was devised by a faculty member.

9. The term 'moratorium' is Erik Erikson's. See Erikson (1968).

10. The commutation can be direct and unmediated. This is so, for example, in the case of elementary and high school teachers in Ontario and other jurisdictions who can upgrade their salaries through accumulating (part-time) university course credits, subject to a minimum grade requirement.

11. The rise of cultural studies, particularly in North America, as a self-conscious academic discipline, is a good example of this. While the debate about self-definition (distinctive methodology? object of knowledge? etc) is couched in intellectual terms, it is hard to resist the impression that scarcely spoken (or critically reflected) professional interests are writing the script.

12. These logistical tensions can generate workplace conflict. Thus, a support staff strike in early 1990 at Cambridge's Robinson College provoked by conference schedules brought to the surface complaints that had long circulated among students about the priority these were being given. It should be added that the College had been specially designed to serve this role.

13. It was widely reported in the Western press that during Sandinista election rallies in 1989, free condoms, in the red and black of the Sandinista flag, had been distributed to the crowds: a public health gesture serving as the excuse for a humorous (and humorous-seeming) piece of political promotion.

14. At Trent, a university with 3000 full-time undergraduates, the current (1990–91) library acquisition budget is $600,000 (of which $200,000 is purely to buy books), while the undergraduate expenditure in the bookstore for course texts is one and a half million. The

ratio of the second to the first figure can be expected to be higher at larger enrolment institutions.

15. The decline of background reading implied by relying for evaluation on courses and credits rather than on final exams has reinforced the wider decline of a 'generally educated public' and of books intended for it. In an excellent instance of the genre whose disappearance he regrets, Jacoby (1987) attributes this to the university expansion and the turning of public intellectuals into professional academics writing only for one another.

16. For insight into the relation between McLuhan's public career and his intra-academic standing, see Theall (1971: 63–5, 153–5).

17. An example is the detective-story writer Michael Innes, in 'real life' J.M. Stewart, an English literature scholar, and fellow of Christ Church, Oxford.

8
THE PROMOTIONAL CONDITION OF CONTEMPORARY CULTURE

'There must be some way out of here' said the Joker to the Thief.

Bob Dylan

The category of promotion

In the same breath that cultural theorists, from Adorno to Jameson, have acknowledged the pervasiveness of advertising in the culture of late capitalism, they have limited the force of that insight by assimilating it to a critique of commercialism in general, and by circumscribing what advertising refers to precisely by using that term.

Advertising is commonly taken to mean *advertisements*, paid for and recognizable as such, together with the process of their production and dissemination. In that restricted sense, however vast and ubiquitous a phenomenon, advertising is certainly only one aspect of a wider process of cultural commodification: institutionally, a subsector of the culture industry; textually, a delimited sub-field within the larger field of commercially produced signs. At the same time, the word has a more general meaning. Originally, to animadvert to something was just to draw attention to it; whence to advertise came to mean to publicize, especially in a favourable light. By extension, then, the word refers us not only to a type of message but to a type of speech and, beyond that, to a whole communicative function which is associated with a much broader range of signifying materials than just advertisements *stricto sensu*. Whether as senders, receivers, or analysts of cultural messages we all recognize that advertising in this second, generic, sense exceeds advertising in the first. But it is hard to grasp the full significance of advertising for contemporary culture unless these meanings are clearly separated. A starting-point for the present study, then, has been to give the functional or expanded sense of advertising a name of its own: *promotion*.

The term has two semantic advantages. The first, reflecting its colloquial usage, is its generality, which directs our attention to the way in which all manner of communicative acts have, as one of their dimensions, and often only tacitly, the function of advancing some kind of self-advantaging exchange. *Promotion* crosses the line between advertising, packaging, and design, and is applicable, as well, to activities beyond the immediately commercial. It can even (as in 'promoting public health') be used in a way which takes us beyond the domain of competitive exchange altogether. For current purposes, though, I have confined it to cases where something, though not necessarily for money, is being promoted for sale – while recognizing that the metaphorical diffusion of the word, wherein it has come to mean any kind of propagation (including that of ideas, causes, and programmes), reflects a real historical tendency for all such discourse to acquire an advertising character. The second advantage stems from the word's derivation. Promotion (as a noun) is a type of sign, and the promoted entity is its referent. From this angle, the triple meaning of the Latin prefix 'pro' usefully highlights the compound and dynamic character of the relationship between promotion and what it promotes. A promotional message is a complex of significations which at once represents (moves in place of), advocates (moves on behalf of), and anticipates (moves ahead of) the circulating entity or entities to which it refers.

Given that definition, the thesis I have been exploring can be simply stated: that the range of cultural phenomena which, at least as one of their functions, serve to communicate a promotional message has become, today, virtually co-extensive with our produced symbolic world.

This may seem hyperbolic, until we start to enumerate the sorts of promotional message, and, associated with them, the circuits of competitive exchange, which are actually swirling about. As we have seen, these include not only advertising in the specific and restricted sense, that of clearly posted 'promotional signs'. They also include the whole universe of commercially manufactured objects (and services), in so far as these are imaged to sell, and are thus constructed as advertisements for themselves. A special case of the latter (in my terminology: 'commodity-signs') is cultural goods. These, indeed, are typically cast in a doubly promotional role. For not only are cultural goods peculiarly freighted with the need and capacity to promote themselves. Wherever they are distributed by a commercial medium whose profitability depends on selling audiences to advertisers they are also designed to function as attractors of audiences towards the advertising material with which they are intercut. In the organs of print and broadcasting, information and entertainment are the flowers which attract the bee. In this sense, too, the non-advertising content of such media can be considered, even semiotically, as an extension of their ads.

But this is not all. The multiply promotional communicative organs constituted by the commercial mass media (and even, via sports sponsorships and the like, by the organs of 'public broadcasting') are also transmissive vehicles for public information and discussion in general. Through that common siting, non-promotional discourses, including those surrounding the political process, have become linked (Bush in Disneyland on prime time news) to promotional ones. It is this complex of promotional media, too, which mediates the communicative activity of all secondary public institutions – aesthetic, intellectual, educational, religious, etc – to what used to be called 'the general public'. Furthermore, even if not directly commercial themselves, these secondary institutions also generate their own forms of promotional discourse, whether, as in the case of university recruitment campaigns, because they have become indirectly commodified, or, as in the case of electoral politics, because they have a market form which is analogous to the one which operates in the money economy.

There are several respects, finally, in which competition at the level of individuals generates yet a further complex of promotional practices. In part this is an outgrowth of the commodification of labour power, and more particularly, in the professional and quasi-professional sectors of the labour market, of the way in which differentially qualified labour power commands a differential price. Hence the dramaturgical aspects of careers and careerism. In addition, however, as Veblen and many others have described, the promotionalization of the individual also extends into the sphere of consumption, both through fashion and more generally through the way in which status competition is conducted through the private theatre of projected style. At a quite different level of social practice (though, as in the TV ads for Towers department stores, 'everything connects'), the entry, on increasingly symmetrical terms, of (unattached) women and men into free (or non-parentally supervised) socio-sexual circulation has also created a mate/companion/friendship market which generates its own forms of competitive self-presentation. Lastly, when any instance of individual self-promotion spills over from the private realm to become a topic of public communication, whether unintentionally, as a personal drama that makes the news, or deliberately, as the amplified staging of a career (sporting, political, artistic, intellectual, etc), inter-individual competition gives rise to yet a further form of promotional practice: the construction of celebrityhood. This itself enters into the realm of public promotion not just as self-advertising, but as an exchangeable (and promotable) promotional resource both for the individual involved and for other advertisers.

It is tempting to summarize these developments by saying that in late capitalism promotion has become, as Frederic Jameson (appropriating the term from Raymond Williams) has argued of postmodernism (1984: 57), a 'cultural dominant'. Given the provenance of that term, however, and the peculiarity of promotion itself as a cultural category, such a formulation will only do if carefully qualified.

Raymond Williams (1982: 204–5) originally developed his distinction between 'dominant', 'residual', 'oppositional' and 'emergent' culture in the context of class-cultural analysis. For him, the interplay of these complexes was conditioned by (and in turn conditioned) that of the emergent, dominant, and oppositional classes whose positions and sensibilities were expressed in them. In taking over this terminology Jameson gave it a different sociological spin. His problematization of postmodernism focused not on class dynamics, but on the structuring effects of 'third stage' capital on social relations as a whole. This has evident parallels with the approach to the rise of promotion being taken here. Still, in Jameson's hands, as in Williams', the notion of 'cultural dominant' remains linked to a notion of culture as (collective) expression. It refers us to the impact of (ascendant) cultural values on the styles, themes, and inflections of artistic, pop cultural, architectural, etc, symbolic domains. In late capitalism, he writes (1984: 57), postmodernism has replaced modernism as 'a new systemic cultural norm'.

The problem is that promotion – unlike any cultural movement – is not only not a class phenomenon, it is not an expressive one either. To be sure, it is embodied in significations, and it is ramified by socialization practices, psychological strategies and habits, and cultural/aesthetic norms and values. But in the first instance, promotion is a mode of communication, a species of rhetoric. It is defined not by what it says but by what it does, with respect to which its stylistic and semantic contents are purely secondary, and derived.

I can put the matter more precisely, perhaps, by saying that promotion has become a key, structuring element of what Scott Lash (1990: 4–5 and passim) has termed contemporary society's 'regime of signification'. He defines this as a combinatory structure, parallel to the material economy (conceived of as a 'regime of accumulation'), which comprises two sub-formations. The first is the 'cultural economy', which itself consists of a combination of four elements: (a) the relations of symbolic production (its property regime), (b) conditions of reception, (c) a mediating institutional framework, and (d) the means of symbolic circulation. The second is the 'mode of signification', involving a determinate set of relations (for example the realist model of representation) between the signifier, signified, and referent of symbolic objects. In general, while allowing for a certain 'relative autonomy', the causal assumption is that the second complex of relations is shaped by the first.

The case of promotion fits the model well. In a promotional message the relation between sign and referent has been (re)arranged in such a way that, first, the former is an anticipatory advocate of the second, and second, within the construction of a promotional image, the boundary between sign and object is blurred. What the suffusion of promotion throughout all levels of social communication has amounted to, then, is a change in the prevalent mode of signification. Moreover, this transformation has itself been associated with changes in the mode of production and circulation of signs (commodification, the rise of the culture industry, and the commercial mass media), that is, with changes in the cultural economy. Indeed, while Lash's model (which he deploys in a fresh attempt to account for the rise of postmodernism) allows for a certain degree of autonomy of the mode of signification from the cultural economy, the causal relation in the case of the late capitalist rise of promotion is direct and virtually unmediated.

But here the notion of a 'regime of signification', a structure of structures, definable in itself, which can enter into interactive relations with the (capitalist) economy proper, reveals a limitation. For the rise of commercialized culture, in symbiotic relation with mass media advertising, has itself been intrinsic to a more general process of capitalist development. Not only has culture become a sector of consumer goods production just like any other produced object of human use. Industrialization and mass production have also, and again for purely economic reasons, led to an expansion of the sphere of commodity circulation, of which the culture industry, via advertising, has itself become a heavily subsidized adjunct. In addition, and further complicating the picture, the rise of inter-individual and non-commercial promotion has registered the effects of a parallel, and only indirectly related, socio-cultural process in which social life in every dimension has increasingly come to assume a commodity or quasi-commodity form.

In trying to locate the place of promotion on the sociological map, in other words, the very distinction between the symbolic and material economies, between the regime of accumulation and the regime of signification, cannot be clearly drawn. And for good reason. Promotional practice is generated exactly on the boundary, a locus which implies the dissolution of the boundary itself.

What the rise of promotion as a cultural force signals, in fact, is not simply a shift to a new mode of producing and circulating signs (cultural commodification), but an alteration in the very relation between culture and economy. Baudrillard (1981), following Debord (1977), has depicted this movement ('the union of sign and commodity')[1] as a merger, although it might be more accurate to depict it as a takeover, since culture has lost its autonomy thereby, while the (market) economy has hypostatized into an all engulfing dynamic. The result is a mutation: still capitalism, but a capitalism transformed. In effect, during the course of advanced capitalist development the globalization and intensification of commodity production have led to a crucial economic modification in which (a) with mass production and mass marketing the moments of distribution, circulation, and exchange have become as strategic as technical improvements in production for profitability and growth and (b) through commodity imaging the circulation and production processes have come to overlap. In which context (with disturbing implications for even an updated Marxism) it has further come about that the ('superstructural') domain of expressive communication has been more and more absorbed, not just as an industry but as a direct aspect of the sale of everything, into the integral workings of the commodified economic 'base'.

This has been a complex transformation, and it evidently did not occur all at once. There have been many phases and stages: from industrialism and the first consumer-oriented urban centres to the radio/film age, coca-colonization and the electronic malls of commercial TV.[2] Whence a further caveat. Besides eschewing an expressionist view of its object, any thesis about the changed weight of promotion within 'late' capitalist culture must also be careful to avoid too sharp a sense of periodization.

Promotion has culturally generalized as commodification has spread, as consumer goods production has industrialized, leading to the massive expansion of the sphere of circulation, and as competitive exchange relations have generally established themselves as an axial principle of social life. But there has been no catastrophe point, no single historical juncture (for example in the 1950s and 1960s) at which we can say that promotion, having previously been 'emergent', finally became a 'dominant' structuring principle of our culture. It is a question, rather, of a cumulative tendency; a tendency, indeed, of very long standing, since, as Bourdieu (1977: 177) has reminded us, the market as a principle of socio-cultural organization predates capitalism and, even in 'primitive' societies, the symbolic and material economies are to some degree 'interconvertible'. Nor can the process of promotionalization be said to be complete. As with commodification as a whole, the advance of promotion has been uneven, both internationally and also within leading capitalist countries themselves. Even in Baudrillard's America, the mirage runs out at the desert and there are low-intensity zones.

Both for the present and historically, then, all that can be safely asserted is that *pari passu* with the development of the market, promotion is a condition which has increasingly befallen discourses of all kinds; and the more it has done so, the more its modalities and relations have come to shape the formation of culture as a whole. But what condition? What are the characteristics of a culture whose communicative processes have come to be saturated in the medium of promotion? What qualities does it exhibit, more precisely, just by virtue of that fact?

Promotion as a cultural condition

The guiding thesis of Horkheimer and Adorno's essay on the culture industry in *The Dialectic of Enlightenment* was that 'culture now impresses the same stamp on everything' (1972: 120). In support, they cited such tendencies as the monopolistic centralization of cultural production, the standardization of cultural produce (which reflects and transmits the rhythms of industrial mass production), the classification of goods and consumers ('Something is provided for all so that none may escape'), the sensate emphasis of style over work, and the promiscuous, mid-market, merging of serious art and distractive entertainment.

In the first instance, their thesis was ironically aimed against conservative laments about the cultural chaos that would ensue from specialization and the decline of organized religion and other ideologically unifying remnants of pre-capitalist society. But it also ran dialectically counter to the analysis of classical sociology. For if, as Durkheim and Weber had asserted, cultural modernity entailed the rational differentiation of social activities and sectors, including, within the cultural sphere, those of art, science, ethics, and religion, then, through the homogenizing impact of commodification, that same movement could be shown to contain the seeds of its own reversal.[3]

Now, implicit in Horkheimer and Adorno's account, though they do not consider it as an independent factor, is that one of the ways in which commodification has been a culturally homogenizing force is through the similar ways in which, whatever the medium and genre, the products of the culture industry present themselves to us as objects and sites of a promotional practice.[4] The point is worth drawing out. It is not just that such diverse vehicles of symbolic expression as pop records, political candidates, philosophical texts, art galleries, news magazines, and sporting events, are all intensively advertised, and that this draws attention to what, as promotables, they all share: the de-sacralized status of publicly circulating, and privately appropriable, items of commercial exchange. The marketing imperative feeds back into their actual construction; so that, for example, the use and build-up of promotional names and the adoption of majoritarian entertainment values have become a common feature of all marketed discourse, regardless of whether its manifest function is to inform, inspire, solidarize or just to entertain. Moreover, this homologous proliferation of self-promotional forms goes beyond the cultural sphere. Not only are the same forms – imaged commodities as advertisements for themselves – to be found throughout the whole world of commercially produced goods. From the clothes we wear, to the parties we vote for at election time, wherever in fact a market of some kind operates, everything mirrors back the same basic signifying mode.

However, the rise of promotion has entailed more than just the boundary-crossing spread of similar rhetorical forms. In a multitude of instances, promotion in one sector has come to dovetail with promotion in another. Bush's campaign appearance at Disneyland advertised that company, just as Disney's $13 million hyping of *Dick Tracy* two years later incidentally boosted the sales of ('Breathless') Madonna's latest album, not to mention audience receipts from the world tour which launched it. In addition, promotional messages borrow their imaging ideas and techniques from one another, whether through direct quotes (in the cola wars), through the logic of positioning wherein a market is segmented into differentially imaged niches, or, more diffusely, by circulating the same stock of promotionally tried-and-tested motifs and social types.

Promotion in different spheres, then, multiply interconnects – both in terms of the common pool of myths, symbols, tropes, and values which it employs, and through the way in which each of the objects to which a promotional message is attached is itself a promotional sign, and so on in an endless chain of mutual reference and implication. Following McLuhan's reference to Poe's sailor (1967: v), I have described the symbolic world which results as a giant vortex in which, for producers and receivers of culture alike, all signifying gestures are swallowed up. But having in mind the *promesse de bonheur* which the discourses of promotion continually proffer, and defer, that vortex can also be thought of as a maze.

In fact, an infinite maze: in which there is no final destination, no final reward, and where the walls are pictures (and pictures of pictures) of ever-multiplying varieties of cheese.

Thus, and this is my first point, we can say that the extension of promotion through all the circuits of social life is indeed a force for cultural homogenization, but only if we add the rider that the outcome is not a mere repetition everywhere of the same. For it brings into being a vast web of discourse which is at once continuous from one part to the next, yet asymmetrical with regard to what (and how many) purchasable entities are being aided thereby in their competitive circulation. Overall, then, the sameness of rhetorical form which promotion everywhere installs is counter-balanced by a semiological complexity which makes every point in the flow as intriguing in its formal construction as it is boringly void of deeper content. As Daniel Boorstin has noted, this seductive quality frustrates any merely demystifying critique. 'Information about the staging of a pseudo-event simply adds to its fascination' (Boorstin, 1961: 38).[5]

A second respect in which promotion shapes the signifying materials of a culture in which that mode has generalized is that these materials become pervasively instrumental in character. The point of promotion is to effect a valorizing exchange, and its whole communicative substance is directed to that end.

Again, instrumentalism is a trend about which traditional social theory has had much to say. The notion that in the transition to modernity means-ends rationality became an end in itself, both in the economy, through science-based production, and in the state, through law and bureaucracy, passed from Weber and Heidegger to the Frankfurt thinkers, and thence to Habermas, through whom it has remained a central preoccupation of contemporary thought. For post-war critics of consumer culture, particularly in the United States, the same problematic has framed a corresponding interest in how, through the applications of behavioural psychology, psychoanalysis and the like, the needs and purchasing decisions of consumers are manipulated from above. In that spirit popular writers from Vance Packard to Brian Key have joined with philosophical ones like Marcuse to generate a picture of advertising as the cultural arm of a totally administered society. Such analysis falters, however, when it comes to demonstrating, whether in the case of selling soap or selling politicians, that such manipulation is really scientific, and, more to the point, that it actually works. As Schudson (1986: 210) notes: 'Advertising may shape our sense of values even where it does not greatly corrupt our buying habits.'

In any case, the cultural problem presented by the instrumental character of advertising, or indeed of promotion in any of its forms, is not just a question of the freedom-violating devices through which goods are sold, needs are shaped, or political order maintained. Beyond this external instrumentality, the discourse of promotion is instrumental vis-a-vis itself. If we consider that speech acts have two functions, the performative (aiming at an external change of state in the listener) and the referential (aiming at the communication of a meaning), then what characterizes promotional speech is the thoroughness with which the former is subordinated to the latter. The case is similar to propaganda, though there is a difference. The effectiveness of promotion is not measured by the extent to which its claims and perspectives are actually believed. What matters is simply the willingness of its audience to complete the transaction promotion aims to initiate. And in this, the casualty is not so much 'truth' as the very meaningfulness of the language material (whether verbal, visual or auditory) which promotional messages mobilize to that end.

Because of their calculatedly supporting role, in other words, the ideals and myths conjured up by the words and symbols used to endow a product, institution or personality with imagistic appeal are emotionally, and existentially, devalued. The effect is complementary to the one Roland Barthes (1972) focused on in his analysis of myth. There – for example in the French *lycée* teacher's use of the Latin tag 'ego nominor leo' (my name is lion) to indicate a grammatical rule – a first-order meaning (who cares about the lion?) is effaced before a second-order one (grammatical correctness) conjured up by the first-order sign as a whole. In promotion, these second-order meanings themselves fade in the extrinsic (and profaning) use to which they are put. The Paradise myth evidently packs less of a spiritual punch in a cigarette ad than in an act of worship. In turn, because of the associative responses which advertising itself engenders, this cheapening of the symbolic currency becomes general and feeds back. Even in a church, it is hard to hear 'paradise' without thinking of the multitude of goods – starting with song and film titles – to which that idea, and the many ways of rendering it, have been promotionally linked.

Such devaluation applies, moreover, not only to the plane of the signified, but also to that of that of the signifier. When Billie Holliday's poignant rendition of 'Summertime' is played as the voice-over for a VW ad, its own mystique as a 'classic' performance, which is inextricable from her own as a tragic figure, is diminished in the very act wherein that of the car is associatively enhanced. Fear of a similar effect has led to the banning in British commercials of direct references to royalty. Paradoxically, then, while the vast apparatus of selling uses established social and psychological values to move the merchandise, and thus incidentally serves as an ideological transmitter as well, that very linkage, which makes the rhetoric of ideology itself rhetorical, dis-cathects the moral, political, etc, categories and symbologies of ideological discourse as such.

I have been speaking, so far, about the way that the rise of promotion has been associated with the generation and diffusion of a certain kind of language material. But it is important to consider as well the effect of promotion on the things it promotes. At first sight, promotion stands apart from its object as an external instrument in that object's circulation. However, the (self-interested) exchange of buyer–seller information is an intrinsic aspect of any market. Promotion of some kind – even if it is only a matter of heaping apples on a road-side table to indicate that they are for sale – is necessary to complete an object's instantiation as an item of exchange. In the developed state, moreover, where commodities are designed to have symbolic appeal as part of their own selling operation, the unity of this process is replicated in the very form of the object. There, what is promoted cannot be disentangled from what promotes it, even in principle.

Haug (1986) has coined the term 'commodity aesthetics' to describe this reflexive effect. But, adopting Marx's language of prostitutes and pimps, he still sees the promotional dressing up of commodities as an externality; indeed, as an unnatural embellishment which both mystifies what circulating objects really are – items of human use – and distorts our needing/desiring relation to them. However, for things implicated in a competitive market to be given a self-promotional form is not merely a decorative – and dissimulating – addition. It changes their very being. An object which happens to circulate is converted into one which is designed to do so, and so is materially stamped with that character. In the case, say, of a Morphy-Richards iron, or even of a Wedgwood vase or a GM car, the distinction between a commodity – only marked as such by its invisible price – and a (self-advertising) commodity-sign may not seem to be of great consequence. For it is only the outward appearance of the latter which is semiotically inscribed, while the bundle of performance characteristics which define what such objects 'really' are remains the same. This cannot be said, though, when the imaged commodity (or quasi-commodity) is already, at the level of its actual use, a complex of signs. When a piece of music, or a newspaper article, or even an academically written book about promotional culture, is fashioned with an eye to how it will promote itself – and, indeed, how it will promote its author and distributor, together with all the other produce these named agencies may be identified with – such goods are affected by this circumstance in every detail of their production.

The necessary and determinate extension of a commodity or quasi-commodity into a promotional sign, and the reincorporation of this into the constitution of the promoted entity itself, manifests, in the clearest fashion, what Derrida has called the logic of the supplement. Promotion is the significative supplement of the commodity. It transforms what it doubles and extends. Furthermore, just as (in Derrida's account) the transformative supplement of writing has been part of language since its oral origins, so too has promotion always been an aspect of even the most undeveloped form of market. The absorption of the circulating object into the circulating sign through 'commodity aesthetics', for all that it has been a real historical process, builds on, develops, and extends a characteristic of the commodity form which is inscribed in its very origin.

Beyond the impact of generalized promotion on the discourses and objects that make up the external aspects of our symbolic world, a few words are needed, finally, on what this development has implied for the subjectivity of those whose communicative activity is mediated by it.

No reflection on the contemporary situation of 'the subject' can avoid reference to the debate which has raged for the last three decades about that category. The initial challenges of structuralism and deconstruction were aimed against radical currents of thought which deployed a vocabulary of history, praxis, and freedom against the alienating and reifying tendencies of a developed capitalism.[6] However, the critique of that humanist vocabulary by Barthes, Althusser, Foucault, and Derrida joined forces with those who used it (against the system) in questioning the inflated individualism which they all took to be an ideological foundation of the established order. As a result, two different kinds of theses about the 'death of the subject' have tended to get confused. The first is a historical thesis, advanced by the early Frankfurt thinkers,[7] to the effect that the (industrial capitalist) organization of production has led to the disorganization of the (classical liberal) subject. At issue, here, is the actual decline, fragmentation, and alienation of the producing and consuming individual in the face of a market-oriented socioeconomic development whose justifying rhetoric falsely promised a moral and political progress predicated on the individual's emancipation as a (responsibly) free being. The second is a philosophical thesis deriving from Nietzsche's reflections on the Cartesian ego. This has questioned whether it is meaningful to talk about the subject at all – especially as an integrated entity which is the real author of its own thought and practice – since, in whatever social and historical situation, the thinking, believing, acting, self, both actually and as a concept, is constituted by, and in the medium of, language.

To propose that contemporary subjectivity is shaped by the cultural determinations I have been describing is evidently to place oneself in the register of the former, that is within a narrative of the (male/bourgeois/ Protestant) individual's disautonomizing decline. To which it should be added, however, that the second, poststructuralist, thesis is not irrelevant to the question of how to factor in the mediating implications of promotion, since promotion itself is a communicative phenomenon. Thus the question of what has happened to the subject as a result of the spread of promotion turns, at least in part, on what has happened to the signifying practices and materials by which the individual subject has come to be enveloped.

The literature on advertising has tended to focus on this question from the side of reception, in which the most highlighted effects have been those which derive from the continual interpellation of subjects as consumers. That is: the growing prevalence of an anomic, feed-me, orientation to the world, and a psycho-economy of needs, desires and beliefs which is expressed in a totemic and fetishizing attitude towards branded goods.[8] As many commentators (Reisman, 1950; Reiche, 1970; Lasch, 1976) have noted, the ideological complex represented by consumerism has also been associated with the emergence of a modal character type – anxious, schizoidal, other-directed, oral-dependent, etc – which exhibits the psycho-pathological features of what Freud dubbed the 'narcissistic personality'.

To this catalogue, I would add only one further point. It concerns not the psychology or anthropology of consumption but the impact on individual consciousness of promotional culture as a whole. If we accept that the symbolic universe reconstituted by the rise of promotion has been de-referentialized – a quality which stems, on the one hand, from promotion's instrumentalization of values and symbols, and on the other from its perpetual deferral of the promoted object, together with any closure of the gap of desire which that object's final arrival might bring – then the promotionally addressed subject has been placed in a novel cultural predicament: how to build an identity and an orientation from the materials of a culture whose meanings are unstable and behind which, for all the personalized manner in which its multitudinous messages are delivered, no genuinely expressive intention can be read. Schizophrenic disintegration and the consumerized conformism of the Pepsi Generation are only the most extreme poles of a possible response. More common is a sensibility which oscillates between a playful willingness to be temporarily seduced and a hardened scepticism about every kind of communication in view of the selling job it is probably doing. In that light, cynical privatism and mass apathy – an index of which is the falling participation rate in American elections – can even be construed as a sign of resistance: for Baudrillard, (1983b), the only form of resistance still open to the media-bombarded 'silent majority'.

But the envelopment of the individual by promotion must be grasped from both sides of the promotional sign. It is not enough to look at this question only from the side of reception, that is to look at subjects only as readers/listeners addressed by a certain kind of speech. We must also take account of the way in which the contemporary subject has become implicated in promotional culture as a writer/performer of its texts.

Of course, only a minority play a directly authorial role in the imaging and marketing of commercial produce. Fewer still are the named creators or performers of cultural goods, though these have an exemplary importance since media stars are our equivalent of mythic heroes, providing the most salient paradigms of how individual praxis contributes to the shaping of our world. But the list grows if we also include all those playing a more specialist or subordinate role in commercial promotion, as well as those engaged in non- or quasi-commercial forms of promotional practice like electoral politics, or the public relations side of hospitals, schools, and churches. In any case, from dating and clothes shopping to attending a job interview, virtually everyone is involved in the self-promotionalism which overlays such practices in the micro-sphere of everyday life.

At one level or another, then, and often at several levels at once, we are all promotional subjects. Nor can we practically choose not to be. The penalty of not playing the game is to play it badly; or even, inadvertently, to play it well. Sincerity has become a prized virtue in a society where phoniness is a universal condition. Hence the cult of the natural and unaffected – a cult which is catered to even in the transparently artificial world of show business when, for example, David Bowie in the early 1980s put Ziggy Stardust and the Thin White Duke behind him and reincarnated as himself.

This example illustrates an even more fundamental point. Individuals who self-advertise are doubly implicated in such practice. They are, that is, not only promotional authors but promotional products. The subject that promotes itself constructs itself for others in line with the competitive imaging needs of its market. Just like any other artificially imaged commodity, then, the resultant construct – a persona produced for public consumption – is marked by the transformative effects of the promotional supplement. The outcome is not just the socially adapted self of mainstream social-psychology, a panoply of self-identified roles attuned to the requirements of the social position(s) which a person has come to occupy. It is a self which continually produces itself for competitive circulation: an enacted projection, which includes not only dress, speech, gestures, and actions, but also, through health and beauty practices, the cultivated body of the actor; a projection which is itself, moreover, an inextricable mixture of what its author/object actually has to offer, the signs by which this might be recognized, and the symbolic appeal this is given in order to enhance the advantages which can be obtained from its trade.

While in other respects their writings are now dated, the social phenomenologists, from Sartre to Goffman, who pondered these matters in the late 1950s (against a drum-beat of concerns about conformism, alienation and anxiety), drew attention to a real issue. The contemporary subject, and nowhere more than in the competitively mediated zones of work and play where our personal self-presentations directly affect our inter-individual rates of exchange, is faced with a profound problem of authenticity. If social survival, let alone competitive success, depends on continual, audience-oriented, self-staging, what are we behind the mask? If the answer points to a second identity (a puppeteer?) how are we to negotiate the split sense of self this implies?[9]

Intersubjectivity, too, is infected by doubt. Knowing how our own promotional moves will be read, how can we make credible to others the imaged egos we want to project as truly our own? And conversely: how can we decipher aright the self-stagings which are similarly projected towards us? To be sure, the result need not be total moral chaos. An ironic distantiation is always possible, and signalling this, or just mutually acknowledging it to be the case, enables us, despite the promotional enactments normally dissimulated on the surface of our discourse, to preserve dialogical respect. Nonetheless, public acts of communication will always be distorted, and properly distrusted, in a social universe in which market forms, and the promotional dynamics to which they give rise, are universally operative. Inauthentic writers are constantly being counterposed to cynical readers: a relationship in which the latter always need to be convinced, while the former must find ways to obviate that resistance when crafting messages for release.

From top to bottom, in short, promotional culture is radically deficient in good faith. For those with sensitive moral digestions, this description will seem too weak. Considering the sugar coating which pastes a personal smile, and a patina of conformist values, over the pervasively self-interested motives which underlie virtually all publicly communicated words and images, the total impression it makes (against which, of course, we screen ourselves through wise inattention) is not merely vacuous, but emetic in its perpetual untruth.

Exit?

The transformist impulse within the tradition of critical social theory from which I have drawn joins with the affirmative conventions of promotional culture itself to direct me to close these reflections on a note, if not of optimism, then at least of openness to what a better future might bring. In so doing, I will not disavow the bleakness of the diagnosis. The spectre of totalitarianism has evidently receded in advanced industrial societies. In two respects, though, a meditation on the place of promotion in contemporary society faces even more difficulties when it comes to thinking our way towards a more liberated, civilized, and organic path of cultural development than was the case for Horkheimer and Adorno when they wrote their gloomy analysis of the culture industry under the shadow of Auschwitz and Mickey Mouse in the early 1940s.

The first is bound up with what both opponents and celebrants of the Thatcher–Reagan era have concurred in describing as the global triumph of liberal capitalism. Not only have the Stalinist regimes of the East collapsed, but also state socialism as a credible project for the Western left. As well, even proponents of a 'third way' – whether cast in the form of socialist democracy, or of a mixed economy with a devolved public sector – have come to seem hopelessly out of touch with a march of events dominated by free trade, the privatization of state enterprise, and the globalization of corporate capital. With markets as with procreation, it seems, you can't be a little bit pregnant.

The correlative development of a culture increasingly made up of endless ads, and driven throughout by the dynamics of commodities and their competitive circulation, has also established itself on a world scale. And to this, the only alternative which currently presents itself is the type of solution represented, most dramatically, by the revival of Islam. That is: the renewed imposition, in a developmental crisis of modernization, of
traditional/authoritarian blockages to market circulation which a
f mine has aptly (and approvingly) characterized as
It is hard to think of this as more than a temporary (and
halt. In any case, a reactive fundamentalism, which has its weak

First World echoes in born-again Christianity, can have little appeal for those whose vision of social progress has itself emerged from the expectations generated out of the partial freedoms delivered by the market, for example in a more egalitarian and emancipated relation between the sexes.

The second difficulty stems from the very character of the phenomenon under discussion. The way in which the promotional mode has extended to all facets of social communication suggests that commercialism, and the market principle more generally, is an even more engulfing cultural force than was supposed by the Frankfurt thinkers. I can illustrate this with a trivial incident from a recent late night chat show on British TV.[11] The interviewee was a member of the fictional heavy metal band *Spinal Tap*, as featured in the satirical movie of that name. The first half of the interview was 'in character', like an episode from the movie itself. The second half, after a chuckle, got down to the serious business of trade talk. It transpired that *Spinal Tap* (one of the songs from the movie's soundtrack had already been a minor hit) were now really on tour, lip-synching their numbers to live audiences in the midst of the same preposterously exaggerated gothic sets as had graced their equally simulated performances on screen. Having performed in Seattle, they were about to try their hand in London. (The fact that they were not a great success can be attributed to the fact that by the late 1980s heavy metal had been eclipsed by rap as the music of choice for working-class youth, so that the parodic effects were blunted.)

Retroactively, then, the original movie's (pseudo-promotional) savaging of the music business had been turned into actual promotion for an 'act' which was itself designed to promote the re-released video and accompanying record. Echoing this, the interview's mid-point switch from a fake conversation to a real one registered only the transition from the promotional satirization of promotion to promotion itself. Not even satire, then, is immune from a process it may seek to destroy through laughter. And the same can be said of other forms of critique as well. Once we are communicating at all, and especially in public, and therefore in a medium which is promotional through and through, there is no going outside promotional discourse. These very words are continuous with what they are seeking to distance themselves from. To paraphrase what Derrida remarked of textuality in general: there is no *hors-promotion*.

That said, discourse is not the whole of being. And when we look at things in wider perspective, we can see that the extensive and intensive penetration of culture by promotion has not been without its elements of tension and conflict.

Two levels of contradiction can be identified. The first involves what may be termed contradictions of circulation. Here, there is a clash between the promotional imperative inherent in the market's lust-to-expand, and the resistance exercised by the moral, aesthetic or religious mechanisms which, in the interests of the current order, surround certain symbols, entities or sites of potential publicity so as to secure their exclusion from profane processes of circulation. Contradictions of this kind are evident in the uneasiness which, since John Stuart Mill, has attended the development of electioneering, in the clash of campaigns for and against legalizing street prostitution, and in the controversies which break out (though I am not remotely suggesting that this was Rushdie's motive) when an author enhances his name by dancing pirouettes through the revealed truths of a militant world religion. The second type of contradiction is at the level of mass psychology. This concerns the tendency of a promotionalized culture to become depleted of the (existential and cosmological) meaningfulness which those implicated in it, just because it is a culture, seek to derive from its symbolic material. In this direction lie the worried hunches not only of conservative thinkers like Daniel Bell or Robert Nisbet, but also of more liberal ones like Anthony Giddens (1990), that late capitalism is drifting towards a fully fledged spiritual-cum-ideological crisis.

These two sources of tension generate the space and energy for a kind of politics. Normally, as in the instances cited, it is localized and intermittent. However, and without wishing to reduce very complex events and processes to a simple formula, modern history has also shown us, as in inter-war Europe and in North America during the 1960s, that a condensation of the contradictions of circulation and of depleted ideological meaning can create the conditions for a massive cultural revolt. All of which implies that, while history never repeats itself, the spread of commodification is associated with ongoing cultural contradictions which go to the roots of capitalism's processes of social reproduction, and that the activization of these provides a certain room to manoeuvre for those wishing to influence, against the grain of the advancing market, the larger drift of events.

But manoeuvre how? The long-range goal that suggests itself is to enlarge the sphere in which promotion is circumscribed. Even as a gradualist project, it should be emphasized, this is not just a question of retricting bad symbols, but of restricting a bad kind of circulation. At the same time, to speak of restriction alone is not enough. There is an evident danger that any politics of inhibiting promotional circulation can get tangled up in rearguard struggles in which pre-market unfreedoms, associated with repressive–hierarchical definitions of the sacred, are reactively defended or restored. A more radical objective would therefore involve not just rolling back the area of cultural life colonized by competitive exchange, but doing so at the same time as the sacralized categories marking out the boundaries of permissible, competitive circulation were themselves humanistically redefined. This possibility can already be glimpsed in situations of familial or affective intimacy where, against the weight of convention and habit, the creative power of symbolic exchange, and the new forms it can create, can be commonsensically acknowledged and given their due. In the public realm, hemmed in by economic interests, state regulation, and institutional rigidity, a similar recognition would require a transformed consciousness on the part of those who are stewards of socially important institutions and resources, and the translation of such recognition into a transformed practice.

In the long term, any strategy of promotional limitation evidently depends on releasing cultural production from its currently overwhelming commercial imperative. In turn, this implies greater subsidies from taxation for all forms of cultural activity, whether popular, mass or minority, so as to reduce reliance both on advertising revenue and on corporate sponsorships. As well, it implies a sustained effort to revalorize the public realm itself as a space for disinterested expression and communication. That all this is intimately connected to a larger project of restricting the market in favour of cooperation, rehabilitating the public sphere, and dis-alienating secondary institutions, both internally, and vis-a-vis their clients and constituencies, also goes without saying.

At a time of sustained neo-conservative retrenchment, such sentiments will seem dismissibly utopian. If so, I offer no counter-prognoses about when, or whether, contemporary civilization will reopen to buried dreams. Proving the this-sidedness of our (social) thinking is a matter for (political) practice, not theoretical speculation – and who would dare to predict? Meanwhile, in an exercise which has sought merely to depict some of the consequences of blindly pursuing the current market-oriented path, the most that can be hoped for is as modest as the horizons of the time to which it belongs: that while history spins its wheels some hint of what the present dispensation blocks can be kept, at least negatively, alive.

Notes

1. For Baudrillard, however, the crux of the sign-commodity conjunction lies in the totemic and status-differential 'system of objects' which mass-produced consumer goods represent at the point of consumption. Sign-exchange-value doubles exchange-value in the constitution of the commodity, constituting a new term (the sign-commodity) within an expanded, and infinitely commutable, field of 'general exchange'. This model is elaborated throughout Baudrillard's early writings, and receives its most formal treatment in 1981, especially pp 123–9 and 143–63.

2. To which we might now add the promotional conquest of outer space. In saying this I am not just referring to the superpower boosterism of the space race, but to its actual commercialization as a spectacle (logos on spaceships, etc) which the post-Cold War Soviet programme, suddenly starved for cash, has pioneered.

3. Lash, Featherstone, and others have recently taken this argument up again in the context of contemporary discussion about postmodernity and postmodern culture. See Featherstone (1988), and Lash (1990).

4. 'The prevailing taste takes takes its ideal from advertising, the beauty in consumption. Hence the Socratic saying that the beautiful is the useful has been fulfilled – ironically. The cinema makes propaganda for the culture combine as a whole; on radio, goods for whose sake the cultural commodity exists are also recommended individually' (Horkheimer and Adorno, 1972: 156).

5. That advertisements are creative and can be enjoyed, and judged, in aesthetic terms beyond utilitarian criteria about sales effectiveness, has occurred to many, inside and outside the advertising industry. In a recent article, Nava and Nava (1990) highlight the 'interconnections and overlap between commercial and other forms of art in order to expand

our understanding of the ways in which young people exercise critical abilities as audience'. The Cannes Film Festival (whose promotional function is self-evident) includes a competitive section on TV ads. Of course, whether or not advertising has to be regarded (properly speaking) as 'art' depends on whether that category is descriptively and normatively identified with autonomous art, an ideal that rose and fell between the Renaissance and the beginning of this century.

6. For Althusser's decentring assault on humanism and existentialism as the basis for a 'scientific' revolutionary theory, see especially 'Marxism is not a humanism' in Althusser (1969). In a parallel (though not of course identically inspired move) Derrida was equally concerned to rescue Husserl and Heidegger from the left-existentialism to which, through Sartre especially, their work had become linked. See 'The Ends of Man' in Derrida (1986: 109–36).

7. See for example Horkheimer (1972: 235–7).

8. For a discussion of totemism and consumer goods see Leiss et al. (1986), Jhally (1987), and Douglas and Isherwood (1979).

9. The work of Irving Goffman (especially 1959) can be read, in this context, as an interactionist exploration of the promotional self, while that of R.D. Laing and associates can be read as an exploration of the schizophrenogenic consequences.

10. I owe this phrase to my colleague Pradeep Bandyopadhyay, for whom the 'atavisms' however are to be viewed positively, i.e. as a way for non-Western civilizations to assert themselves against the West.

11. The clip was shown shortly after midnight, 22 October 1990, on Channel 3.

BIBLIOGRAPHICAL REFERENCES

Althusser, L. (1969) *For Marx*. London: Allen Lane.

Althusser, L. (1971) 'Ideology and the ideological state apparatuses', in *Lenin and Philosophy and Other Essays*. London: New Left Books.

Althusser, L. and Balibar, E. (1977) *Reading Capital*. London: New Left Books.

Andren, G., Ericsson, L. and Tannsjo, T. (1978) *Rhetoric and Ideology in Advertising: a Content-analytical Study of American Advertising*. Stockholm: LiberForlag.

Ang, I. (1985) *Watching Dallas: Soap Opera and the Melodramatic Imagination*. London and New York: Methuen.

Apter, D. (1965) *The Politics of Modernization*. Chicago: University of Chicago Press.

Attali, J. (1980) *Bruits: essai sur l'économie politique de la musique*. Paris: Presse Universitaire de France.

Bagdakian, B. (1984) *Media Monopoly*. Boston: Beacon.

Baran, P. and Sweezey, P. (1968) *Monopoly Capital: An Essay on the American Economic and Social Order*. New York: Modern Reader.

Barthes, R. (1972) *Mythologies*. New York: Hill and Wang.

Barthes, R. (1978) 'The rhetoric of the image', in *Image–Music–Text*. New York: Hill and Wang.

Bartow, E. (1952) *News and These United States*. New York: Funk and Wagnalls.

Baudrillard, J. (1968) *Le systemes des objets*. Paris: Gallimard.

Baudrillard, J. (1970) *La société de consommation*. Paris: SGPP.

Baudrillard, J. (1972) *Pour une critique de l'economie politique du signe*. Paris: Gallimard.

Baudrillard, J. (1976) *Echange symbolique et la mort*. Paris: Gallimard.

Baudrillard, J. (1981) *Towards a Critique of the Political Economy of the Sign*. Translated by C. Levin and A. Younger. St Louis: Telos.

Baudrillard, J. (1983a) *Simulations*. New York: Semiotext(e).

Baudrillard, J. (1983b) *In the Shadow of the Silent Majority*. New York: Semiotext(e).

Bayley, S. (1986) *Sex, Drink and Fast Cars: the Creation and Consumption of Images*. London: Faber & Faber.

Bell, D. (1976) *The Cultural Contradictions of Capitalism*. New York: Basic Books.

Benjamin, W. (1970) 'The work of art in an age of mechanical reproduction', in H. Arendt (ed.) *Illuminations*. London: Jonathan Cape.

Berger, J. (1972) *Ways of Seeing*. Harmondsworth: Penguin.

Berger, J. (1987) *The Capitalist Revolution: Fifty Propositions about Prosperity, Equality, and Liberty*. Aldershot: Gower.

Berman, M. (1982) *All That is Solid Melts into Air*. New York: Simon and Schuster.

Blau, P. (1886) *Exchange and Power in Social Life*. New Brunswick (USA): Transaction.

Bloom, A. (1987) *The Closing of the American Mind: How Higher Education has Failed Democracy and Impoverished the Souls of Today's Students*. New York: Simon and Schuster.

Bone, H. (1955) *American Politics and the Party System*. New York: McGraw-Hill.

Boorstin, D. (1961) *The Image: or What Happened to the American Dream*. London: Weidenfeld and Nicolson.

Boulding, K. (1956) *The Image*. Ann Arbor: University of Michigan Press.

Bourdieu, P. (1977) *Outline of a Theory of Practice*. Translated by R. Nice. Cambridge: Cambridge University Press.

Breton, A. (1974) *The Economic Theory of Representative Government*. London: Macmillan.

Brooks, J. (1969) 'The fate of the Edsel', *Business Adventures*, New York.

Buck-Morss, S. (1989) *The Dialectic of Seeing: Walther Benjamin and the Arcades Project*. Cambridge and London: MIT Press.

Burke, P. (1978) *Popular Culture in Early Modern Europe*. London: Temple Smith.

Burton, A. (1976) *Josiah Wedgwood: a Biography*. London: André Deutsch.

Christian, W. (ed.) (1980) *The Idea File of Harold Adams Innis*. Toronto: University of Toronto Press.

Curran, J. (1977) 'Capitalism and control of the press', in J. Curran, M. Gurevitch and J. Woollacott (eds) *Mass Communication and Society*. London: Edward Arnold. pp 195–230.

Debord, G. (1977) *The Society of the Spectacle*. Detroit: Black and Red.

Derrida, J. (1976) *Of Grammatology*. Baltimore: Johns Hopkins University Press.

Derrida, J. (1986) *The Margins of Philosophy*. Brighton: Harvester.

Dinnerstein, D. (1976) *The Mermaid and the Minotaur*. New York: Harper & Row.

Douglas, M. and Isherwood, B. (1979) *The World of Goods*. New York: Basic Books.

Downs, A. (1957) *An Economic Theory of Democracy*. New York: Harper & Row.

Ehrenreich, B. (1983) *Hearts of Men: American Dreams and the Flight from Commitment*. Garden City: Doubleday.

Emery, E. (1950) *History of the American Newspaper Publishers' Association*. Minneapolis: University of Minnesota Press.

Emery, E. (1954) *The Press and America: An Interpretative History of Journalism*. Englewood Cliffs, NJ: Prentice-Hall.

Enzensberger, H. (1988) *Dreamers of the Absolute*. London: Century Hutchinson.

Erikson, E. (1968) *Identity, Youth, and Crisis*. New York: Norton.

Ewen, S. (1976) *Captains of Consciousness: Advertising and the Social Roots of the Consumer Culture*. New York: McGraw-Hill.

Ewen, S. and Ewen E. (1982) *Channels of Desire: Mass Images and the Shaping of American Consciousness*. New York: McGraw-Hill.

Featherstone, M. (1988) 'In pursuit of the postmodern: an introduction', *Theory, Culture & Society* 5: 195–215.

Finer, A. and Savage, G. (eds) (1965) *Josiah Wedgwood: Selected Letters*. London: Cory, Adams and McKay.

Fleming, J. (1962) *Robert Adam and His Circle in Edinburgh and Rome*. London: John Murray.

Forty, A. (1986) *Objects of Desire: Design and Society from Wedgwood to IBM*. New York: Pantheon.

Foster, H. (1984) *The Anti-aesthetic: Essays on Postmodern Culture*. New York: Bay Press.

Freidan, B. (1963) *The Feminine Mystique*. New York: Norton.

Freud, S. (1964) *The Future of an Illusion*. Garden City, NY: Anchor.

Galbraith, J. (1971) *The Affluent Society*. Harmondsworth: Penguin.

Geddes, N. Bel (1932) *Horizons*. Boston: Little Brown and Co.

Giddens, A. (1990) *The Consequences of Modernity*. Cambridge: Polity in association with Basil Blackwell.

Gitlin, T. (1985) *Inside Prime Time*. New York: Pantheon.

Goffman, E. (1959) *The Presentation of Self in Everyday Life*. Garden City, NY: Anchor.

Goffman, E. (1979) *Gender Advertisements*. New York: Harper.

Gouldner, A. (1976) *The Dialectic of Ideology and Technology: The Origin, Grammar, and Future of Ideology*. London: Macmillan.

Gramsci, A. (1971) *Selections from Prison Notebooks*. Translated and edited by Q. Hoare and G. Nowell Smith. London: Lawrence and Wishart.

Haug, W. (1986) *Critique of Commodity Aesthetics: Appearance, Sexuality and Advertising in Capitalist Society*. Cambridge: Polity.

Head, S. (1956) *Broadcasting in America*. Boston: Houghton Mifflin.

Heskett, J. (1980) *Industrial Design*. New York: Oxford University Press.

Hobsbawm, E. (ed.) (1983) *The Invention of Tradition*. Cambridge: Cambridge University Press.

Horkheimer, M. (1972) *Criticial Theory: Selected Essays*. New York: Seabury.

Horkheimer, M. and Adorno, T. (1972) *Dialectic of Enlightenment*. New York: Herder and Herder.

Horowitz, G. (1977) *Repression: Basic and Surplus Repression in Psychoanalytic Theory: Freud, Reich and Marcuse*. Toronto: University of Toronto Press.

Horowitz, G. and Kaufman, M. (1987) 'Male sexuality: toward a theory of liberation', in M. Kaufman (ed.) *Beyond Patriarchy: Essays by Men on Pleasure, Power and Change*. Toronto: Oxford University Press. pp 81–102.

Innis, H. (1953) *The Bias of Communication*. Toronto: University of Toronto Press.

Jacoby, R. (1987) *The Last Intellectuals: American Culture in the Age of Academe*. New York: Basic Books.

Jameson, F. (1984) 'Postmodernism, or the cultural logic of capital', *New Left Review*, No. 146: 55–92.

Jamieson, K. (1984) *Packaging the Presidency*. New York: Oxford University Press.

Jewett, R. and Lawrence, J. (1977) *The American Monomyth*. Garden City, NY: Doubleday Anchor.

Jhally, S. (1987) *The Codes of Advertising: Fetishism and the Political Economy of Meaning in the Consumer Society*. London: Frances Pinter.

Juergens, G. (1966) *Joseph Pulitzer and the New York World*. Princeton, NJ: Princeton University Press.

Kaplan, A. (1987) *Rocking Around the Clock: Music Television, Postmodernism and Consumer Culture*. New York: Methuen.

Katz, E. and Lazarsfeld, P. (1955) *Personal Influence: The Part Played by People in the Flow of Mass Communication*. Glencoe: Free Press.

Kelly, A. (1965) *Decorative Wedgwood in Architecture and Furniture*. London: Country Life.

Kelly, A. (1975) *The Story of Wedgwood*. London: Faber & Faber.

Kerr, C. (1966) *The Uses of the University*. New York: Harper.

Kline, S. and Leiss, W. (1978) 'Advertising, needs, and commodity fetishism', *Canadian Journal of Political and Social Theory* 2(1).

Kristeva, J. (1984) *Revolution in Poetic Language*. New York: Columbia University Press.

Kroker, A. and Cook D. (1986) *The Postmodern Scene: Excremental Culture and Hyper-aesthetics*. New York: St Martins.

Laclau, E. (1977) *Politics and Ideology in Marxist Theory: Capitalism, Fascism, Populism*. London: New Left Books.

Lansbury, G. (1925) *The Miracle of Fleet Street: the Story of the Daily Herald*. London: Victoria House Printing Co. and the Labour Publishing Co.

Lasch, C. (1976) *The Culture of Narcissism: American Life in an Age of Diminishing Expectations*. New York: Norton.

Lash, S. (1990) *The Sociology of Postmodernism*. London: Routledge.

Leiss, W. (1972) *The Domination of Nature*. New York: George Braziller.

Leiss, W. (1978) *The Limits to Satisfaction*. London: Marion Boyars.

Leiss, W., Kline S. and Jhally S. (1986) *Social Communication in Advertising: Persons, Products and Images of Well-being*. Toronto: Methuen.

Lévi-Strauss, C. (1969) *The Elementary Structures of Kinship*. Boston: Beacon.

Leymore, V. (1975) *Hidden Myths: Structure and Symbolism in Advertising*. London: Heinemann.

Luntz, F. (1988) *Candidates, Consultants and Campaigns*. Oxford: Basil Blackwell.

Luxton, M. (1980) *More Than a Labour of Love: Three Generations of Canadian Women's Work in the Home*. Toronto: Women's Press.

McGinniss, J. (1969) *The Selling of the President, 1968*. New York: Trident.

McKendrick, N. (1960) 'Josiah Wedgwood: an eighteenth century entrepreneur in salesman-ship and marketing technique', *Economic History Review*, 2nd series, XII(3): 408–33.

McKendrick, N., Brewer, J. and Plumb, J. (1982) *The Birth of a Consumer Society: The Commercialisation of Eighteenth Century England*. London: Hutchinson.

McLuhan, M. (1963) *The Gutenberg Galaxy: The Making of Typographic Man*. Toronto: University of Toronto Press.

McLuhan, M. (1965) *Understanding Media*. New York: McGraw-Hill.

McLuhan, M. (1967) *The Mechanical Bride: Folklore of Industrial Man*. Boston: Beacon.

McPherson, C.B. (1964) *The Political Theory of Possessive Individualism*. Oxford: Oxford University Press.

Mandel, E. (1978) *Late Capitalism*. London: Verso.

Mankowitz, W. (1952) *The Portland Vase and the Wedgwood Copies*. London: André Deutsch.

Mankowitz, W. (1953) *Wedgwood*. London: Barrie and Jenkins.

Marcuse, H. (1969) *Eros and Civilisation: a Philosophical Enquiry into Freud*. London: Sphere.

Maroney, H. (1985) 'Embracing motherhood: new feminist theory', in A. Kroker, M. Kroker, P. McCallum and M. Verthuy (eds) *Feminism Now*. Montreal: New World Perspectives.

Meteyard, E. (1865) *The Life of Josiah Wedgwood* (2 vols). London: Hurst and Blackett.

Mill, J.S. (1948) 'Considerations on representative government', (Vol. IX, London: 47) in R. McCallum (ed.) *On Liberty and Considerations on Representative Government*. Oxford: Basil Blackwell.

Mingle, J. and Associates (1981) *Challenges of Retrenchment*. San Francisco: Jossey-Bass.

Mitchell, J. (1976) 'Women and equality' in J. Mitchell and A. Oakley *The Rights and Wrongs of Women*. Harmondsworth: Penguin.

Moorhouse, H. (1986) 'Racing for a sign: defining the "hot rod" 1945–1960', *Journal of Popular Culture* 20(2): 83–96.

Morris, A. and Sizer, B. (eds) (1982) *Resources and Higher Education*. Guildford, Surrey: Society for Research into Higher Education.

Nava, M. and Nava, O. (1990) *MOCS* No. 1 March 1990.

Newman, J. (1947) *The Idea of a University*. New York: Longman-Green.

O'Connor, J. (1973) *The Fiscal Crisis of the State*. New York: St Martin's.

O'Connor, J. (1984) *Accumulation*. New York: Basil Blackwell.

Ogilvy, D. (1973) *Confessions of an Advertising Man*. New York: Ballantine.

Ong, W. (1982) *Orality and Literacy: The Technologising of the Word*. London: Methuen.

Plato (1973) *Phaedrus*. Translated by W. Hamilton. London: Penguin.

Plato (1988) *Gorgias*. Translated by W. Hamilton. London: Penguin.

Plumb, J. (1973) 'The royal procelain craze', in J. Plumb *In the Light of History*. Boston: Houghton Mifflin.

Postman, N. (1987) *Amusing Ourselves to Death: Public Discourses in the Age of Show Business*. London: Methuen.

Poulantzas, N. (1969) *Pouvoir politique et classes sociales*. Paris: Maspero.

Reiche, R. (1970) *Sexuality and Class Struggle*. London: New Left Books.

Reisman, D. (1950) *The Lonely Crowd: A Study of the Changing American Character*. Garden City, NY: Doubleday.

Riley, J. (1988) *Liberal Utilitarianism: Social Choice Theory and J.S. Mill's Philosophy*. Cambridge: Cambridge University Press.

Rogers, L. (1949) *The Pollsters*. New York: Arnold Knopf.

Rothschild, E. (1974) *Paradise Lost: The Decline of the Auto-industrial Age*. New York: Vintage.

Roszak, T. (1969) *The Making of a Counter-culture: Reflections on the Technocratic Society and its Youthful Opposition*. Garden City, NY: Doubleday.

Sahlins, M. (1976) *Culture and Practical Reason*. Chicago: University of Chicago Press.

Scholem, G. (1974) *Major Trends in Jewish Mysticism*. New York: Schocken.

Schrank, J. (1977) *Snap, Crackle and Pop: The Illusion of Free Choice in America*. New York: Delta.

Schudson, M. (1986) *Advertising: The Uneasy Persuasion. Its Dubious Impact on American Society*. New York: Basic Books.

Schumpeter, J. (1950) *Capitalism, Socialism and Democracy*. New York: Harper and Brothers.

Schwartz, T. (1974) *The Responsive Chord*. New York: Anchor.

Sennett, R. (1977) *The Fall of Public Man*. London: Faber & Faber.

Silk, G., Anselmi, A., Robert, H. Jr. and MacMinn, S. (1984) *Automobile and Culture*. Los Angeles: LA Museum of Contemporary Art.

Sinclair, J. (1987) *Images Incorporated: Advertising as Industry and Ideology*. London: Croom Helm.

Skolnick, M. (1984) *'Please Sir, I Want Some More': Canadian Universities and Financial Restraint*. Toronto: OISE Press.

Smythe, D. (1981) *Dependency Road: Communications, Capitalism, Consciousness and Canada*. New Jersey: Ablex.

Swanberg, W. (1961) *Citizen Hearst: A Biography of William Randolph Hearst*. London: Longman-Green.

Theall, D. (1971) *The Medium is the Rear-view Mirror: Understanding McLuhan*. Montreal and London: McGill-Queens Press.

Thomas, J. (1971) *The Rise of the Staffordshire Potteries*. Bath: Adams and Dart.

Tuchman, G., Kaplan, A. and Benet, J. (eds) (1978) *Hearth and Home: Images of Women in the Mass Media*. New York: Oxford University Press.

Tunstall, J. (1977) *The Media are American: Anglo-American Media in the World*. New York: Columbia University Press.

Venturi, R., Brown, D. and Izenour, S. (1972) (revised 1988) *Learning from Las Vegas*. Cambridge: MIT Press.

de Vries, L., van Amstel, J. and Laver, J. (eds) (1968) *Victorian Advertisements*. London: Murray.

Wernick, A. (1986) 'The post-Innisian significance of Innis', *Canadian Journal of Political and Social Theory* 10:(1–2) 128–50.

White, T. (1961) *The Making of the President 1960*. London: Jonathan Cape.

Williams, G. (ed.) (1976) *John Stuart Mill on Politics and Society*. London: Harvester.

Williams, R. (1976) *Keywords: a Vocabulary of Culture and Society*. London: Fontana.

Wiliams, R. (1982) *The Sociology of Culture*. New York: Schocken.

Williams, R. (1989) *The Politics of Modernism: Against the New Conformists*. London: Verso.

Williamson, G. (1909) *The Imperial Russian Dinner Service: a Story of a Famous Work by Josiah Wedgwood*. London.

Williamson, J. (1978) *Decoding Advertisements*. London: Marion Boyars.

INDEX